Reinventing the Soul

Reinventing the Soul

Posthumanist Theory and Psychic Life

MARI RUTI

OTHER

Other Press
New York

Parts of this book appeared in an article entitled "From Melancholia to Meaning: How to Live the Past in the Present," *Psychoanalytic Dialogues*, 15(5):637–660, 2005.

Production Editor: Mira S. Park

This book was set in 11pt. Berkeley Book by Alpha Graphics in Pittsfield, NH.

Library of Congress Cataloging-in-Publication Data

Ruti, Mari.
    Reinventing the soul : posthumanist theory and psychic life / Mari Ruti.
      p. cm.
    Includes bibliographical references and index.
    ISBN 1-59051-123-9 (978-1-59051-123-7) (pbk. : alk. paper) 1. Soul.
2. Philosophical anthropology. 3. Poststructuralism. 4. Parapsychology.
I. Title.
    BD421.R88 2006
    128—dc21

                                             2005015170

Contents

Acknowledgments

Many individuals have contributed to my ability to complete this project. My most profound gratitude belongs to Judith Feher-Gurewich who, like the fairy godmother with the magic wand, brought this book into existence from what in retrospect seems like a disjointed conglomerate of notes and fragments. It is Judith's unparalleled understanding of, and passion for, Lacanian psychoanalysis, as well as her keen and uncanny capacity to repeatedly hand me the missing piece of the riddle, that have made this book what it is. I feel infinitely fortunate in having received such dedicated and personalized attention in the conceptualization of my first book. Needless to say, all errors and misjudgments are my own.

I also want to thank my long-term advisor, colleague, and friend, Alice Jardine, who had faith in this project already when I did not myself yet have a clear sense of where I was headed. Alice's trust in the convoluted workings of my mind, and her encouragement in the early days of the project when it was all too easy to lose confidence, made all the difference in the world. David Eng, who read two different versions of the entire manuscript, and whose patient and insightful comments proved more helpful than I can express, taught me that it is possible to gracefully combine a dazzling intellect with the kind of spirit of generosity that represents the best of what academia has to offer.

My colleagues at the Harvard Committee on Degrees on Studies of Women, Gender, and Sexuality—Kathy Coll, Brad Epps, Afsaneh Najmabadi, Katy Park, Juliet Schor, and Kath Weston—have taught me the true meaning of loyalty, collegiality, and mentorship. Without their unfailing support and sound advice I would have never been able to finish this book, let alone flourish as a newly minted intellectual. I am also grateful to Nancy Banks, Steph Gauchel, and Christianna Morgan who, through their efficient reliability and consistent good cheer, helped me carve out the mental space that I needed to finalize this book.

Many thanks also to my new colleagues at the University of Toronto English Department—particularly Michael Cobb, Jeannine DeLombard, Neil Dolan, Alexandra Gillespie, Colin Hill, Linda Hutcheon, Mark Levene, and Dan White—for allowing me to retreat into my writing in the first few months of my appointment (when I really should have been fully and enthusiastically present). I also wish to thank Teresa Brennan for her encouraging comments, Eric Downing for Nietzsche and for giving me my first deep thrill of intellectual excitement, Barbara Johnson for her inimitable aura that compels one (despite oneself) to try even harder, Julia Kristeva for teaching me to appreciate the clinical side of psychoanalysis, Lynne Layton for providing an example of a truly well-rounded intellectual, David Plunkett for endless conversations about Heidegger and Foucault, Jessica Rosenberg for gently nudging me to write more precisely, and Michael Tan for his thoughtful assistance with the first draft of this book. I am deeply indebted to Nico Carbellano for years of theory-talk and laughter (who knew that theory could be so funny?), for her humbling brilliance, and for her priceless suggestions in the final stages of this project. Thanks also to Stacy Hague, Elaine Lindenblatt, and Mira Park at Other Press for their constructive editorial assistance.

The following individuals made my life possible during the time that it took me to write this book: Megan Boler, Sean Carroll, Doreen Drury, Michael Knisley, Marjorie McClung, Jennie McKnight, Noriko Murai, Richard Ogden, Stephanie Poggi, Jean Russo, Bob Samiljan, Shauna Shames, Melina Shannon-DiPietro, Josh Viertel, and Billy Yeskel. You have been my rock, my raft, and my lifeline—I owe you everything. Thanks also to Katia Dianina, Melissa Feuerstein, Francine Latil, Louisa Shea, and Rebecca Wingfield for many evenings of much-needed frivolity and lightness. Special thanks to Maggie Schmitt who, in her enigmatic way, induced me to write this book.

This book arises from and tries to articulate something fundamental about the leap that I have made from a working-class background without books, learning, or running water to a Harvard Ph.D. (and beyond). The distance that lies between the three-house village in southern Finland where I grew up and the life that I now lead is incomprehensible, even to me. I would consequently like to thank my parents, Jukka and Ritva Ruti, for not having ever asked for explanations. They have worked harder than anyone should need to so that I could roam free. I have written this book in part to justify—and to have something concrete to show for—the fact that I was given the kinds of opportunities that they never had. This is the kind of debt that only grows larger with the passage of time.

Mari Ruti
March 1, 2006

Preface

This is a book about psychic life from a posthumanist perspective. It arises from my conviction that posthumanist theory—by which I mean French poststructuralism, Lacanian psychoanalysis, and their multiple derivatives—contains a great deal more insight about the affirmative potentialities of the psyche than is commonly acknowledged. My objective is to unearth the creative and transformative dimensions of posthumanist theory so as to arrive at a better understanding of what it means to live in the world as a creature of consciousness,[1] as a creature who possesses the capacity to contemplate the meaning of life and the immanence of death, and to ask itself what makes its life worth living. For the most part, we tend—I

---

1. By "consciousness" I do not mean a pure form of self-reflexivity. Marx already proposed that consciousness is always a social entity in that it is inevitably "burdened" with the materiality of existence. By this Marx meant not only that consciousness is determined by the material relations of production that govern a given society, but also that human beings have consciousness only insofar as they have access to language. As he put it: "Language is as old as consciousness, language is practical consciousness that exists also for other men, and for that reason alone it really exists for me personally as well" (1846, p. 158). Posthumanist theory has developed this insight to great advantage, and it is in this spirit that I use the term "consciousness" in this book.

certainly do—to go about our daily activities in ways that prevent us from fully experiencing the world. We spend much of our lives ignoring the issues that matter to us the most, either because such issues seem too difficult to face directly, or because we keep chasing the elusive and magical moment—that perfect calm in the eye of the storm—that we imagine will allow us to regather our scattered selves for long enough to be able to focus our energies. Similarly, we spend much of our lives ignoring the details—the way raindrops play upon the calm surface of a lake, the hundred shades of green upon a hillside, or the perfect line of a lover's collarbone—that make up our daily realities. It is almost as if the impossibility of living passionately in the present was built into the very structure of our lives, making it difficult to remain cognizant of the fact that life is not a mere prelude to another existence that might allow us to think about and experience all the things that we do not have time to think about and experience at present, but rather our sole chance to do all the thinking and experiencing that we wish to engage in.

In this book, I take seriously the idea that it would be a shame to let life pass us by without fully experiencing it. At the same time, I make a concerted effort to consider the kinds of structural inequalities that make it difficult for many of us to think beyond our daily survival. In this sense, this book is about the possibilities that life offers us, as well as about the various barriers—psychic, societal, and economic alike—that prevent us from fully exploring these possibilities. It is a book about inner potentiality at the same time as it is a book about psychic pain, the concrete realities of having to live with this pain, and the invaluable lessons that such pain at times teaches us about ourselves and our strength. Most importantly, it is a book about what it means to live purposefully, not in the sense of being able to formulate a coherent life narrative, but rather in the sense of being able to distill the poetry out of at least some of the relentlessly prosaic moments that make up our everyday existence.

On the most basic level, I am interested in what it means to live well. I want to say right away that I recognize that this is a question that we can ask with any degree of decency only in the context of lives that are devoid of acute forms of exploitation, such as war, violence, or extreme poverty. I also realize that it is a question that may not be important to everyone. But it is to me. And I ask it in part because it has rarely been asked in the context of the kinds of posthumanist critical theories of subjectivity and psychic life that I wish to discuss in this book. Indeed, what makes this book different from most other books that explore the age-old question of what it means to be human, and to shape and be shaped by the various beings, objects, and entities of the world, is the fact that I approach this question from a deeply constructivist rather than a traditionally humanistic perspective.[2]

I also approach it from within a strong commitment to progressive politics. Having been trained primarily in Lacanian psychoanalysis, post-68 critical theory, and deconstructive feminist and queer theory, my thinking about subjectivity has been profoundly influenced by, and owes its allegiances to, the work of the two or three generations of constructivist thinkers who have taught us that the demise of the humanist self in all of its disguises holds tremendous potential for those of us who have throughout Western history been excluded from the rights and responsibilities of full subjectivity. At the same time, the fact that I have boldly entitled this book *Reinventing the Soul* is meant to signal that I believe that progressive critical theory needs to reassess its relationship to humanist philosophy, and to salvage out of it the concepts, ideals, and sites of intensity that might help us produce the kinds of theories of psychic life that resonate with the subject's attempt to live in the world in meaningful ways.

I have chosen to call this book *Reinventing the Soul* because I believe that the deconstructive gesture should never stop at the level of critique, but should be able to provide a viable alternative to the idea, model, or concept that it criticizes and takes apart. In other words, if we are to theorize away the humanist soul (or the metaphysical notion of interiority), then we should be able to replace it with a posthumanist set of hypotheses that conveys something constructive about human interiority and psychic life. I think that by far the worst that could happen—if it has not already happened—would be for posthumanist criticism to be perceived as a form of theorizing that empties and devitalizes the human subject. To the extent that such a (mis)conception gains ground, it strengthens the appeal of traditional paradigms of subjectivity and psychic life, feeding the increasing

---

2. Constructivist theories of subjectivity presuppose that we do not possess an innate, essential, or unchangeable core of subjectivity, but that our selfhood is socio-culturally and normatively constituted through complex processes of language acquisition and socialization. Rather than being guided by an enduring kernel of subjectivity from which our entire being would somehow enigmatically radiate, our identities are always fundamentally open to outside influences. This implies that our sense of self, far from being stable and consistent, by necessity evolves in response to the various intersubjective and socio-cultural stimuli that surround us.

conservatism of American society and academy alike, and leaving progressive critics greatly disadvantaged.

In the political terrain, the far right has done well in recent decades in part because it has been highly successful in presenting the voters with what appears to be a coherent set of values. I may disagree with every single "value" that is part of the conservative package—and I may complain bitterly about the overly simplistic articulation of these values—but as long as I am incapable of countering them with my own alternative system of values, I will be unlikely to win anyone to my cause. Posthumanist critics within the academy are obviously not in the business of fishing for votes, but the situation is somewhat analogous in that we are frequently perceived to be thinkers who pronounce the death of traditional values without being able to present anything affirmative in their place. In the same way as the political right has seized the opportunity to define "morality," "family," and even "values" themselves, traditional academic discourses seem to possess a monopoly on concepts such as the soul. This, I think, is extremely dangerous, for as long as we allow others to fill the vacuum that creates the hunger for meaning in the first place, we relinquish our capacity to impact the way in which individuals understand themselves and the world in which they live. While the relationship between theory and the "real" world is rarely straightforward, the theories that we devise do occasionally filter down to the level of lived experience. What then is the message that we would like to impart? Why should we leave so much of what is exciting and invigorating about life to the traditionalists?

I am aware of the many sophisticated objections that could be raised against placing the word "soul" in the title of a posthumanist book—and will return to some of these later—but as matters stand at present, I am less interested in poststructuralist purity than I am in destabilizing the image of posthumanist theory as a mode of analysis that presents a barren, hollowed-out, and disempowering vision of psychic life. That said, it is obviously prudent to acknowledge that the soul is a particularly risky and volatile concept in that it can be interpreted (and misinterpreted) in countless directions. I would consequently like to specify right away that although I am looking for a substitute of sorts for the traditional religious and philosophical concept, the notion of the soul that this book advances is neither theological nor metaphysical, but psychoanalytic, derivative of Freud's theories of psychic energy and desire. Indeed, the simple fact that the Greek word for soul (*psyche*) resides at the very heart of psychoanalysis makes it possible to think about analysis as a particular way of understanding and caring for the soul (cf. Lear 1990, p. 4n). It also guides us to think about the soul not as what transcends the realm of the human, but rather as what must always respect and attempt to decipher what is distinctively human, including the fact that we are by necessity creatures of desire. The soul in this book is therefore not—as it frequently is in theological or metaphysical accounts—a means of renouncing desire, but rather what reflects the power and particularity of the subject's desire.

This book follows a dual trajectory. First, I would like to reconceptualize what it means for human consciousness to encounter the world—including the collective structures of sociality and meaning-production that mediate our relationship to the world. My sense is that recent posthumanist theory has developed in an unnecessarily grim direction, portraying the subject's relationship to the world primarily in terms of what the subject lacks and fails to be rather than what it might possess and aspire to become. The discourses of lack, alienation, and social subjection that dominate contemporary theories of subjectivity tell us that in order to become functioning members of society, we must internalize many of its rules and regulations—including what wounds, oppresses, and subjugates us. What has been much less thoroughly investigated is the idea that we also possess the power to become acquainted with its sources of richness and potentiality, with the various channels of possibility that enable us to grow and develop as individuals. I would consequently like to shift posthumanist discourse in a more affirmative direction by focusing on questions of creative agency, psychic transformation, and the subject's dynamic relationship to the socio-symbolic structures that surround it. Since we are by definition social beings, it seems counterproductive to emphasize the hegemonic aspects of collective structures without simultaneously considering how these structures enable and sustain us. My goal throughout this book, therefore, is to highlight the ways in which human beings relate to the world in active rather than merely passive ways—as creators of meaning rather than as helpless dupes of disciplinary power.

Second, I would like to consider the mechanisms of psychic resourcefulness that allow the subject to survive when sociality fails. As much as I believe in the enabling dimensions of sociality, and as much as I would like to dissociate the notion of sociality from the notion of hegemonic power, I cannot deny that the two frequently coincide. Moreover, as much as I believe in the power of loving intersubjective and communal ties to sustain the self against oppressive circumstances, I recognize that there are situations where such sustenance is simply not forthcoming. I would consequently like to reflect on what happens when the world sinks back rather than steps forth in the face of one's demand for love and attention. How does the self adequately care for itself even when communal and/or social support is lacking? How does the dispossessed subject protect itself against becoming a desperate and beseeching supplicant in relation to an indifferent, unyielding, or ungenerous world? How does it manage to approach the world from a position of radical alienation without falling into a state of inconsolable and brokenhearted abjection?

I would like to propose that the logic of the posthumanist soul implies the possibility of the kind of self-sufficiency that is not a matter of either narcissism or defensive autonomy, but rather of psychic richness and resilience. I think that there is a strong tendency in contemporary progressive theory to hear the call for self-sufficiency as a call for individualism and Emersonian self-reliance. One of my objectives is to transcend the conceptual poverty of this framework, and to depict self-sufficiency as a matter of the subject's ability to develop a relationship to itself that is multidimensional enough to sustain both meaningful intersubjective ties *and* periods of solitude, self-reflexivity, and introspective stillness—that is open enough to connect with others yet robust and self-contained enough to survive the withdrawal of the other.

I admit that I am greedy. I want to hold onto the constructivist ethos of contemporary theory, yet I also want to think about the kinds of more "humanistic" concerns that have for the most part been sidelined in recent posthumanist criticism. Because poststructuralist and other constructivist theories initially came into being as a critique of humanism—as a critique of traditional notions of identity, meaning, and representation—they tend to fairly consistently reject and ridicule concerns and modes of inquiry that are associated with humanism. This, I think, is a mistake, for it leads posthumanist theory to ignore many of the most interesting aspects of human existence. For instance, while poststructuralism has provided a complex account of the various regulatory processes that contribute to the crystallization of identity positions, it does not always speak persuasively enough about the real-life demands of inhabiting these positions. In other words, our increasingly sophisticated understanding of the self as ideologically saturated has not necessarily enhanced our ability to consider those facets of inner experience that are most closely related to the subject's attempt to weave a convincing narrative of what it means to live in the world in imaginative and ethically compelling ways. This, I feel, is too large a

concession on the part of those of us interested in the future and continued viability of progressive critical theory, which is why I have written this
book as a first attempt to consider how we might reorient constructivist
criticism toward a more agentic analysis of subjectivity and psychic life.

I am also greedy in the sense that I would like this book to be accessible to readers across the academic disciplines without at the same time
losing the interest of the specialists. I have consequently striven to write it
in clear and nontechnical language while still retaining the tone and conceptual complexity of a scholarly text. I have found this to be a demanding
task, as it is in many ways easier to speak to one's peers than it is to con-
verse with readers who do not all share the same critical vocabulary. I have
also found this manner of writing strangely disconcerting in that it leaves
the text naked and exposed in ways that a more obscure style by definition
eludes. Difficult and obscure texts continue to fascinate and motivate me,
and I understand the theoretical reasons—such as the desire to defy the
notion of transparent and commonsensical meaning—for writing them. But
the process of writing this book has taught me to recognize the high stakes
of writing with a degree of lucidity as well, for such writing makes it impossible to hide behind discourse, making the gaps and failings of one's
reasoning readily discernible to the reader. As paradoxical as this may
sound, I have discovered that writing clearly is not necessarily a matter of
displaying mastery (as poststructuralist thinkers sometimes imply), but
rather of having to be entirely up front about the fact that mastery is always inevitably an impossible ideal.

If I have chosen lucidity over obscurity in this book, it is in part because I would like to make constructivist critical theory available to a wider
audience. Since the goal of this book is to bring constructivist theory closer
to the kinds of concerns that have to do with concrete life-words and experiences, it seemed important the write it in comprehensible language. I
have over the years met countless individuals whose primary resistance to
constructivist criticism stems from the fact that they perceive it to be an
elitist and arrogant endeavor. Their opposition, in other words, has less to
do with the content of this criticism than with the fact that it seems to weave
overly complicated discursive webs around concepts and ideas that are not
in themselves necessarily very difficult at all. I would never wish to disparage the kind of writing that finds pleasure in the rhythm, tempo, and
playfulness of language, for my own writing is often driven precisely by
this pleasure. Yet I also understand the aggravation of following an endless spiral of signifiers that do not in the end lead to anything particularly

glistening or substantial; in such instances, the display of fireworks far outstrips the object of celebration.

What may make this book somewhat challenging to read is that, perhaps more than is customary in academic writing, my theoretical "position" shifts considerably as my argument develops. For instance, although I start out by being quite critical of poststructuralist theories of subjectivity and psychic life, any reader who proceeds to Chapter 3 will discern that this is in many ways a thoroughly poststructuralist book. Similarly, whereas Chapter 1 stages a critique of Judith Butler, Chapter 2 defends aspects of Butler's theory. This is not so much a question of inconsistency or wishy-washiness on my part as it is of my relentless effort to stay true to the complexity of my subject matter. The issues that I discuss in this book do not lend themselves to stable assessments that would allow me to take sides in any clear-cut manner; the fact that I do not agree with parts of Butler's theory, for instance, does not mean that I cannot find other parts of it quite convincing. My argument opens out gradually and in many directions at once, thus asking a great deal of patience and forbearance on the part of the reader. I can only hope that the unruliness of this text—its sites of tension and seeming incongruity—is also where its innovative energy resides.

Thinking about how I would like this text to be read, I keep returning to the idea that I mean it as a sympathetic reassessment of the legacies of poststructuralism. I also mean it as an attempt to think about the future of critical theory—about the kinds of questions that I hope will in coming years preoccupy those of us interested in issues of subjectivity and psychic life. These two aims are obviously intimately intertwined in that it is only by rethinking the legacies of poststructuralism that it is possible for critical theory to adjust its terrain of inquiry in such a way as to be able to ask new kinds of questions. In the most general of terms, one could say that my objective in this book is to engage in a form of self-criticism designed to help us reevaluate the major terms and assumptions of constructivist theory so as to expand the territory of progressive thought. It is precisely because I cannot imagine working without a strongly constructivist notion of subjectivity that I find it frustrating that poststructuralist theory is so frequently aligned with a radically impoverished conception of what it means to be human. By refocusing on the psyche, and by returning to some basic questions about the potentialities of human life, I hope to deepen our understanding of the subject as a dynamic participant in the molding of its existence.

Introduction

> Socrates pointed out that we are unique among creatures in being
> able to address a fundamental question: How shall I live? This
> question was, for him, so important that he famously claimed that
> the unexamined life was not worth living. It is arguable that the
> citizens of Athens put Socrates to death for goading them to think
> about what their own lives meant.
>
> Jonathan Lear, *Love and Its Place in Nature*

HOW SHALL I LIVE?

The question that Socrates posed so long ago—How shall I live?—is one
that has largely fallen out of fashion among those of us thinking about
subjectivity and psychic life from a constructivist perspective. This is not
merely a matter of theoretical oversight, but represents an important
dimension of the way in which poststructuralist and other forms of
constructivist criticism have over the years defined and defended their
ideological borders. Indeed, the constructivist emphasis on the fractured,
decentered, and alienated self has made it difficult to think about the
"meaning" or "value" of life without feeling that one has been hoodwinked
and seduced by the sirens of humanist metaphysics. It is then with a
mixture of excitement and trepidation that I present to you this book that
attempts to honor the major insights of constructivist theory while at the
same time foregrounding the kinds of concerns over the meaning and
value of life that have in recent decades been designated—and quite often
denigrated—by the label "humanistic." I will call these concerns, for lack
of a better word, "existential."

I use the term *existential* here in a loosely phenomenological[1] sense, as a means of referring to a mode of being in the world that is consciously concerned with the shape of its own destiny. If we assume that being human entails, among other things, the ability to ask ourselves what our lives mean and how we should best live them, it becomes impossible to theorize the self in any profound manner without reflecting on the fact that each of us is in one way or another capable of creatively grappling with the myriad potentialities of our being. How should I live? What is truly important? What do I value? How do I make sense of suffering? Of loss, hardship, and affliction? How do I face the injustice and violence of the world? How do I meet its infinite richness and potential? How do I reconcile the various facets of my being? Retain self-respect in the face of my conflicting desires? Knowing my life to be impermanent and fleeting, how do I learn to live it wisely, with compassion and integrity? These are just some of the questions that continue to motivate individual life choices. But they are also questions that for the most part exceed the interpretative conventions of progressive critical theory. This, I think, is unfortunate. And, as I hope to illustrate in this book, it is also entirely unnecessary in that there exists no convincing theoretical reason for divorcing issues of existential meaning and value from constructivist paradigms of subjectivity.

In its most ambitious formulation, the aim of this book is to stretch the limits of constructivist criticism to accommodate notions of psychic agency and enablement, inner renewal and restoration, metamorphosis and transformation, existential potentiality and self-actualization, as well as creativity and imaginative capacity. I begin from the premise that the fact that the subject is socially constructed does not mean that it is therefore empty, or that it does not experience its existence as entirely real and compelling. After all, the whole point of socialization is that cultural norms are internalized in such a way that they become an integral component of the subject's psychic life; our identities may be constructed, but we certainly live them as our "reality." That is, while the directives that we live by may originate in the larger socio-symbolic order within which we exist and evolve, over time we come to experience these directives as nuggets of

---

1. Phenomenology studies phenomena in the world as they are experienced by human consciousness. Heidegger posits that phenomenology means "to let that which shows itself be seen from itself in the very way in which it shows itself from itself" (1927, p. 58). Existential phenomenology in turn examines themes of human existence that arise from the subject's engagement with the world—from its status as a "Being-in-the-world."

wisdom that emanate from within our own being. This is one reason that it is sometimes very difficult for us to change. Even though the psychic patterns that give consistency to our identities are not given or predetermined in any essential sense, they have often become so deeply ingrained that we experience them as who we "are"—as a highly charged site for the unfolding of psychic and affective meanings. Likewise, the nonessential nature of cultural realities does not prevent us from living these realities in tangible and profoundly life-determining ways.

What this suggests is that those of us working with posthumanist paradigms of subjectivity cannot assume that existential questions—questions about the best way to live, for instance—carry any less weight now than they did prior to 1968. The fact that the self is socio-culturally constituted, that it is alienated rather than self-identical, does not mean that it does not long to live its life meaningfully. No matter how sophisticated our critical insights into the ideological seductions, exclusions, and manipulations through which we come to inhabit particular subject positions, no matter how refined our understanding of the systems of signification and power that rob us of self-determination, and no matter how elaborate our efforts at cultural demystification, it is virtually impossible to exorcise, on the level of concrete lived experience, the appeal of a life well lived. Who among us does not strive to live life to the fullest? Who does not hunger for psychic and affective profundity? Who can resist the allure of a unique calling, the promise of passion, beauty, and creative insight?

The self's constructed status does not in any way exempt it from the challenging task of negotiating a rewarding life for itself. Yet, perhaps because the attack on interiority resides at the very heart of the poststructuralist project, it remains difficult for constructivist theory to articulate a strong enough account of existential concerns. While I cannot imagine that the intention of early poststructuralist thinkers was to drain the subject of all "human" content—to disregard what it means for the subject to face its own mortality, for instance—the manner in which poststructuralist theory has been disseminated within the American academy makes it relatively common to fixate on theories of signification and power without in any way wrestling with the existential implications of what it means to live in this world.

I want to be careful here. There are important ways in which theories of signification and power—such as Judith Butler's influential analysis of social subjection, performativity, and parodic repetition—are intensely interested in what it means to live in the world. Among other things, Butler seeks to reveal the manner in which normative assumptions about gender and sexuality delimit the realm of what qualifies as "human," thereby rendering some lives culturally unintelligible from the start. In this sense, Butler's work arises from the desire to expand the social and psychic parameters of what constitutes "a livable life," and thus to increase the life possibilities of those consigned to the sexual margins (Butler 1990, p. xxvi). More generally speaking, poststructuralist theory frequently articulates a strongly ethical impulse to loosen the strictures of what society deems right and proper, and therefore to create a space for alternative definitions of identity. This ethical impulse—often veiled or unstated yet readily discernible to those of us invested in constructivist theory—is one of the main reasons that I remain profoundly respectful of the gains of poststructuralism even as I endeavor to move beyond its customary borders.

One of the challenges that poststructuralist theory has had to face is the difficulty of supporting its ethics with a convincing enough model of agency.[2] Post-Foucaultian and post-Lacanian theories often struggle with this issue, at best providing a precarious opening for the subversive reiteration of hegemonic meanings, and at worst solidifying the status quo by insisting that any act of subversion merely plays into, and thus enhances, the authority of dominant paradigms. Although I agree in principle with the idea that subjectivity necessarily emerges within a discursive network of power relations, and that resistance can consequently only be understood in the context of this network's attempt to co-opt the individual's every effort to evade it, there is something too depressingly bleak about the conception of an all-encompassing power structure which, affording no escape, merely keeps displacing the individual from one fold of symbolic power to the next. Similarly, while I fully accept the Lacanian assertion that subjectivity is founded on the kind of constitutive lack that is inherently irredeemable, I would not want to confuse this foundational alienation—alienation that makes happiness in any absolute sense an ever-elusive dream—with the idea that psychic agency in all of its forms is impossible.

I also would not want to conflate lack in the Lacanian sense with the intensely demoralizing effects of encountering an unfair and profoundly discriminatory world. Because constructivist theories of subjectivity are centered around the notion of irremediable alienation, they can all too easily

---

2. I would like to specify that when I refer to "poststructuralism," I am most often talking about Anglo-American adaptations of French poststructuralism. In instances when I mean to allude to French poststructuralism itself, I state so explicitly.

(often without meaning to) perpetuate a vision of psychic life that is deeply disempowering to those whose inner abjection arises from painful socio-economic or intersubjective realities. While the posthumanist investigation of constitutive alienation on the one hand represents an important advance over humanist conceptions of unitary subjectivity, on the other hand it can make it more difficult to effectively respond to the tangible realities of more insidiously selective forms of psychic injury. The latter are undoubtedly also constitutive in the sense that over time they become an integral part of the individual's psychic makeup. Yet the fact that they result from the particularities of hegemonic power—from the unequal ways in which individuals are interpellated into the dominant order—rather than from any inherent necessity of subject formation means that they remain open to restorative intervention.

While I would not want to imply that constructivist theory has neglected the psychic consequences of these more circumstantial forms of wounding—quite the contrary, I recognize that it is to the theorizing of the past few decades that we owe our ability to think through the complex relationship between psychic and social realities—I would nevertheless venture to say that in its insistent critique of humanist notions of subjectivity, poststructuralist theory has been better at naming lack in the Lacanian sense than at providing affirmative solutions to the inner malaise that ensues from the alienating effects of oppression (cf. Flax 1990, Layton 1998, Oliver 2001).

Posthumanist theory sometimes has trouble viewing healing as an ideologically viable preoccupation. Yet without a notion of healing, it is difficult to act on the kinds of concerns that result from the experiential dimensions of injustice. Anne Anlin Cheng has argued persuasively that when it comes to understanding the psychic effects of oppressive economic and socio-cultural conditions, agency consists of a "convoluted, ongoing, generative, and at times self-contradicting negotiation with pain" (2000, p. 15). This implies that a theory attuned to the realities of oppression in both its material and immaterial manifestations should not only draw attention to the psychic devastation that can accompany any given individual's encounter with adversity, but should also highlight the more transformative moments of overcoming. What are the means of empowerment at the disposal of individuals coping with the scars that result from a long history of marginalization? How might we begin to chart out a posthumanist account of psychic restoration without at the same time surrendering our awareness of identity as always inherently destabilized? What are the theoretical lines of inquiry that would allow progressive critical theory to take seriously the existential dimensions of human life without compromising its constructivist edge?

Recent criticism has expended enormous amounts of energy in outlining the complex dynamics of oppression. But it seems to me that those who find themselves in oppressive circumstances do not necessarily find it particularly difficult to understand the causes and modalities of their oppression. The poor person who finds herself in an unremitting state of anxiety usually has little trouble connecting her anxiety to her poverty. The African-American man who finds himself mistreated in a restaurant, board room, or college campus is likely to connect the mistreatment to his skin color. The Asian-American woman who finds herself fetishized by her white male lover will be prone to suspect that this fetishization is related to her ethnicity. The female-to-male transsexual who finds himself scrutinized on the subway on his way to work will not find it difficult to relate the scrutiny to his choice of gender. And the butch lesbian who finds herself the object of homophobic slurs outside her apartment will know the reason for those slurs. What is infinitely more demanding than recognizing the causes of one's oppression is the fact of having to emotionally deal with the anxiety, mistreatment, fetishization, scrutiny, or hate speech that is the concrete manifestation of this oppression.

By this I do not mean to suggest that the roots of oppression are always self-evident. Quite the contrary, they are often exceedingly difficult to decipher, particularly as the multiple axes of oppression that may at any given point in time conspire against an individual tend to overlap and intersect in ways that can be virtually impossible to unravel. I am merely arguing that there is a whole lot of work to be done over and above the work of understanding how oppression functions, and that it is this more restorative work that lies ahead for constructivist criticism.

What I am saying is that if I am interested in questions of creative agency and psychic potentiality in this book, it is not because of any nostalgia for the seamlessness of the humanist self, but rather because I would like to find affirmative ways of thinking about the kinds of psychic ruptures which, for too many individuals of our time, represent the legacy and lived reality of power relations. I believe that it is essential to think constructively—as well as deconstructively—about the inner processes that allow the subject to live in the world in imaginatively enabled ways. In more concrete terms, I am interested in the inner mechanisms that allow individuals to translate their states of lack and abjection into psychically livable reali-

ties. Poststructuralist criticism offers us a powerful analysis of the hegemonic systems that entrap us in repressive subject positions, but it does
not always tell us a whole lot about how we might be able to lead a worthwhile existence despite our interpellation into such positions. I obviously
recognize the power of dominant systems to fix subjectivities in normative ways. Yet I think that it is even more important to locate the sites of
ingenuity and resilience that allow individuals to prevail over their experiences of hardship. What do we make of the fact that the more subjectivity has ceased to be restricted to a small subsection of the population,
the more it has come to connote subjection rather than autonomy (cf.
Flax 1990, Layton 1998)? How do we productively address the fact that
the notion of the alienated self is the kind of luxury that those striving
for sheer survival—those struggling to hold together the various fragments
of their lives in ways that provide a basic level of existential security—
cannot always afford?

NARRATIVE AGENCY

Poststructuralist theory has come under attack in recent years from conservative and progressive directions alike. It is consequently important for
me to specify that I do not agree with criticisms that accuse it of political
quietism, ethical relativism, or individualistic complacency. Although the
poststructuralist questioning of the socio-symbolic and discursive processes
of subject formation has made it difficult to build a political platform around
any notion of coherent, unitary, or fixed identity, it has given us a deeper
understanding of the ways in which politics is inevitably built into the very
fabric of subjectivity.[3] Equally importantly, poststructuralism has revealed
that the Western drive to force people, concepts, and forms of knowledge
into neat categories has historically gone hand in hand with extreme forms
of violence. As a result, while poststructuralism has frequently been repri-
manded for lacking an ethical charge, I would contend that its ethical genius resides in its recognition that the quest for absolute truth and firm
categories of knowledge all too easily produces and reproduces normativity
in its most brutal forms. In this sense, the valorization of ambiguity and

---

3. For an excellent overview of some of the main criticisms of poststructuralism, as
well as of the responses to these criticisms by poststructuralist thinkers, see Butler and
Scott 1992.

uncertainty that poststructuralist thinkers so often exhibit should be understood as an ethics of a sort.

I do not then doubt the political or ethical commitment of poststructuralist theory. This theory has been extremely successful in showcas-
ing the manner in which traditional humanistic notions of subjectivity tend
to perpetuate an insidious structure of taken-for-granted knowledge that
validates the experiences of some while systematically denigrating those of
others. It is, in other words, not at all fortuitous that much of the most
groundbreaking theorizing about subjectivity has in recent decades taken
place in academic fields—feminist and queer theory, ethnic and cultural
studies—inhabited by those who have historically been marginalized by
the Western philosophical tradition. This opening up of the theoretical
terrain has been immensely important, not only because it has made "subjectivity" available to formerly deprivileged groups and individuals, but also
because it has delivered us from the reductiveness of essentialist identity
categories. It has in fact given us the conceptual tools with which to understand how the very categories and conventions of knowledge that we use
to describe identities are ideologically and socio-culturally conditioned.
Similarly, it has allowed us to sharpen our awareness of the ways in which
factors such as race, ethnicity, gender, sexuality, religion, education, and
economic status contribute to the constitution of a person. As the "universal" Man of Metaphysics has gradually yielded to a polyphony of subject
positions, we have come to see that the subject is always an astonishingly
complex and particular reality.

Constructivist criticism has forged an invaluable conceptual space
beyond humanist metaphysics, and in so doing, has promoted the personal
and political viability of those excluded from more canonical discourses.
In addition, the radical denaturalization of identity that it has achieved
has allowed us to comprehend a great deal about the polyvalent, contradictory, and often quite precarious nature of subjective and psychic realities. At the same time, when critics of poststructuralism charge it of
emptying the psyche of depth and substance, and of promoting a fragmented and surface-oriented conception of subjectivity, intellectual hon-
esty demands that I admit that it is possible to trace a consistency of
theoretical effects and strategies that has over the decades produced this
impression. I would, for instance, have to concede that constructivist
theory may have erred too far on the side of nonmeaning at the expense
of meaning. It has focused on alienation and the breakdown of meaning
more than on the creative and innovative potentialities of the psyche. It

has emphasized the performative dimensions of identity without a whole lot of regard for matters of psychic meaningfulness or existential wisdom. And it has developed highly formalistic theories of psychic life that frequently seem to have little to do with the manner in which individuals experience their everyday lives.

Let me clarify right away that I do not wish to return to a transparent notion of the relationship between subjectivity and experience. This book is not, in other words, intended as a theoretical justification of identity politics, for I remain utterly persuaded of the validity of the constructivist critique of essential identities. The feminism that I adhere to, for instance, is closely aligned with the efforts of poststructuralist and queer theories to destabilize our understanding of both gender and sexuality. At the same time, I believe that our experiences do inform—in deep and fundamental ways—how we conceptualize ourselves as individuals and how we interact with the world around us; the fact that our identities are multiple and ever-shifting does not mean that we do not possess a strong sense of ourselves as grounded in our past and present circumstances.

One way to better account for the importance of experience from a posthumanist perspective might be to recognize the distinction between the subject as a discursive position—as an economically and socio-symbolically situated entity—on the one hand, and the subject as an intricate psychic reality with specific needs, desires, and motivations on the other. While these two "subjectivities" are clearly mutually interdependent—the subject's needs, desires, and motivations are obviously in large part shaped by its discursive positioning (and vice versa)—the failure to distinguish between the two misses the fact that the subject can be "alienated" without losing its existential aspirations (cf. Benjamin 1998, p. 87). The subject's decentered status, in other words, does not in the least diminish the poignancy of its various psychic states; the subject's inner experiences of pleasure or pain, joy or sadness, anticipation or anxiety are not in any way invalidated by the poststructuralist critique of the unitary self. Rather, such affective states may be exactly what enables the subject to make sense of the complexities of its inherently fragmented and self-contradictory status; it is precisely because the subject's psychic life is never fully determined by its discursive positionality that it becomes possible for it to counter the economic and socio-symbolic forces that seek to constitute it as a hegemonically determined identity. This insight is something that posthumanist thought has been relatively slow to recognize, with the result that it tends to focus on inner divisions without at the same time adequately examining those creative and transformative potentialities of the psyche that might allow the subject to survive these divisions.

Being able to think about inner survival in the constructivist context calls for the capacity to conceptualize psychic potentiality without reverting to metaphysical notions of ontological fullness. As a result, one of my aims is to delineate the ways in which theories of psychic potentiality can be highly compatible with posthumanist models of fluid and polyvalent subjectivity. More specifically, I would like to demonstrate that one way to think about psychic potentiality from a constructivist perspective is to acknowledge that while collective systems of meaning-production restrict the subject's capacity to name itself in any absolute or definitive manner, they simultaneously open a space for potentially enabling existential narratives. I will try to show that such narratives are important because they create the conditions for active self-constitution—for transformative acts of reinterpretation and self-mythologization. Needless to say, such efforts at meaning-production manifest themselves in drastically different, even apparently antagonistic, ways in various contexts. Even within one socio-cultural setting, it would be difficult to establish any common parameters to the lived experience of personal meaning-making. However, it seems safe to posit that, in one way or another, meanings get made and that, whatever the realities of ideology and disciplinary power, most of us would like, however precariously, to position ourselves as their makers.

Many posthumanist thinkers are accustomed, in the aftermath of Lyotard's (1979) critique of Western master narratives, to think about narrativization with a degree of suspicion, as a means of aspiring to the kind of inner coherence that denies the power of the unconscious to disrupt subjective realities and, in so doing, upholds the authority of the rationalistic humanist self. Such a conception links narrativization to an epistemological and ideological violence that seeks to reduce the multiplicity of psychic realities into one overarching paradigm of unitary subjectivity. My aim in this book is to take the notion of narrativization in a different direction and to align it with psychoanalytic practices of free association and narrative self-constitution which, while granting meaning to the subject, do not aspire to any degree of self-mastery. To the extent that psychoanalysis relies on an inherently open-ended process of signification for the production of subjective meaning, the narratives that it engenders are always necessarily fragmentary, incomplete, and paradoxical. As a result, although the purpose of clinical processes of narrativization is often to translate unconscious desire into conscious meaning, they are by no means aimed at constructing an immutable account of inner experience. Indeed, it is precisely because definitive psychic integration remains unattainable that the psychoanalytic project remains viable in the first place, for it is only insofar as the psyche resists coherence that it stays open to transformation.

The type of narrative agency that I have in mind consequently has little to do with the confident self-representations of the humanist subject, but rather aims at forms of meaning that can be experienced as empowering even as they are recognized as provisional and inconsistent. If we understand agency quite simply as the individual's creative capacity to respond both to the difficulties and opportunities of the world, it is evident that there is nothing about it that implies a unitary or essential form of subjectivity. Quite the contrary, it becomes clear that it is precisely insofar as the subject is constructed that it possesses agency in the first place in the sense that it can aspire to reconstruct both itself and its surroundings. Along related lines, the constructedness of the self does not in any way diminish its existential responsibility, but rather brings this responsibility into sharper focus by asking it to actively consider how it is that it would ideally like to live; the fact that the subject is in some degree able to manipulate the contours of its existence not only ushers in all the anxieties and ambiguities of existential "choice" but also foregrounds the ethical implications of its actions, thereby forcing it to recognize its accountability vis-à-vis the world. In this sense, the self's actions in the world are not in any way less ethically charged under the constructivist model than they are in more metaphysical philosophies.

WHY PSYCHOANALYSIS?

While this book draws quite promiscuously on a number of different discourses—including poststructuralist criticism, continental philosophy, and recent feminist and queer theory—its approach is predominantly psychoanalytic. This is because I find psychoanalysis to be distinctive among contemporary theories of subjectivity in that it advances a profoundly constructivist and anti-essentialist notion of psychic life while simultaneously recognizing and taking seriously the countless ways in which inner realities can be experienced as "real" and "fixed." As human beings, we are compelled to face the return and repetition of the past, even when this past is less than ideal. The fact that psychoanalysis deals with psychic pain and suffering, and that one of its primary objectives is to liberate the individual from compulsive forms of repetitive (and therefore seemingly "fixed") behavior, forces psychoanalytic thinkers to confront the manner in which the psyche, however constructed, frequently displays stunningly enduring characteristics. By this I obviously do not mean that psychoanalysis understands identities to be stable, for the clinical practice of analysis is based on the idea that identities are inherently malleable and open to renewal. At the same time, analysis foregrounds the often quite excruciating ways in which identities can feel stuck in the past. In this manner, it draws attention to the more stubbornly entrenched aspects of psychic life—to how the play of signification cannot be understood independently of the subject's psychic history and its ongoing experiences in the world.

Psychoanalysis also manages to address ideals of psychic potentiality and self-actualization without resorting to teleological accounts of self-constitution. While more metaphysical approaches often present self-actualization as a matter of transcending the world—of escaping the immanence of materiality so as to arrive at some loftier sphere of ideality and self-overcoming—psychoanalysis regards self-actualization as a matter of the subject's ability to make the most of its unique and tangible positionality in the world. Jonathan Lear (1999) points out that psychoanalysis studies the highly idiosyncratic route that the subject takes through the world rather than the universal route that might take it away from the world (p. 165). This implies that psychoanalysis is, among other things, interested in questions of individuation—in how best to honor and develop the subject's inner potentialities in all of their particularity. Lear in fact proposes that one of the most significant features of analysis is that it can enhance the subject's capacity to ask the right kinds of questions about what makes its life worthwhile, as well as to find answers that allow it to embark upon the complicated task of reshaping its existence along more gratifying lines. In this sense, analysis caters to those who suspect that they may not be answering the most important of life's questions well enough, or who feel that their attempts to answer these questions have somehow been fundamentally distorted. Analysis is then an effort to unravel these distortions—to get to the bottom of the subject's psychic "commitments" not only on the level of conscious belief but also unconscious wish and fantasy (p. 162).

Psychoanalysis thus teaches us to think about self-actualization as a matter of the individual's ability to fully experience the world. Self-actualization, in other words, is not a function of the subject's capacity to rise above its everyday realities, but rather of its ability to meaningfully engage with these very realities. This manner of characterizing matters may seem foreign to those academics whose understanding of psychoanalysis is derived from Lacan, for it is hardly customary to present Lacan as a theorist of self-actualization. I should perhaps then divulge right away that one of my goals in this book is to extract from Lacan a theory of psychic potentiality and self-actualization that can operate outside the realm of psychoanalysis—as a general philosophy of life. I will try to show that Lacan offers us a rendering of psychic potentiality that is largely devoid of the metaphysical baggage that this concept historically carries. What is more, Lacanian analysis—indeed, psychoanalysis at large—is able to treat the notion of psychic potentiality in a remarkably concrete manner, adding a practical twist to the abstract deliberations of philosophical inquiry.

The larger question that I would like to raise in this context is the following: Since humanist philosophers did not possess the insights regarding psychic life that those of us living in the post-Freudian world do, might it not be possible to use psychoanalysis to advance the project of these philosophers while at the same time avoiding their worst pitfalls? Philosophy aims to generate knowledge about the world, as well as to contemplate the preconditions of this knowledge. Traditionally it also often sought to change the way people lived their lives, what they valued, and how they went about making important decisions. Arguably, this more applied side of philosophy has been all but lost over the last few decades of scholarly deliberation. How then might psychoanalysis meet the hunger for philosophical insight that continues to burn both within and beyond the walls of academic cogitation?

I would like to propose that one of the strengths of Lacanian psychoanalysis is that it shows us that even though we are creatures of lack and alienation, we are capable of living in the world in meaningful ways. I am convinced that if Lacan is so focused on lack, it is not because he wants us to fall into a state of despair, but because he wishes us to recognize the manner in which lack gives rise to all the creative and imaginative capacities of the psyche. After all, it is lack—the fact that there exists an empty slot in the puzzle of life—that makes movement and modification possible by preventing the subject from ever becoming entirely self-contained. This implies that it is lack that sustains a space for future possibility—for the subject's capacity to transform, evolve, and grow in new directions. I would consequently like to argue that Lacan demonstrates that we are beings of potentiality only insofar as we are beings of lack; if there was no lack, there would be no psychic life. Lack, moreover, is what connects the subject to the world by making it a subject of desire. As such, it holds the subject open to its surroundings in ways that allow for a dynamic interchange between it and the world.

Ultimately, what is at stake in my reading of Lacan is our ability to reconceptualize the relationship between lack and potentiality. Whereas recent constructivist criticism has tended to construe the subject's lack-in-being in relatively debilitating terms, as what causes alienation and psychic subjection, phenomenological thinkers from Heidegger to Merleau-Ponty regarded the subject's inner "nothingness" as the basis for its creative un-veiling. From this phenomenological point of view, the subject's lack was not the opposite of psychic potentiality but rather its very precondition. I would like to argue that this more affirmative understanding of lack is still readily discernible in Lacanian theory, and that it is only in post-Lacanian criticism that lack has lost its generative dimensions.

I do not mean here to suggest that the Lacanian conception of lack is identical to phenomenological notions of nothingness. Yet I also find it entirely counterproductive to position Lacanian theory against phenomenology, as if the two had nothing whatsoever in common. Although it is true that phenomenological accounts of subjectivity do not possess a strong enough understanding of the unconscious, it is not at all the case—as has sometimes been assumed in the aftermath of Sartre's popularization of Heidegger—that they uphold a fully agentic and rationalist self. Pre-Sartrean phenomenology exhibits an almost mystical appreciation for the mysteries of life, for its sites of ambiguity and unknowability, which means that it cannot possibly resort to metaphysical notions of self-mastery. It is, for instance, clear that Heideggerian phenomenology, like Lacanian psychoanalysis, offers a sophisticated critique of Cartesian philosophy. Conversely, as Kaja Silverman (2000) has recently pointed out, it is apparent that the Lacanian notion of lack carries a strong trace of the Heideggerian concept of nothingness.

In Chapter 3, I will try to demonstrate that Heideggerian phenomenology and Lacanian psychoanalysis are both profoundly preoccupied with the unfolding of the individual's psychic potentialities. More specifically, I will argue that Heidegger and Lacan reveal that the subject's lack-in-being, far from exhausting its creative potentialities, is what allows these potentialities to materialize in the first place. Above I mentioned that I see absolutely no reason to divorce constructivist paradigms of subjectivity from concerns of existential meaning and value. In Chapter 3, I will advance this argument a step further by positing that Lacan, *precisely insofar as he provides us with a constructivist theory of subjectivity*, is in fact better equipped than more traditional philosophers to give us a sophisticated understanding of what it means for the subject to realize the full extent of its existential potential.

Psychoanalysis recognizes the human being as a creature of lack who nevertheless needs to live in the world in relatively coherent (and non-psychotic) ways. This is to say that psychoanalysis acknowledges the importance of being able to provide some constructive answers to Socrates's question about the best way to live even as it stresses the power of the unconscious to undermine both the question and the answers provided. Along related lines, though it might seem reasonable to assume that the Lacanian emphasis on the subject's lack-in-being precludes considerations of psychic renewal and restoration, I would argue that the very opposite is the case. The fact that Lacan refuses to envision the relationship between lack and restoration in a manner that would be immediately and intuitively comforting to us should not blind us to the therapeutic implications of his theory.

The uncertainty regarding these more therapeutic aspects of Lacanian analysis arises from the fact that Lacan views restoration not as a matter of overcoming lack, but rather of learning how to dwell productively within and through this lack. The goal of analysis for Lacan is not to fill or cover over the subject's sense of alienation, but rather to translate this alienation into something that can be meaningfully articulated; "healing" is therefore not about suturing the subject's sense of lack, but rather about teaching it to transform this lack into a manageable psychic reality. In this manner, Lacanian psychoanalysis deftly deconstructs the dichotomy between lack and restoration—between alienation and inner potentiality—that has frequently prevented constructivist criticism from addressing issues of psychic renewal. This insight allows us to understand how posthumanist criticism might be able to make room for the more affirmative dimensions of subjectivity and psychic life without giving in to a futile search for secure foundations. Lacan shows us that renewal and restoration are not a matter of inner wholeness or triumphant homecoming, but rather of the subject's capacity to mobilize the creative potentialities of its psychic life.

But is it not precisely psychoanalysis that is responsible for the dispirited account of subjectivity that characterizes much of posthumanist criticism? Is it not Lacan's strongly anti-humanist structuralism that has shaped the manner in which we read and interpret the psyche? Absolutely. But I would like to argue that if this is how psychoanalysis, particularly Lacanian analysis, has been deployed within the American academy, it is because academic critics have by and large not been particularly interested in the clinical aspirations of analysis (except insofar as they have criticized the relationship between Freud and his hysterics). Critical theories of subjectivity most often treat psychoanalysis as a source of insight about language and the unconscious, and obviously they are correct to do so. However, psychoanalysis is also a technique aimed at curing symptoms, at making people feel better about their lives. Most academic debates overlook this, with the result that they tend to suck the life out of psychoanalysis, turning it into something quite mechanical when it should in fact be full of affect—of pain, suffering, love, pleasure, and desire. Tears and laughter—the relentless tussle of living—is what psychoanalysis is about, in addition to signifiers.

Because psychoanalytic discourses within the academy rarely touch upon the therapeutic dimensions of analysis, they often miss out on the lessons that analysis—and I will try to show that Lacanian analysis is no exception here—can teach us about psychic potentiality and self-actualization. I would in fact go as far as to propose that this neglect of the clinical side of analysis is one reason psychoanalytic theories have recently lost much of their footing within the academy. In the early years of constructivist criticism, psychoanalysis functioned as an invaluable tool for understanding the intricacies of subject formation, and allowed us to evaluate and criticize received notions of gender and sexuality. However, theories of subject formation, as well as of gender and sexuality, have progressed so swiftly during the last two decades that it is no longer necessary to draw on psychoanalysis to develop constructivist theories of identity. This being the case, if psychoanalysis is to stay relevant and reclaim its rightful place within the academy— as I think it should—we need to concentrate on what is distinctive about analysis, namely that it is a *practice* as well as a theory of subjectivity and psychic life. By this I of course do not mean to imply that psychoanalytic theories of subject formation are no longer of interest to us. I am merely suggesting that shifting our focus to the clinical side of analysis gives us access to exactly those "juicy" details of existence that other constructivist theories have not always been able to conceptualize in convincing enough terms. In this manner, psychoanalysis may be able to provide insight into some of the most persistent impasses of posthumanist theory.

REINVENTING THE SOUL

By far the most difficult part of writing this book was managing the considerable uncertainties and hostilities around the term "soul." While interlocutors outside the academy seemed to possess a strong intuitive understanding of the fact that by the term I wished to evoke a certain ethos of inner depth, versatility, and creative capacity, academic readers tended to react with a degree of resistance, pointing out—correctly enough—that the word carries no currency in contemporary critical thought. The advice I kept receiving was that it would be more prudent and less provocative to write the book without the term. This advice made me restless. I tossed and turned. I came very close to losing my nerve. In the end, I kept the term, for I came to the conclusion that since one of the main goals of this book is to resist the solidification of critical theory into well-worn patterns of investigation that exclude alternative venues of thought, it would be a rather ironic display of spinelessness on my part to give in to the pressure to take the safer and more predictable path.

I admit that I found the resistance to the notion of the soul—which at times reached an astonishing pitch and venomous intensity—to be intriguing in itself. I quickly came to realize that, being neither American nor religious, I had vastly underestimated the extent to which the soul in American culture carries a distinctively religious connotation.[4] Let me then take the occasion to clarify that although the conception of the soul that this book advances draws on the rich descriptions of inner vitality and animation that can be found in numerous belief systems around the world, I do not mean the term in a theological, and least of all, in the Christian, sense; although there may well be a spiritual dimension to this book, it is not one that can be contained within the parameters of organized religion. Along related lines, it is hardly my intention to resuscitate the metaphysical ideal of the transcendent spirit, but merely to ask *why there exists, in posthumanist thought, no adequate equivalent to the humanist soul.* The objective of this book,

---

4. During the final rounds of revising this book, it dawned upon me that many of the problems that I have encountered in writing it result from the fact that the Christian paradigm is fundamentally foreign to me. Having reached adulthood in one of the most secular societies in the world, I have always found Christianity to be simply one of the many (distantly discerned) religious traditions that populate the world. This is why the idea that the soul might be regarded as specifically Christian has consistently taken me off guard. I of course know that the soul is a part of Christian mythology. But does this mean that it is inherently or exclusively Christian? It may shock the reader to find out that when I settled on the soul as the major metaphor of this book, it never occurred to me to connect it with Christianity. This was clearly a blind spot of enormous proportions on my part, particularly after twenty years in the United States. At the same time, I feel that the idea that the soul should automatically be associated with Christianity only reinforces a strangely Christian-centric vision of human existence.

as its title suggests, is to *reinvent* the soul rather than to perpetuate its conventionally humanistic definitions. How better to stretch the limits of posthumanist theory than to breathe life into a concept that has for so long functioned as one of its main punching bags?

The image of breath is fitting here in that the soul has historically often been associated with breath and breathing. Many different traditions have over the centuries developed a concept of an inner force, energy, or principle that gives life to and individualizes the body. While each tradition uses a different name for what in the West has come to be called the soul, a privileged position is frequently assigned to the notion of breath as a source of life. For instance, the Egyptian *ka*, the Hebrew *nephesh* and *ruah*, the Greek *psyche* and *pneuma*, the Latin *anima* and *spiritus*, the Sanskrit *prana*, and the Chinese *ch'i* all convey the metaphoric intertwining of breath and spirit.[5] That these different traditions view breath as what carries and communicates spirit suggests that it may be fruitful to think about the soul as a form of energy that on some very fundamental level relates to the individual's capacity to keep breathing in the face of life's challenges. The soul in this sense is what sustains the individual's inner agility and resourcefulness. But if this is the case, what does it mean that so many of us these days sprint through life in a distinctively hurried, harassed, and breathless kind of way?

In *Coming to Writing*, Hélène Cixous (1977) likens the birth of creativity to the astonished flutter of a soul gasping for air, to something akin to the sensation of blood returning to a body part that has gone numb because one has inadvertently cut off one's circulation—the pins and needles of energy rushing back to a lifeless limb. This image is in many ways emblematic of the main concerns of this book insofar as I am interested in the psychic processes that allow individuals to arrive at a sense of inner revitalization even when their external circumstances seem to militate against

---

5. The *Oxford English Dictionary* defines the soul as the "animating and vital principle of life in man." Similarly, the *American Heritage Dictionary* states: "The animating and vital principle in human beings, credited with the faculties of thought, action, and emotion, and often conceived as an immaterial entity." Secondary definitions in both sources refer to the intellectual and/or spiritual powers of man, or conceptualize the soul as the seat of emotions, feelings, and sentiments. For an overview of the complex history of the soul in the various belief systems of the world, see the nine articles (under "soul") in *The Encyclopedia of Religion*, vol. 13. For an explanation of the significance of "breath and breathing," see the same work, vol. 2. For Semitic, Hebrew, Greek, and Christian conceptions of the soul, see also *The Encyclopedia of Religion and Ethics*, vol. 11. For a more philosophical outline, see *The Routledge Encyclopedia of Philosophy*, vol. 9.

the possibility of such revitalization. Indeed, if I am drawn to the soul as a matter of being able to breathe freely, it is because I think that contemporary life, with its frenzied and often quite anxious rhythm, tends to induce the kind of tensing up of the body and mind that constricts the fluid flow of breath. I also believe that hardship and psychic trauma in their various forms—from racism, sexism, homophobia, and socio-economic exploitation to intersubjective strife—frequently interfere with the individual's ability to lead a supple and imaginatively enabled existence. In this sense, our vitality is threatened by a whole host of external forces that can result in states of psychic paralysis and inflexibility—that cause the kind of inner impoverishment and soullessness that make it impossible for us to pursue fulfilling existential trajectories.

It is, moreover, possible for entire societies to display symptoms of soullessness. If soullessness on the individual level manifests itself in the subject's inability to find psychic meaning and value, as well as in the difficulty of forming open and caring connections with others, on the societal level it could be argued to perpetuate the kinds of inegalitarian structures which, when they do not literally kill people, break the spirit of the disadvantaged. It may also be related to the rationalist attempt, so common in our highly instrumentalist culture, to deny and flee from the messages of the unconscious—to live life without pausing to consider the implications of the fact that we cannot ever be fully in control of our psychic destinies.

This last point is particularly important to me, for I understand the unconscious to be not only what disrupts our conscious plans and designs, but also, and more importantly, what forces us to pursue our lives with a degree of appreciation for the unpredictable. Indeed, if the notion of the soul drove my inquiry from the very beginning of this project, it is because I felt thwarted by the fact that human interiority is frequently talked about in contemporary critical theory in ways that downplay rather than expand upon its more enigmatic and inscrutable qualities—qualities that in more traditional discourses dealt with the unfathomable depths of the psyche. Posthumanist theory is notorious for criticizing humanist philosophy for having propagated the false assumption that we have immediate and transparent access to ourselves and our lives; yet it could be argued to harbor its own version of transparency in the sense that it often valorizes surface over depth in ways that make it difficult to attend to the more opaque layers of psychic life. The "meanings" that the poststructuralist psyche produces may be fashionably erratic and contradictory, but there is nothing secretive or reserved about them; no excavation of depths is necessary, as everything throbs readily on the surface.

I have fixated on the soul in part because it provides an apt metaphor for thinking about those aspects of the self that are more reticent and introverted, that reside in the shadowy regions of the invisible, intangible, and nonreferential world, but that nevertheless constitute as significant a portion of our lives as do the more voluble concerns of everyday existence. These hidden components of the self do not necessarily reveal themselves according to the logic of common sense, but rather express themselves in the tension of our conflictual longings, in the violence of our affects and urges, as well as in the inexplicable compulsions that propel us in directions that we do not foresee or understand, and whose significance only reveals itself gradually, in the protracted uncoiling of an entire lifetime. Needless to say, these more elusive dimensions of subjective experience are no less permeated by socio-discursive power than their more conspicuous counterparts. But they are also something that an analysis of socio-discursive power *alone* is unlikely to touch or awaken. My hope is that I will be able to capture in the pages of this book—even if it must by necessity be in the most tentative of critical sketches—something of this interior world in which we find ourselves so radically "other."

I like to think of the soul as a dynamic entity that connects the individual to the world at the same time as it provides a space for self-reflexivity. Indeed, if the psyche is understood to carry the responsibility for negotiating the subject's relationship to its surroundings by, on the one hand, processing incoming external stimuli and, on the other, channeling internal drives and energies into sociality—the psyche in this sense functioning as the permeable boundary, the amorphous space of mediation, between the biological body and its cultural inscriptions—then might it not be appropriate to characterize the soul as the specific dimension of the psyche most insistently concerned with the subject's attempt to find its place and purpose in the world? In this sense, the soul relates to those aspects of the psyche that are most directly linked to the individual's endeavor to infuse the necessities of daily life with forms of meaningfulness and value that translate to inner satisfaction.

I also like to think of the soul as being indicative of the subject's ability to meet its internal tensions and conflicts in such a manner that they do not deplete its psychic resources, but instead generate energy that allows it to pursue its path with confidence and anticipation. Soulfulness is therefore most convincingly expressed by the kind of imaginative agility that enables the individual to discern how a painful experience—one of loss, frustration, disappointment, failure, or disenchantment, for instance— might function as a valuable rite of passage that ultimately, over time, empowers rather than debilitates. Soulfulness, in other words, entails the subject's capacity to recognize how abundance at times flows from lack, opportunity from loss, how an impediment or delay might in the end work to its advantage, how it is, in short, that its most volatile experiences often provide its most inspiring and life-enhancing existential openings. More-over, as we will see toward the end of this book, it implies the subject's ability to sit still with its pain or sorrow, for without this graver side the soul cannot gain its affective range—cannot, in other words, accumulate the sinuous intensity that accounts for the weightiness of its psychic effects.

THE FUTURE OF CRITICAL THEORY

When I first embarked upon the task of writing this book, I wanted to answer the basic question: What lies beyond poststructuralism? My sense was that poststructuralist criticism had exhausted its freshest energy, and that if critical theory was not to meet an untimely demise, it was necessary to find new sources of vitality. Indeed, it was quite obvious that the posi-tion of progressive critical theory within the academy was already quite tenuous. It was as if the defenders of tradition were wiping their brows with a deep sigh of relief over the fact that the academy had finally over-come its "high theory" fad. This turn against theory was all the more dis-turbing in that its architects seemed to assume that those who do not theorize are somehow wholly outside of theory, as if there existed an idyl-lic realm of living and thinking that escapes the convoluted cynicism of critical thought. The fact that there really is no possible way to operate outside of theory—and that it is precisely when one thinks that one has nothing to do with theory that one is most securely (and naively) caught in its tentacles—did not appear to diminish the glee of the anti-theory forces that seemed content with the idea that texts, authors, and experiences were once again available to us as generous and relatively unproblematized sites of meaning.

Riding this anti-theory wave, my first impulse was to defend the con-tinued relevance of poststructuralism. Yet I did not want to do so without trying to understand its weaknesses as well as its strengths. If the wake of poststructuralism was experienced by many as a "void" or a "crisis," then what was it that poststructuralism had failed to accomplish? What factors might have led to the growing disillusionment with critical theory? And what should we be able to do better in the new era?

There is no such thing as the death of theory. There are highs and lows, peaks and valleys, periods of exuberance and others of hibernation. The pendulum always swings back in the end. It is a question of timbre and timing—of finding the right frequency. I confess that when I first set out to discover the "beyond" of poststructuralism, I in many ways picked a highly inopportune moment to do so in the sense that poststructuralism was under siege, and those attacking were, from my point of view, on the wrong side of the fence. On the one hand, I knew that if I wished to approach my topic with any degree of conviction, I would have to allow myself to step outside of the familiar bounds of poststructuralist criticism. Indeed, how could I possibly expect to find the "beyond" of poststructuralism if I kept myself squarely within the conventions of the very paradigm that I was hoping to surpass? On the other hand, I knew that the danger of being misunderstood as part of the conservative backlash was strong.

This danger was exacerbated by the fact that I was writing my first book, which meant that I could not rely on the trust that more established scholars tend to wield among their peers; it is far easier to criticize and modify what one has helped to build than it is to enter the game during the last inning only to demand a change in the ground rules. I knew, for instance, that my insistence on the importance of lived experience could easily be confused with the idea that raw and untheorized experience is somehow more valid than our ability to question the terms and categories of knowledge that we use to describe such experience. And, indeed, in the early stages of this project I kept running in circles (not scoring any home runs, mind you) because my every effort to break out of the recognizable mold of poststructuralist criticism was read as a "betrayal" of the constructivist cause, or worse, as an attempt to revive traditional humanist ideals of core subjectivity and autonomous self-constitution. The idea that I could be fully committed to constructivist models of subjectivity and psychic life yet still interested in some of the same questions as the so-called "canonical" thinkers appeared to be beyond the realm of possibility. As much as I had expected to struggle with this problem, I admit that it became somewhat difficult over time to ignore the sensation of having somehow fallen into a wholly Foucaultian network of discipline and punish. The one and only thing that seemed protected from deconstruction was deconstructive criticism itself. Rarely prone to bouts of paranoia, I nevertheless increasingly came to feel that the professionalization of my field, with its attendant definitions of acceptable and unacceptable styles of inquiry, was actively keeping me from pursuing my inspiration.

This conflict between professionalization and inspiration is of course a common one, for it constitutes one of the major paradoxes of the academic process of knowledge validation: we wish to advance knowledge, yet we simultaneously seek to ensure that this "advancement" takes place according to the relatively narrow rules and regulations that govern each discipline. In *History After Lacan*, Teresa Brennan (1993) describes the professionalization of the American academy in terms of well-established "fixed" reference points which, when obediently adhered to, provide legitimacy, approval, and security, but which make it difficult for scholars to venture into less well-charted terrains of knowledge production. This, Brennan asserts, explains why American critics rarely choose the boldly "propositional" mode—a mode characterized by confident and far-reaching theories, hypotheses, and lines of questioning—favored by many French intellectuals, but instead remain within the "secondary" mode of meticulous research, exegesis, and criticism. While the American preference for the secondary mode may curtail excessive hubris and unfounded claims to originality, it creates an awkward division of labor whereby the Americans find themselves humbly commenting on and improving the theories produced by the French. As Brennan puts it, "They have the insights, we fill them out, gain Ph.D.s, and have something to say at conferences" (p. xiii).[6]

In this book, I have done my best to resist the temptation to fall into this rather embarrassing pattern of servitude. Although I certainly do a great deal of commenting on Nietzsche, Foucault, Lacan, Kristeva, Irigaray, and Cixous, among others, I have also claimed for myself the right to use the propositional tone when it seems appropriate. The challenge, as Brennan herself acknowledges, is to find a way of combining the two modes so as to be able to produce solid scholarship without killing everything that is daring about it. The risks of this type of writing are greater—you can easily fall flat on your face—but so are its rewards. For me, the risks of the propositional mode were worth taking because they seemed the only means

---

6. There are obviously many brilliant American critics who have been able to break out of this mold. The point, in other words, is not that American critics are not capable of the propositional mode, but merely that the American academic system actively discourages scholars from pursuing this mode. Only those who have managed to rise to the level of academic superstardom seem exempt from this delimitation.

of preserving the seeds of inspiration that had originally steered me to my topic, and that sustained my efforts throughout the long process of translating thoughts into sentences, paragraphs, and chapters.

But if it is inspiration that I am after, perhaps I am altogether in the wrong field. Perhaps I should be writing poetry or fiction instead of theory. One commentator on an early version of this book in fact kindly informed me that my entire endeavor was misguided because—how could I have missed it?—inspiration died in the nineteenth century. This comment gave me pause. What was I being told? I wondered. That in the name of anti-humanist exactitude, I was to write texts that were as flat and devoid of inspiration as possible? That in the name of academic austerity, I was to deprive myself of everything that possessed the potential to infuse my writing with life and vibrancy?

Austerity is often the precondition of genius, but as Nietzsche tells us in no uncertain terms, there is a world of difference between the kind of austerity that leads to creativity and the kind of self-flagellating austerity that produces nothing but debilitating inertia. I would argue that inspiration might not be such a bad thing in the context of the strong push toward increasing professionalization that characterizes the American academy. While I do not wish to imply that professionalization in itself is necessarily a problem—the rapid proliferation of knowledge has in fact made it impossible to stay current in one's field without a degree of specialization and a sustained vigilance to new developments in the discipline—it seems clear that we pay a high price for professionalization when it begins to narrow the field of analysis and to place obstacles on interdisciplinary writing. One of the most frustrating dilemmas of academic work is that it seems commonly acknowledged that the most groundbreaking inquiries often challenge disciplinary boundaries, yet professionalization has made it more and more difficult to engage in such inquiries. And—I will say what many of us down in the trenches are thinking—it is frequently young academics who are forced to sacrifice their intellectual passions for the tedium of tidy topics designed to ensure timely promotion and tenure.

I have positioned myself at the intersection of psychoanalysis, philosophy, and critical theory in part because I want to believe that all three are committed to living in a state of awe and wonder in relation to what is intricate and unknowable about human existence. My hope is that there is something about this state of awe and wonder that is capable of resisting the pull of professionalization (cf. Lear 1999, p. 4). For the same reason, I have also consciously aligned myself more closely with the figure of the public intellectual than with the professional scholar. This is a choice that many academics struggle with, as each alternative brings its own unique pleasures, and it is sometimes very difficult to accurately pour these pleasures into the measuring cups of life and work. It is difficult to weigh the pros and cons in any meaningful manner. For me, the decision came down to the choice between securing the future and living in the present, and I chose to live in the present, guided by the kind of desire that cannot but be "true" on the level of the unconscious even when it complicates things on the rational level. The tone of this book is intentionally speculative—I paint in bold and broad strokes rather than with the precision of close readings (although these are not absent either)—not only because I believe in the value of the "big picture," but also because metatheoretical reflection is what most captivates me as a thinker and writer. Some of the sacrifices that this type of writing demands—such as the impossibility of engaging in detailed analyses of secondary literature—I have made deliberately. Others are no doubt unconscious, and discernible only to the reader.

In this text, I am much more interested in providing a provocative point of departure for further debate around some of my principal preoccupations than I am in offering a fully developed theory of subjectivity and psychic life. I do not in fact even want to pretend to be able to provide such a theory. I see this book as a kind of protracted introduction to a whole host of issues and concerns that have been marginalized in recent decades of constructivist criticism, and I present my arguments in the spirit of a work-in-progress, as a means of contributing to an ongoing conversation about the future direction of progressive critical theory. Moreover, since my aim is to work between categorical divisions rather than to perpetuate them, I have for the most part stayed away from staging attacks on individual thinkers. While I obviously find some accounts more persuasive than others, I know that no theory of psychic life can provide a complete or comprehensive understanding of human experience. It is always possible to discredit an argument, to discover the one detail, flaw, or blind spot that unravels the whole. But this is in many ways the easy way out in the sense that it is much less demanding to quibble over disagreements than it is to build something of solid substance. What interests me is not who is right or wrong, but rather what each thinker can bring to the table that is useful.

I admit to an ardent desire for wide-ranging scholarship that manages not only to stimulate our minds, but also to touch us on a more visceral level. The stakes of this desire are high in that it revolves around the

capacity of constructivist critics to engage with some of the most persistent conundrums of human existence without leaving us empty-handed.
This is not a matter of returning to Wordsworth's England to revive a conception of inspiration, but rather of trying to comprehend what inspiration might mean in the contemporary context—for *us*.

THE LIVABLE LIFE

It would be difficult to write a book about subjectivity and psychic life
without it containing an echo—however muted—of one's personal experience. In the case of this particular text, the echo is clearly audible, and
motivates much of what is contained in its pages. The way I have framed
my inquiry, as well as the manner in which I monitor which issues become central and which fade into the background, reflects the fact that I
have lived my life as a continuous quest for transformation. This is to say
that I have consistently poured my energies into the seemingly interminable attempt to shed the socio-economic uncertainties of the past for a
less anxious, and therefore more livable, present. By "uncertainties" I mean
not only the immediate and often quite unmediated terror that arises from
the lack of material resources, but also the psychic consequences of sustained periods of such terror—how one views oneself and one's place in
the world, how one is perceived by others, how hope weaves its way in
and out of one's life in a shaky and strangely tremulous manner, what it
means to speak from a place of silence, and what it feels like to be continuously relegated to a place of weakness when one knows oneself to be (by
necessity) strong and resilient.

There may be few things in life that stoke one's desire for a vibrant
sense of psychic potentiality more than the exasperated realization that such
potentiality is, for purely practical reasons, beyond one's reach. One often
hears it argued that questions of existential meaning and value are too individualistic to be of interest to progressive thinkers, yet I think that one
of the most devastating aspects of living in difficult economic or socio-
cultural conditions is that these questions are by definition foreclosed. If I
am so interested in Socrates's question about how to live, it is in part because I have witnessed too many others not being able to ask it, or being
forced to turn away from it for fear that the answers would only heighten
their sense of being condemned into a place of impossibility. Indeed, it is
a question that I myself have been able to ask only in the last few years, in

the context of writing this book, and often with the impotent sense of guilt that tends to plague those of us fleeing from the demons of the past.

This guilt runs as follows: Who am I to sit here in the luxurious company of my books and ponder the meaning of life when those I have left behind never had the chance to do so? And do not tell me that they did not want to, that the meaning of life was not a priority for them, for I know that it was. And do not tell me that they were under the spell of "false consciousness"—that the wish to meditate upon the meaning of life constitutes an empty and illusory pursuit of a bourgeois ideal—for I believe that the longing for moments of respite and reflection speaks to something more complicated than a mere cultural norm. I am intimately familiar with the difference between having the time and conceptual space to hear one's thoughts on the one hand and not being able to attain such a refuge of contemplation on the other. This difference cannot possibly be measured by reference to some bourgeois accomplishment.

In the early stages of this project, the question of how to live—which then felt quite exotic and outlandish, even a bit illicit in all of its opulent grandeur—invariably fetched the same seemingly self-evident answer: I should live my life in such a way as to ensure that I do not under any circumstances fall back upon my past. More recently, toward the end of the writing process, the question began to elicit less defensive answers, increasingly turning on my capacity to determine what I mean by what I have been calling the "livable" life. I of course know that any notion of the livable life cannot but be entirely relative, but as the reader no doubt deserves something concrete to hold onto, let me say that today, at this particular moment, the livable life for me means (at least) the following: the absence of war, violence, abject poverty, and oppression; the capacity to define, for oneself, how one understands the livable life; a sense of future possibility; the chance to develop one's potentialities in imaginative ways; a life that includes meaningful employment, that allows for pleasure and play, that contains oases of rest and energized tranquility, that feels animated rather than dejected, and that enables one to meet the inevitable obstacles of existence with a degree of resourcefulness; the ability to form rewarding interpersonal and communal ties; a passionate sense of engagement with the world; an ease of body, mind, and spirit; contemplative wisdom; and—how could it be otherwise?—space and time to breathe (deeply, from the soul).

I keep coming back to the idea of rest and breathing space. Lauren Berlant points out that what is striking about working class fantasies of the so-called "good life" is precisely the quest for resting places, for a sense of solidity, permanence, and social belonging—the ability not only to "make a life," but to return to what appears secure and familiar.[7] Poststructuralism has taught us to consider the yearning for resting places as a regressive form of homesickness for a utopian state of stability. But it seems important to recognize that rest only comes to be regressive from the point of view of valorizing restlessness and mobility—something that in itself is a normative stance (even if it aspires to counter-normative status). Indeed, does not the incessant celebration of mobility feed right into the economic demands of capitalism in that it normalizes speed and constant turmoil, and encourages the uprootedness, dislocation, and disconnectedness of individual life-worlds, thereby producing hyper-efficient workers detached from all intimate connections and the distracting demands of sociality?

The pursuit of resting places may well endorse a certain kind of sociocultural normativity, but I would not want to kid myself into thinking that by aspiring to mobility instead I would somehow automatically escape the vicissitudes of normativity. The larger issue here is that a great many of our conclusions about subjectivity and psychic life depend on how we define "normativity." One of my arguments in this book is that contemporary constructivist theory at times conceptualizes normativity—and therefore what is desirable for the simple reason that it falls outside of normativity—in such rigid terms as to actually diminish our capacity to effectively theorize many of the most pressing concerns of psychic life. For instance, the fact that constructivist theory frequently conceives of profundity in opposition to performativity, materiality in opposition to metaphoricity, stability in opposition to inner fluidity, the imagination in opposition to signification, and existential meaningfulness in opposition to the incessant play of meaning, consistently casts important aspects of human existence outside of posthumanist criticism, excluding, among other things, the possibility of rigorous constructivist insights regarding what it means to exist in the world as a creature of creative capacity. From whose point of view is rest regressive? Who can afford mobility? Do rest and mobility signify the same way for everyone? On what basis do we decide what constitutes "buying into the hegemonic system"?

---

7. All references to Berlant are from a talk entitled "Capitalism, the Children, and Compassion: *La Promesse* and *Rosetta*" that she gave at the Harvard Humanities Center Gender and Sexuality Studies Seminar on March 19, 2004. Quoted with permission.

I would argue that there are situations and vantage points from where it becomes possible to see the quest for resting places as a form of resistance—resistance to various forms of economic or socio-cultural displacement, for instance—rather than of normative complacency. This should not be interpreted to mean that I wish to supplant the ideal of mobility by that of rest in any general sense, for I recognize the matter to be highly context-specific. I would not, for instance, want to imply that queer theory should drop the concept of performativity fluidity, or that postcolonial studies should return to a taken-for-granted vision of a stable "home," or that Gloria Anzaldúa (1987) should abandon the invigorating hybridity of the *mestiza* consciousness. I merely want to point out that "mobility" is not an ahistorical or universal ideal in the sense of fulfilling some eternal Platonic schema. It is an ideal that post-68 theory has—sometimes for very good reasons—set up as an ideal, and it is essential to keep in mind that there are situations in which, as Berlant aptly puts it, mobility becomes a nightmare rather than a dream. It is also important to recognize that those who find it difficult to sustain incessant mobility as a way of life are not necessarily dupes of a dominant cultural norm, but rather articulate a need for security which, in many instances of social marginalization, makes perfect sense.

There is, in my view, no contradiction in criticizing the normative power of fixed identity categories while simultaneously acknowledging the desire of individuals to live their lives in ways that feel safe and reliable. There is also no reason whatsoever to assume that the longing for resting places either requires or produces a unitary and coherent subject in the metaphysical sense. I have already suggested that the subject's constructed status does not mean that existential questions are of no interest to it. Similarly, the fact that the subject seeks spaces of respite and non-conflict does not imply that it therefore embodies the ideal of an essential core identity. There is, I think, a strong tendency in posthumanist theory to string together a whole variety of terms—such as "core," "innate," "essential," "unitary," "coherent," "stable," "constant," "permanent," "non-conflicted," "immobile," "restful," "normative," and "hegemonic," for instance—as if they were immovably bound together by some invisible internal logic. But the fact is that it is quite possible to be non-conflicted without being essential or unitary. It is possible to be restful without being permanent. And it is certainly possible to aspire to a livable—and perhaps even the "good"—life without being normative.

Fantasies of the good life are of course not without danger. Berlant remarks that the promise of the good life can be so seductive that individuals come to mistake the *striving* for such a life—the incessant work and effort imagined necessary for its realization—for the life itself. In this manner, Berlant argues, subjects tend to reproduce "what we should not name the good, but 'the bad life'—that is, a life dedicated to moving toward the good life's normative zone but actually stuck in what we might call survival time, the time of struggling, drowning, holding onto the ledge, treading water, *not-stopping*." This suggests that economic and socio-cultural oppression not only leads individuals to read a perpetual state of crisis as entirely normal and banal, but—even more tragically—as the very precondition of the good life; while the subject believes that it is possible to earn the good life through the successful traversing of crisis, the crisis in the meanwhile grows to be a permanent and commonplace part of life. From this perspective, the economics of scarcity is characterized by a vicious cycle that causes individuals to reproduce the very social forms that fail to secure "the basic dignities of ordinary existence" in the first place (Berlant). The individual's attachment to the promise of the good life is thus at once over-optimistic and frustrated, making life seem the most precious and worthwhile precisely when it is most grueling. In this sense, socio-economic privation is doubly insidious in that even as it dangles the ever-elusive promise of the good life, it effectively closes off the future.

I have written this book because I fear the devastating psychic, affective, and physical toll that is exacted by this kind of life—a life that is lived as an ongoing state of crisis, as an endless vacillation between anticipation and disappointment. I also dread the constriction of psychic space, the squandering of inner potentialities, and the painful sense of lost opportunity that can (but does not always) ensue from a life rendered difficult by circumstance. And I am quite frankly terrified of the sensation of being caught up in the alluring intrigue of future release and redemption, all the while knowing that the future remains scaled down to the task of "getting through the day" (Berlant). This state of double consciousness is not at all contradictory, but merely reflects the psyche's tendency to disavow, even as it recognizes, what it does not want to see. Indeed, this kind of disavowal is in many ways built right into the economics of scarcity insofar as there is rarely an opportunity to pause to reflect upon one's predicament, except perhaps in fleeting and all-too-fragile moments snatched from the claws of time and toil. The interminable effort to produce and reproduce the basic material conditions of one's life, the numbing pace of work and survival, as well as the ever-present "monster in the mind"—as I like to call psychic anxiety—make it difficult to carve out the mental space to confront one's future. And why would one want to, if all that it holds is more of the same?

THE OTHER SIDE OF LACK

I have written this book because I am haunted by the fear of pouring my energies into endeavors that leave no space for creativity—that result in a sense of inner exhaustion rather than of vitality and multidimensionality. In *A Room of One's Own*, Virginia Woolf (1929) describes the way in which poverty corrodes the soul "like a rust eating away the bloom of the spring, destroying the tree at its heart" (p. 38). By this Woolf means to convey the dread and bitterness that bred in her under conditions of material deprivation. Woolf goes on to explain that she inherited a small fortune around the same time as women won the vote in England, and that of the two—the vote and the money—the money was by far the more important because it lifted the state of anxiety that had for so long poisoned her existence. This lifting of anxiety is, viscerally speaking, what I would like to communicate by the idea that the soul enables us to breathe freely. While I cannot quite join Woolf in saying that there is no force in the world that can take away my newly found material security (p. 38), I know exactly the sense of relief that she is talking about, not because I have inherited a fortune but because I know what it means for a difficult past to open to a more livable present. This book is in many ways a testimony to this fact, for it only became possible for me to write it once this transition from the past to the present had begun—once silence yielded to the realization that I too had the right to speak. This is why, more than anything else, this is a book about metamorphosis—about why it is that the past does not always determine the future.

I cannot pretend that the past is not with me, silencing me, placing barriers upon me, shaming me, and causing me to fall when everything and everyone tells me that I should thrive. If anything, I know that the past tends to resurface in the present with a tremendous degree of passion and persistence. But I also believe that it is possible to learn to live with the past in such a way that it does not paralyze the present. This is why one of the principal ambitions of this book is to elucidate the mechanisms of psychic resourcefulness that empower the subject to constructively surmount the impediments to its sense of agency. I would like to comprehend how individuals not only survive their experiences of lack, privation, and abjection, but manage to translate these experiences into a source of existential insight—into something potentially valuable. Lacan once stated that the soul can best be understood as what enables the subject "to bear what is intolerable in its world" (1975, p. 84). Though Lacan may on some level be mocking the Christian ideal of earthly endurance, his statement resonates with me insofar as I am looking for psychic modalities that might allow the subject to come to terms with those aspects of its existence that, for one reason or another, feel unbearable.

Above I emphasized that it is often difficult for individuals to change. But the fact that change is difficult does not mean it is impossible, which is why I think it is important for constructivist criticism to take seriously the processes of inner transformation that arise from, and are enabled by, the fact that creative and imaginative potentiality is a large part of who we are as human beings. I am talking here about the kinds of transformations that truly make a difference. Poststructuralist theory tends to present the subject as constantly in motion in ways that imply that transformation is something that simply happens to the subject, whether it so wishes or not, and that there is little qualitative difference between the various transformations that take place during the subject's lifetime. I readily concede that transformation is an inherent dimension of the human condition, and that it is impossible for any of us to arrive at a definitive telos or resting point. But I also think that this particular way of portraying change can all too easily water down the meaning of the word. If everything is endlessly mutable in the poststructuralist sense, how do we isolate and analyze the changes that actually mean something?

In this book, I am primarily interested in psychic transformations that are meaningful precisely because they are not self-evident or uniformly available. My starting point is therefore in many ways exactly the opposite of how recent constructivist criticism has envisioned the psyche. Poststructuralist theories often depict the psyche as mercurial and restlessly mobile, yet irrevocably caught up in hegemonic processes that make any genuine change impossible. I, on the other hand, would like to present the psyche as relatively fixed (by hegemonic processes, among other things), yet infinitely inventive and capable of far-reaching transformation. This means that the creative capacities that interest me are a matter of depth as well as of surface. They exact an effort even as they bring pleasure. And they enable the subject to actively participate in the production of meaning even as it is forced to make its way in the world of preexisting meanings.

I have chosen this particular approach because I believe that those of us interested in progressive critical theory and political practice need an affirmative lens through which to analyze the realities of hegemonic power in ways that, rather than reiterating the endless inescapability of abjection, provide a more constructive platform for the subject's attempts to attain a degree of agency and inner integrity. The five chapters that follow are all in one way or another organized around the idea that lack (or, depending on the context: abjection, absence, constraint, limitation, melancholia, psychic pain and suffering, etc.) carries the potential for creativity, meaning, value, beauty, and (sometimes, if we are lucky) inspiration. By this I do not mean to suggest that lack is always a source of something valuable— sometimes lack only leads to more lack—but rather that the individual who has learned to transform lack into meaning or value has gained possession of one of life's most precious gifts. Since no life remains untouched by lack (although some lives obviously have more of it than others), the difference between a livable life and an unbearable one may well hinge on the individual's capacity to live with lack in dynamic and resilient ways. In instances when the subject's lack or suffering results from inequalitarian economic or socio-cultural structures, it is obviously most effectively treated by modifying the relations of power that distribute pain and pleasure in uneven ways. But until such a modification takes place, psychic survival is still a necessity. Moreover, there are forms of lack and suffering that no creature of consciousness can escape. Regarding these latter, there is perhaps no better cure than being able to discover the kernel of creative possibility that this lack or suffering may contain.

Chapter 1 explores the possibilities for creative agency—as well as for psychic potentiality and self-actualization—that transpire from the fact that the subject by necessity participates in a social world. My aim is to develop an affirmative alternative to the post-Foucaultian tendency to conceptualize subjectivity as an effect of hegemonic power. I read Nietzsche to show that agency in the constructivist context might best be understood in terms of the kinds of mythologies of being that grant the subject a sense of imaginative empowerment without resorting to ontological models of interiority. I also return to Foucault to demonstrate that as much as he accentuates the socio-historical and discursive constraints within which subjectivity unfolds, he nevertheless believes in the subject's ability to actively participate in the molding of its existential predicament. By drawing a parallel between what Nietzsche describes as the practice of "giving style" of one's character and Foucault's examination of the "art of living" that developed during the Roman empire, I illustrate that Foucault, no less than Nietzsche, is interested in the innovative potentialities of the psyche. The purpose of this comparison is to reveal that, for both Nietzsche and Foucault, creativity is a function of self-limitation rather than of unbounded freedom. This in turn provides a useful framework for comprehending how the fact that the subject cannot escape its socio-historical positionality might not impede its access to agency, but rather make this agency possible by providing the limits or boundaries within which it can be meaningfully negotiated. My point is that while collective structures of sociality and meaning-production undoubtedly place restrictions on subjective enactments, they simultaneously make it possible for such enactments to take on significance. After all, what could the subject's "agency" mean outside of sociality?

Chapter 2 connects the soul to Freud's notion of psychic energy, delineating the ways in which contemporary Western society—and particularly the structures of inequality that characterize this society—can deplete the individual's inner vitality. I argue that such inner impoverishment is an important concern for constructivist critical theory because it erodes the subject's ability to meaningfully engage with the potentialities of its being. I compare Kelly Oliver's analysis of trauma with Judith Butler's model of performative subjectivity to reveal the context-specific nature of progressive politics. I also consider Cynthia Willett's attempt to reorient Western philosophy from questions of autonomy toward a more socially informed account of self-actualization. Although I agree in many ways with Willett's community-oriented slant, I wonder about her tendency to idealize what it means for individuals to participate in communities. I maintain that the historical overvaluation of autonomy cannot be effectively countered by an equally narrow overvaluation of sociality. A stronger distinction between loving and harmful forms of sociality, I suggest, might enable us to better understand why autonomy has been such a persistent ideal throughout Western philosophy. I propose that self-actualization may in the end have less to do with the choice between autonomy and sociality than with the intensity with which the subject is able to experience the various aspects of its life—the autonomous and social alike. Through a reading of Audre Lorde, I illustrate that self-actualization is less a matter of what we do than of how completely we are able to immerse ourselves in what we are doing. The chapter ends with a consideration of passionate eros as a particularly seductive, if volatile, site for the exploration of inner potentiality. This final section of the chapter paves the way for the more psychoanalytic chapters that follow.

Chapter 3 sketches a Lacanian theory of psychic potentiality. By focusing on the clinical aspects of Lacanian psychoanalysis, I illustrate that while much of post-Lacanian criticism has fixated on the alienating effects of constitutive lack, it is possible to discover in Lacan an account of creative capacity. By highlighting the productive relationship that exists between the subject's lack-in-being and its imaginative enablement, I interpret the Lacanian symbolic as a versatile locus of meaning-making and psychic possibility which, though certainly easily co-opted by disciplinary power, should not be equated with this power. I maintain that conflating the symbolic with Foucault's concept of regulatory power divests Lacanian theory of all of its more empowering dimensions. I also compare the Lacanian notion of lack with Heidegger's concept of nothingness to demonstrate that lack is not what destroys psychic potentiality, but rather what allows this potentiality to materialize in its various forms. By relating Lacan's insights on the "poetic function" of language to Heidegger's ideal of "poetically dwelling" in the world, I propose that potentiality for Lacan is a matter of the subject's ability to exchange the enticements of its imaginary world for the meaning-making capacities of the signifier. I argue, in other words, that it is only by accepting lack as the condition of its existence that the Lacanian subject begins to act in inspired and ethically accountable ways. I conclude the chapter by reflecting on what Lacan might still be able to offer feminist and queer theory. By shifting our attention from the hegemonic aspects of the Lacanian symbolic to its more creative dimensions, I hope to present a persuasive account of the continued relevance of Lacanian analysis to progressive critical theory.

Chapter 4 investigates the idea that one of the most important objectives of psychoanalysis is to enable the subject to develop an imaginatively supple relationship to its own past. Ideally, analysis empowers the subject to read the losses and impasses of its past as valuable pieces of its attempt to redefine its future. I suggest that one of the most effective ways to accomplish this goal is to enhance the subject's capacity to overcome melancholy fixations. I try to provide a balanced understanding of melancholia in that I acknowledge the creative potentialities of melancholia at the same time as I highlight the ways in which it can bar the subject's access to these very potentialities. I recognize that the melancholy subject's refusal to abandon its lost objects may in certain circumstances represent an entirely reasonable response to loss. Yet I also insist that it is only when the subject is able to transcend its melancholy states that it can become a subject of creative agency. By reading Lacan and Kristeva side by side, I illustrate that the subject's ability to move from melancholia to meaning-production is a necessary precondition of such agency. I also bring Cixous in conversation with Lacan and Kristeva to better understand how loss can give rise to inspiration. Finally, I consider Luce Irigaray's discussion of the dynamics of passionate love, as well as Kaja Silverman's analysis of what it means to give an "active gift of love," to develop a conception of love that challenges narcissistic structures of desire. My objective is to reveal that it is only by working its way through melancholia that the subject can develop genuinely loving relationships with others.

Chapter 5 highlights the distinction between debilitating and transformative forms of psychic pain and suffering by focusing on psychoanalytic processes of narrativization and self-mythologization. I contrast Schopenhauer's ideal of ascetic self-renunciation with Nietzsche's more "cheerful" form of asceticism to determine what Nietzsche might be able to contribute to psychoanalytic theories of pain and symptomatic behavior. While psychoanalysis aspires to work through pain until it yields to processes of interpretation, Nietzsche stresses that it is at times important to let suffering "lie upon" oneself. Nietzsche, in other words, believes that it is possible to banish suffering too quickly, before one has had the opportunity to internalize the messages it might be trying to communicate. Nietzsche thus regards suffering as a potentially valuable source of insight and creative agency. Indeed, Nietzsche weaves a profoundly affirmative epistemology of suffering that suggests that those who have learned to "exploit" their suffering have attained a more profound and variegated understanding of the world.[8] He accordingly urges us to acknowledge that a familiarity with the sadder side of existence may be an indispensable precondition of our ability to discern what the really important questions are, and how best to take advantage of the fact that we are capable of asking them in the first place. Within this context, I consider Nietzsche's philosophy of *amor fati*—love of fate—in an attempt to differentiate between passively submitting to one's destiny on the one hand and being able to dynamically engage with the potentialities of this destiny on the other. My aim is to show that Nietzsche presents a preeminently consoling philosophy of life that implies that the suffering we experience can at times become a source of revelation and existential insight.

---

8. I would like to thank Nico Carbellano for the phrase "epistemology of suffering."

Self

> My soul has lost its potentiality. If I were to wish for anything, I
> should not wish for wealth and power, but for the passionate sense
> of the potential, for the eye which, ever young and ardent, sees the
> possible. Pleasure disappoints, possibility never.
>
> Søren Kierkegaard, *Either/Or*

LIVING UP TO ONE'S POTENTIAL

One of my aims in this book is to think through the possibilities for creative agency opened up by the fact that subjectivity is culturally constituted through language—that it by necessity arises within collective structures of sociality and meaning-production. The purpose of this first chapter is to initiate this quest through a reading of Nietzsche and Foucault that is designed to show that a constructivist theory of subjectivity need not be purchased at the price of a disempowered self. My objective is to offer an alternative to those contemporary theories of subjectivity, such as Judith Butler's analysis of subjection, that place a strong emphasis on the ways in which the individual remains trapped in hegemonic social systems. Such theories often draw on Foucault's concept of disciplinary power without fully considering the more affirmative ideas that are equally available in his work. They also tend to rely on a narrow understanding of Lacanian psychoanalysis that foregrounds Lacan's examination of the alienating effects of signification at the expense of his more constructive pronouncements regarding the innovative potentialities of

the signifier.[1] As a result, they frequently talk about the relationship between the self and the world as if only the self was permeable and the world
was, in contrast, impermeable and entirely hegemonic. I would like to
develop a more balanced interpretation of the self–world relationship and,
in so doing, highlight the strategies through which the human subject might
be able develop an active and creative relationship to itself.

To state the matter in slightly different terms, I would like to think
about how constructivist theory might be better able to account for what
Kierkegaard in *Either/Or* describes as the soul's "passionate sense of the
potential" (1843a, p. 40). Although it would be possible to interpret the very
ideal of "potentiality" as a clever rule of disciplinary power that holds the
individual imprisoned in normative—and ultimately entirely unattainable—
fantasies of self-actualization, I prefer to understand it as what enables the
subject to remain psychically connected to what is unknown and unknowable about its future. Insofar as being human entails a process of molding
an identity and a way of being in the world, it by definition implies a sense
of potentiality. This sense of potentiality is what keeps subjectivity mobile. As a result, whereas the attempt to "live up" to one's potential might
at times lead to untenable psychic attachments, the alternative—the absence of hope and sense of possibility—seems even less appealing.

The idea that existence implies the gradual blossoming of latent capabilities, and that it is therefore the subject's responsibility to bring to frui-
tion, to the best of its abilities, the full extent of its existential promise,
underlies much of traditional Western thinking about self-actualization. The
limitations of this line of reasoning are obvious from the contemporary perspective, for the belief that the subject's mission is to fully actualize and live
out the possibilities contained, or even implied, in its being all too easily
feeds a preeminently teleological understanding of existential fulfillment.
Perhaps even more problematically, traditional theories of potentiality—
particularly those that draw on the potent legacies of Plato, Kant, and Hegel—
tend to be centered around the search for transcendent meaning in ways that
create firm divisions between matter and spirit, body and soul, passion and
reason, and so on. This means that the Western subject's yearning to exhaust
its potential has often been associated historically with the upward gaze, with
the subject's attempt to rise above the trivialities of ordinary life so as to as-
cend to a nobler and more spiritually exalted realm of experience.

---

1. I will return to this aspect of Lacan in Chapter 3.

It is then hardly surprising that posthumanist theories have not been particularly interested in pursuing questions of potentiality and self-actualization. But the fact that the existential aspirations of contemporary subjectivity cannot be analyzed according to metaphysical conceptions of self-realization does not mean that such aspirations no longer play a part in the individual's psychic landscape. Likewise, the fact that humanist philosophies of potentiality have been dominated by teleological notions of self-actualization does not mean that alternative conceptualizations are not available to us. Indeed, even the Kierkegaardian rendering of potentiality has a great deal to offer to contemporary thought in that it opens to a decidedly fluid and non-essentialist ideal of subjectivity. While Kierkegaard is frequently seen primarily as a precursor to a brand of twentieth-century existentialism that relies on an overly individualistic notion of selfhood, there is arguably also something quite compelling about his vision of subjectivity as a matter of unrealized potentiality in search of variable channels of fulfillment. The fact that Kierkegaard regards subjectivity as a site of perpetual "becoming" rather than of predetermined certainties allows us to think about existence as an open-ended process of encountering the countless possibilities that arise from the subject's capacity to be self-reflexively invested in its future.

In wishing to foreground issues of potentiality and self-actualization I am not interested in a notion of a unified or coherent self. I am also not interested in escaping the human realm in pursuit of some transcendent ideal. And I am most certainly not interested in promoting the American fetishes of wealth, comfort, and worldly success—the dream of being "the best I can be" in the liberal or capitalist sense. Rather, I am invested in the idea that the subject can develop a relationship to itself that is richly textured and multidimensional, that allows it to inhabit the world in ways that feel rewarding and meaningful, and that enable it to connect with others across differences as well as around common interests.

I understand the temptation to argue that questions of self-actualization died with the sovereign self of the humanist tradition, and are consequently either wholly irrelevant to the posthumanist moment or, worse still, ideologically compromising to those of us committed to social justice. However, if we are willing to think about self-actualization as a matter of inner resourcefulness and intersubjective capacity rather than of transcendence, it is obviously not in any way antithetical to progressive political agendas, but rather an essential component of our efforts to create a more egalitarian world. The matter in effect gains a degree of urgency when we consider the fact that existential disempowerment can be particularly prevalent among those struggling to overcome anxieties that result from the lived realities of social injustice. The factors that cause disorientation and despair in the lives of all of us are greatly exacerbated by economic or sociocultural marginalization. As a result, the existential poise that represents a largely inaccessible ideal for even the most privileged may seem even more unsustainable for those compelled to expend their psychic energies in devising and enacting stratagems of social survival.

Oppression attacks the subject's confidence in its ability to navigate the pressures of everyday existence. Perhaps even more fundamentally, it implies that a socially devalued subject could not possibly ever live a meaningful life. It in fact tells such a subject that the very definition of what a meaningful life might look like is something that resides outside of it, in the dominant external world. As a result, paying closer attention to questions of potentiality and self-actualization does not displace our commitment to social justice, but merely modifies our definition of justice by highlighting the ways in which existential empowerment is accessible to some social groups but consistently eludes the grasp of others. This implies that it is not the ideals of potentiality and self-actualization themselves that are necessarily problematic, but rather the exclusionary practices which, first, make these ideals available to some but not to others and, second, place restrictions on what these ideals are allowed to entail, legitimating some definitions but not others. What are the economic, racial, ethnic, gendered, and sexual lines of demarcation that not only place material constraints on our aspirations but, even more disturbingly, limit our very capacity to imagine what it would mean to lead enabled and multidimensional lives?

THE SELF AND THE WORLD

In foregrounding issues of psychic potentiality and self-actualization, I want to refuse the idea that we are—now and for all time to come—beholden to the hegemonic narratives of what these concepts mean. This is why I am disturbed by the fact that constructivist criticism—at least the version of it that circulates in feminist, queer, and other progressive post-Foucaultian venues—often portrays subjectivity in ways that leave little space for creative agency. On the one hand, theorizing subjectivity as an effect of dis-

course rather than of innate inner attributes has offered us a dynamic alternative to static and deterministic models of selfhood and allowed us to
think about the possibilities for social change. On the other hand, the effort to understand how cultural regimes of meaning place limits on subjectivity has tended to produce its own brand of determinism that makes
it increasingly difficult to conceptualize the self as a versatile agent of
meaning-production.

Looking at the history of twentieth-century theory, it is easy to see
how this state of affairs has come about. If it is at all possible to name a
consistent theme that runs through the last few decades of constructivist
criticism, it would have to be the loose consensus that there is no going
back to the universalist self of humanist metaphysics. The humanist self is
of course far from being a timeless entity, presenting a coherent image of
the manner in which human interiority organizes itself in relation to the
world. Even if we adhere to post-Cartesian philosophy, differences of
perspective abound: while Enlightenment thinkers often posited a
self-transparent subject of knowledge, German idealism—the tradition of
Fichte, Schelling, Hegel, and Schopenhauer—was interested in the subject's
dialectical relationship to objects. This latter tradition presents a narrative—
perhaps most memorably captured in the fierce battle-unto-death of the
Hegelian master and slave—that emphasizes the self's dependence on others
for the actualization of its aims. The leap from Descartes's solipsistic subject to Hegel's other-oriented phenomenology is significant. Yet what uni-
fies these divergent approaches is their conviction that it is the human
individual who stands at the center of each and every endeavor—that it is
the thinking, judging, reasoning, imagining, and intuiting self who is the
creator of experience, meaning, and value. In this sense, the humanist tradition works from the self outward, positing a fully integrated consciousness capable of constituting, evaluating, and at times even possessing, the
external world.

The critique of the self-certainties of the humanist subject was well
under way by the end of the nineteenth century. While Marx had done
his best to convince his contemporaries that individual destinies are in
large part dictated by material relations of production that function according to a logic of their own and that consequently put the autonomy
of the self in question, Nietzsche had revealed the inherently ideological
nature of all truth claims, thereby introducing a degree of uncertainty
into all metaphysical endeavors. Most importantly for our purposes, Freud

had theorized the unconscious as a disorderly site of "otherness" within the self that subverts the individual's every effort to project a sense of inner mastery.

However, it is twentieth-century thought that most decisively precipitated the downfall of the humanist self. While structuralism turned to impersonal structures—language, culture, and the incest taboo, for instance—for explanations of social organization and processes of meaning-production, poststructuralism revealed the ways in which these structures themselves are always inherently unstable and in process. Lacan in turn wedded structural linguistics with the best insights of Freud to produce a psychoanalysis wholly divorced from the last traces of biological determinism, and capable of providing a powerful account of the manner in which subjectivity emerges at the intersection of language and desire. More generally speaking, it was the mounting emphasis on language—the realization that the subject can have no relationship to itself, others, or the world except through structures of signification that predate its birth and that will endure long after its death—that triggered the groundbreaking transition from essentialist to constructivist models of subjectivity. Indeed, what most clearly distinguishes twentieth-century theory from earlier philosophies of the self is its insistence on the centrality of language in the constitution of subjective realities.

The shift to constructivist models of subjectivity was nothing short of revolutionary: within the relatively short span of a century, the signifier replaced the soul as the organizing principle of existence—as the seat and origin of psychic meaning. In this manner, the humanist self of full consciousness that had been thought to possess an unmediated access to itself and its meanings was retheorized as a site for the always potentially uncanny and destabilizing disclosure of alterity.

Thus far into this familiar story, all seems well and good. The emergence of constructivist models of subjectivity opened the way for the kinds of theoretical and political advances that I would never wish to trade away. There is, however, one major dimension of this progression of events that I find regrettable, and this is the idea that the subject is by necessity disempowered in relation to collective structures of meaning-making. Looking at the development of twentieth-century thought, it is readily apparent that the more "constructed" the subject became, the more it was drained of creative capacity. This is in large measure due to the fact that language-centered theories initiated a radical reversal in how the self's relationship to the world was conceptualized: rather than viewing the self as an active inventor of meaning, it became customary to underline its precarious marginality in relation to larger systems of sociality and meaning-production (cf. Benhabib 1992, p. 208). This trend finds its culmination in recent post-Foucaultian criticism that tends to downplay the resourcefulness of the psyche in favor of theories aimed at highlighting the ways in which the individual remains irreversibly caught up in disciplinary networks of signification and power.

Butler's analysis of subjectivity, for example, has over time grown less and less open to the idea that the individual might retain a degree of imaginative agency in relation to the world. The pioneering theories of performativity and citationality that Butler developed in *Gender Trouble* (1990) and *Bodies That Matter* (1993) were still explicitly aimed at forging a space for agency from within the realities of disciplinary power. These early texts argued that insofar as the dominant social order cannot contain the subject's ability to enact the parameters of its being in ironic or unfaithful ways, it invariably contains the seeds of its own undoing. The flamboyant or parodic repetition of normative constructs of gender and sexuality, for instance, exposes the performative character of such constructs, and therefore in the long run loosens the restrictions on how gender and sexuality can be lived in the world. Indeed, to the extent that performances are understood to constitute the self rather than merely express a preexisting identity, it makes no sense to talk about authentic or inauthentic, valid or invalid, modes of "being"; the fact that the subject cannot claim grounding in anything beyond its performances defies any attempt to classify it by recourse to some objective measure of truthfulness. This in turn opens a space for transformative and potentially transgressive performances—for ways of seeing and acting differently, and thus of inducing a tear in the fabric of cultural meaning.

The question of agency remains central in Butler's 1997 text *The Psychic Life of Power*. What is different about this later work, however, is that the line between agency and social subjection becomes increasingly blurred and precarious. While Butler's examination of the reiterative strategies of performative subjectivity gestured toward the generative aspects of signification, *The Psychic Life of Power* focuses on the inescapability of hegemonic power in ways that lead Butler to portray subjectivity as being virtually synonymous with subjection. Butler in fact maintains that since we gain social viability only through cultural practices that regulate us—since we are forced to seek the "sign" of our existence in names that are not of our own making—our subjectivity by definition entails a high degree of subjection; insofar as the emergence of subjectivity implies the subject's submission to the hegemonic codes of power, there can be no subject, no social existence, independently of such codes. As Butler puts it: " . . . if the terms by which we gain social recognition for ourselves are those by which we are regulated *and* gain social existence, then to affirm one's existence is to capitulate to one's subordination" (1997, p. 79). In this manner, social categories "signify subordination and existence at once" (p. 20).[2]

Butler recognizes that power is productive rather than merely restrictive in the sense that it quite literally makes the subject. She in fact describes subjection as the "kind of power that not only unilaterally *acts on* a given individual as a form of domination, but also *activates* or forms the subject" (p. 84). However, perhaps because Butler takes Foucault's analysis of the "subjectivation of the prisoner" as paradigmatic of subject formation as such, she ends up all but equating the productivity of power with its disciplinary tendencies. While Foucault himself emphasizes the fact that power gives rise to new kinds of subjective possibilities—and I will return to this later in this chapter—Butler seems to regard power primarily as what subordinates the subject (even as it appears to grant autonomy). Subjectivation, Butler maintains, "denotes both the becoming of the subject and the process of subjection—one inhabits the figure of autonomy only by becoming subjected to a power, a subjection which implies a radical dependency . . . it is clear that the subject produced and the subject regulated or subordinated are one, and that compulsory production is its own form of regulation" (pp. 83–84). Subjection is then "the principle of regulation" (p. 84) according to which the subject is produced as always already subdued and disciplined; autonomy is simply a disguise that covers over the subject's radical dependence on the power that produces it in its own image.

For Butler, social norms are obstinately intractable in part because they provide us with a much-coveted sense of identity and cultural belonging. She proposes that insofar as we yearn for social recognition—insofar as

---

2. Butler's latest book, *Undoing Gender* (2004), takes Butlerian theory in a direction that resonates more closely with what I am trying to accomplish in this book. The present critique should therefore be understood to be specific to *The Psychic Life of Power*.

we desire to be acknowledged in our basic humanness—we tend to form "passionate attachments" to the very conventions that subjugate us (pp. 6–7). Horkheimer and Adorno already argued in *The Dialectic of Enlightenment* (1944) that the "masses" tend to "insist on the very ideology which enslaves them. The misplaced love of the common people for the wrong which is done them is a greater force than the cunning of the authorities" (p. 134). This insight—which Butler so brilliantly democratizes by insisting that the love of hegemonic power is not something limited to the "masses" but rather a universal human predicament—has captured the contemporary critical imagination to such an extent that the central question of inquiry within the theoretical community has in recent years been to understand what it means for the subject to consent to its subordination. As Lauren Berlant remarks, critics have spent a great deal of energy trying to comprehend the dynamics of hope, deferral, and patience that keeps individuals attached to scenes of injustice and subjection even when these scenes remain consistently disappointing. The assumption, as Berlant so succinctly states, is that the individual raised in dominant culture is a "sucker for injustice."[3] What gets eclipsed in these types of analyses, Berlant implies, is the fact that not having a choice about something is not the same thing as consenting to it.

Moreover, the idea that hope is always misplaced, and that there is little that is enriching about collective systems of sociality and meaning-production, leads to a strangely defensive theory of agency, namely the idea that if transformation is possible at all, it can only emerge through the subversive reenactment of the very power that oppresses us—that all we are capable of is more of the same with a slight twist. The belief that systems of sociality and meaning-production are by definition oppressive implies that the subject is forced either to inhabit an inherently hostile world or to seek agency within the gaps or margins of the social order. What this scenario does *not* allow for is the possibility that the individual might be able to participate in the collective structures of the world in agentic and imaginative ways.

Consider, for instance, the dispute between Butler and Slavoj Žižek regarding the idea that there might exist a component of psychic experience that eludes the grasp of disciplinary power. Žižek interprets the

---

3. See footnote 7 of the Introduction.

Lacanian real[4] as an unthematizable "rock" of subjectivity, focusing on the manner in which the real, in evading all efforts of signification, all attempts at discursive approximation, provides a subversive site for the resurfacing of the repressed. The real as the traumatic "kernel" that resists symbolization, but that nevertheless always returns, represents for Žižek a means of conceptualizing the self as not entirely co-opted by disciplinary power (1989, p. 69). Butler in turn argues that Žižek's characterization of the real as inherently rebellious overlooks the tenacity of social power. Butler in fact maintains that Žižek's effort to "freeze" the real outside of discourse results in a "prepolitical pathos" that sidesteps an analysis of how the notion of the real as a site of cultural unintelligibility is produced by the very power that it seems to escape (1993, p. 207). Indeed, for Butler, the suggestions that the subject might have access to a psychic modality—such as the Žižekian rock of the real—that is capable of circumventing social power represent precisely the kind of ideological mystification upon which this power rests.

I am here less interested in the particulars of the debate between Žižek and Butler than in the fact that this debate, on both sides, appears to take it for granted that agency is most directly expressed through the subject's ability to elude the processes of signification that constitute its cultural reality. The crux of the matter seems to revolve around the possibility (Žižek) or impossibility (Butler) of evading the hegemonic stipulates of the signifier, and not, as one might expect, around the creative or transformative potentialities of signification. Although one could make the case that this is merely a semantic difference, and that ultimately one's capacity to evade the signifier's hegemonic meanings amounts to the same thing as one's ability to signify creatively, I think that the distinction is in fact quite important. *As long as critical rhetoric lingers on what the subject as a socially subjected entity should seek to avoid rather than on what it as a creative being could hope to imagine or invent, it remains impossible to think about agency affirmatively.*

Psychic agency demands more than the individual's capacity to evade the signifier's hegemonic law. It calls for the subject's ability to harness its

---

4. The Lacanian real is in many ways the exact opposite of what we in everyday existence think of as our "reality." More properly stated, the real is "reality" in its unmediated form; it is "reality" that feels so immediate that we lack the ability to symbolize it. As such, the real is what remains inarticulable and unrepresentable, what escapes the significatory conventions of the world, and what therefore takes place "in excess" of and disrupts social subjectivity.

imaginative resources in such a way as to give rise to new meanings. Humanist accounts of the imagination spoke confidently about the subject's ability to remold its world. In such accounts, the imagination—often defined as the uniquely human capacity to participate in the production of meaning—was thought to provide an important respite from deterministic models of selfhood. Because the imagination was seen to carry the promise of infinite creative potential, of worlds as of yet undiscovered, it was consistently called upon to sustain the individual's projects of self-actualization. Indeed, not long before the rise of poststructuralism, Sartre still posited that the imagination represents the "whole of consciousness" insofar as this consciousness is able to realize its freedom (1940, p. 216). For Sartre—as for earlier thinkers as varied as Kant, Schiller, Baudelaire, and Oscar Wilde—the imagination was a means of "negating" reality so as to be able to fashion a new and more magnificent alternative.[5] We now know that such imaginative endeavors are inherently ideological in that they take place within the parameters of socio-symbolic power. But does the fact that the imagination cannot be divorced from its cultural underpinnings mean that it cannot be mobilized productively?

Upon entering the posthumanist universe, it is easy to get the impression that the subject, having lost the power to "negate" reality through its imaginative faculties, seeks to negate itself instead (thus the discourse of lack, alienation, and subjection). But why should the fact that the self is inevitably traversed by the signifiers of the social world imply that it is automatically disempowered vis-à-vis this world? As I see it, it is precisely because the self remains open and receptive to the world that it is capable of transforming both itself and the world in the first place; it is the psyche's interaction with the world that makes it creative in ways that then in turn enable it to make a difference in this world. If the psyche is saturated by

---

5. While Kant asserts that the imagination is a powerful agent for creating "a second nature out of the material supplied to it by actual nature" (1790, p. 176), Schiller maintains that it is on the wings of the imagination that the individual is able to leave behind the narrow bounds of the present so as "to strive forward to an unbounded future" (1795, pp. 115–116). Closer to our time, Baudelaire posits that the imagination "decomposes all creation," and with material arranged according to its own principles, "creates a new world" (1859, p. 299). Similarly, Oscar Wilde argues that the purpose of the imagination is "to create, from the rough material of actual existence, a new world that is more marvelous, more enduring, and more true than the world that common eyes look upon, and through which common natures seek to realize their perfection" (1891, pp. 363–364).

the world, the world can similarly be said to be saturated by psychic meaning in the sense that it is always informed by the creations and projections of the psyche; the social world is not merely what forms individuals, but also what exists and takes shape in response to these individuals precisely insofar as they possess psychic lives. The circuits of influence that flow between the social world and the psyche are therefore never unidirectional, originating in the world and winding up in the psyche, but rather circular and reciprocal, allowing meaning to travel in both directions. This explains why the social world, no less than the individual's private world, over time evolves in profound and unpredictable ways.

At first glance, it may seem that the recent constructivist tendency to present the psyche as a vulnerable entity subjected to a hegemonic social world follows quite naturally from the early years of French poststructuralism, for the theories that radiated from post-68 Paris were quite effective in their ability to focus on the ways in which the world enters into and conditions the psyche. Yet I would argue that the post-Foucaultian propensity to fixate on the alienating dimensions of the self–world relationship in fact deprives these earlier theories of their most radical insights. Far from representing the culmination of constructivist theory, the overemphasis on disempowerment hinders our ability to fully engage with the more inspired implications of the fact that meaning by necessity arises between the self and the world. It in fact robs the psyche of imaginative capacities in ways that, to me at least, seem entirely alien to the early sensibilities of French poststructuralism, for French poststructuralism, while certainly driven to discredit the coherent self of humanist metaphysics, was equally driven by a deep appreciation for the richness of meaning.

The work of early poststructuralist thinkers was aimed at the opening up of meaning—the texts of Lacan, Barthes, Derrida, Kristeva, Cixous, and Irigaray, for instance, reveal an intense love of the signifier that celebrates its creative capacities—and much of the euphoria felt within the American critical community upon first encountering this body of work had to do with the wealth of discursive opportunity that it introduced. Not only were writers such as Barthes and Cixous calling for a comprehensive overturn of outmoded and rigid systems of thought, but their writings were infused with the kind of energy that swept the reader into a whirlpool of significatory excess and polyvalence. What was most pioneering about French poststructuralism was precisely its ability to not only argue for, but to display and concretely put into action, the inherent mobility and multiplicity of meaning. This more creative spirit is what has been lost under the more recent emphasis on all-powerful external structures that control the individual's every attempt to participate in the production of meaning.

I am not trying here to rescue a "pure" form of French poststructuralism from its more recent "corruptions," but merely to illustrate that the tendency to downplay creative agency is by no means the only possible adaptation of poststructuralist theory. It seems to me that French poststructuralism presented a model of creativity which, though certainly radically different from the humanist philosophies that preceded it, nevertheless remained ardently devoted to the idea that human beings possess the power to signify in imaginatively exciting ways; the emphasis on the playfulness of the signifier, while accentuating the slippery nature of all processes of meaning-making, at the same time foregrounded the individual's fluid and productive relationship to these very processes.

I therefore find it somewhat surprising that so much of recent constructivist theory has emphasized the impossibilities, rather than the possibilities, of meaning-making. I am baffled by the fact that this theory has focused so strongly on what the subject cannot do—that is, on what it can neither effect nor affect at the level of discourse. I recognize that this approach emerges out of a commitment to social justice that requires a consideration of both material inequality and the psychic experience of powerlessness and subjugation. At the same time—and precisely because I too am committed to social justice—I cannot but feel that the chain of reasoning here functions backward in the sense that oppression cannot possibly be addressed affirmatively by theories that posit the inevitability of psychic colonization. How can we resist oppression if social subjection is presented as everywhere inevitable? Indeed, such theories may paradoxically serve to further abject the already abjected. If we foreclose the possibility of a self capable of both imagining a better world and acting creatively to bring that world into existence, I do not see how we can ever effectively work against our material, discursive, or psychic dispossession.

NIETZSCHE'S METAPHORS

I think that it is a mistake to regard the subject's constructed status as synonymous with its subjection to a hegemonic external world. Quite the contrary, as Nietzsche already showed us more than a century ago, it is precisely the constructedness of the self that allows it to fashion the kinds of personal mythologies of being that contribute to its sense of agency and self-actualization. Indeed, what intrigues me is how and why contemporary theory—which is otherwise so deeply indebted to Nietzsche—has lost sight of the most affirmative dimensions of his philosophy. Why is it that the Nietzschean subject possesses a far greater degree of agency than the subject of contemporary constructivist theory?

The first thing to recognize is that Nietzsche's account of the self–world relationship shares important insights with theories of social subjection, for he argues that the socio-symbolic world is composed of metaphors that over time congeal into the kinds of "facts," "truths," and "realities" that wield an almost tyrannical power over our psychic states. Truth, Nietzsche maintains, is merely "a sum of human relations" which becomes "poetically and rhetorically intensified, metamorphosed, adorned, and after long usage seems to a nation fixed, canonic, and binding" (1873, p. 636). What is at first merely appearance "becomes in the end, almost invariably, the essence and is effective as such" (1882, p. 122). Truths are therefore fictions that are so thoroughly convincing that we come to forget their fictitious origins and instead experience them as compelling psychological realities. For the most part, we live out our social fictions as if they were self-evident truths, and our affective connection to these fictions is such as to make them appear unassailable. Nietzsche's metaphors in fact sink into the very flesh of human existence in ways that make it impossible to divorce them from the emotional demands of this existence; by insisting on the at times devastating actuality of psychic fictions, Nietzsche reminds us that the fictitious origin of "facts" does not diminish their real-life impact—does not alter the fact that they remain a site of human joy, strife, and suffering.

Nietzsche therefore highlights the mechanisms by which social conventions become institutionalized—by which culture manages to obliterate its metaphoric foundations so as to constitute itself as a hegemonic reality. This process of cultural fossilization demands that the representational effort, the labor of producing and sustaining cultural meanings, get obscured by the very credibility of its product; the success of any particular "fact," "truth," or "reality" depends on its ability to cover over the traces of its constructedness so as to pass itself off as what is culturally necessary or desirable. The naturalization process thus not only conceals the rhetorical devices that promote the crystallization of cultural meanings, but also conjures away the particularities of social power, including the intricate disciplinary apparatus that forecloses the possibility of some meanings while endorsing and facilitating others.

Nietzsche therefore foreshadows the insights of contemporary theory regarding the pervasiveness of disciplinary power. Indeed, what Nietzsche portrays as the fossilization of fictions into facts is akin to what Roland Barthes (1957) describes as the cultural process of myth-making. Barthes argues convincingly that insofar as mythologization naturalizes social constructs, it conceals the ideological character of cultural representations, and cloaks the relations of power that inevitably underpin our efforts of making sense of the world. In this manner, mythologies lend legitimacy to already existing social hierarchies, allowing those on top of these hierarchies to pass on their cultural fictions as the "realities" that structure our lives. Barthes's objective, like that of Nietzsche, is to unveil the mythological character of existence, and to denaturalize what we take to be universally true, valid, and reasonable. Indeed, much of the interpretative power of poststructuralism can be traced back to this single insight—derived from Nietzsche—regarding the mythological nature of all "truths."

As a feminist, I have been particularly influenced by those deconstructive endeavors that have interrogated the elaborate collective mythologies that maintain fixed and wounding conventions not only of gender and sexuality, but also of class, race, and ethnicity. I would consequently not wish to argue against the idea that mythologies often injure us in acute and overwhelming ways. Yet I would insist that if we are to follow Nietzsche in maintaining that mythologies possess the power to shape our realities, we should give equal credence to his strong conviction that they also carry the potential to radically restructure these realities. After all, the pervasiveness of disciplinary power is for Nietzsche only half of the story—and the less interesting half for that—in the sense that much of his philosophy is designed to show us how we can live creatively despite our immersion in collective structures of meaning-production.

As much as Nietzsche stresses the processes of reification that elevate metaphors to the status of truths, he at the same time views the metaphoricity of existence as a basis for the innovative reconstruction of social fictions. Nietzsche in fact emphasizes that while merely pointing out the metaphoric nature of "reality" does not prevent it from functioning as reality, it is possible to fashion a new reality simply by formulating a new set of metaphors (1882, p. 122). In this manner, the fact that our beliefs, values, and ideals partake of mythologies by definition holds them open to creative reconfiguration. The notion of mythology cannot therefore be placed in a simplistic adversarial relationship to poststructuralism, let alone feminism or other progressive social movements, for it resides at the very heart of both psychic and cultural transformation. As Barthes (1957) notes, any critical gesture toward demythologization is one that unavoidably remythologizes; there can be no unraveling of myth without the creation of counter-myth (p. 135).

Nietzsche proposes that we who "think and feel at the same time are those who really continually *fashion* something that had not been there before: the whole eternally growing world of valuations, colors, accents, perspectives, scales, affirmations, and negations" (1882, pp. 241–242). Nietzsche thus asserts that what makes us human is our capacity to generate new meanings and values. He moreover emphasizes that it is only because we tend to overlook the fundamentally metaphoric nature of existence that we come to lose confidence in our ability to reshape the world. This veiling over of life's metaphoricity is for Nietzsche indicative of what is insipid and enervated, worn-out and powerless to inspire, and what consequently engenders subjects who are blindly obedient of conventional morality. As a result, what distinguishes the Nietzschean noble—the brave and inventive spirit who is light-footed and persistent enough to reach the top of the mountain—from the so-called "herd" is its ability to resurrect the forgotten "art" of existence so as to live it as a *willed*, rather than as a fossilized, fiction. As Nietzsche famously puts it, "As an aesthetic phenomenon existence is still *bearable* to us, and art furnishes us with the eyes and hands and above all the good conscience to be *able* to turn ourselves into such a phenomenon" (1882, pp. 163–164). By this he means that the metaphoric character of our existence should not in any way trouble us, for it is precisely what allows us to approach the world as creators, inventors, and myth-makers. Indeed, the mistake we make is to fail to recognize that our strength as humans lies *not* in our capacity to discover truth (which is an inherently misguided endeavor), but rather in our talent for spinning all kinds of enchanting fables about the world and about ourselves.

For Nietzsche, we are at bottom artists—individuals capable of great feats of imaginative resourcefulness. He talks about this imaginative resourcefulness in remarkably concrete terms, as a matter of becoming "the poets of our life—first of all in the smallest, most everyday matters" (1882, p. 240).[6] This capacity to take a poetic approach to one's existence is for

---

6. Alexander Nehamas (1985) has discussed this aspect of Nietzsche's philosophy at length.

Nietzsche one of the characteristics of existential nobility. The noble insists on its ability to actively fashion, rather than remain passively fashioned by, the conventions that govern its socio-symbolic universe. Creative agency is therefore a matter of being able to dynamically participate in the construction of the meanings and values that govern the world rather than simply submitting to the familiar and often quite convenient guidelines of the collectivity.

To make the matter even more tangible, Nietzsche likens existence to a dream, and maintains that it is the subject's ability to both recognize the dream as a dream and, in spite of this recognition, to continue the act of dreaming, that sustains its capacity for creative self-fashioning. Since there is no escape from the dream—no essence or thing-in-itself behind the veil of appearances that would provide an existential basis outside of the dream—the best that the subject can do is to enthusiastically throw itself into the task of dreaming. Indeed, it is only the subject who possesses the kind of double vision that is able to behold both the dream and the act of dreaming—to acknowledge the fictitiousness of the dance, yet go on dancing—who belongs to those rare "masters of [the] ceremony of existence" (1882, p. 116) who know how to invent their own particular poetics of existential enablement.

Nietzsche describes self-poeticization as a matter of the subject's ability to "give style" to its character. The self-stylizing subject directs its double vision at the spectacle of the self and reaps genuine gratification from a personal mythology that is felt to be real even as it is known to be illusory. This art of self-stylization is practiced by those "who survey all the strengths and weaknesses of their nature and then fit them into an artistic plan until every one of them appears as art and reason and even weaknesses delight the eye." Self-stylization thus revolves around the subject's artistic dexterity—around its capacity to conceal, disclose, accent, reinterpret, and transform aspects of its being in ways that empower it to read them as parts of a meaningful whole. As Nietzsche explains, the ugly and the unpolished, along with the lovely and the refined, retain their place in the overall design. In this sense, the artistic constitution of the self entails a careful transmutation of all of its characteristics, be it through a courageous sublation of the negative, or a meticulous cultivation of the positive. Style in this sense is not merely a matter of good taste, but infiltrates, inculcates, and inhabits the most profound layers of the individual's psyche. For Nietzsche, the quality of the individual attributes is relatively insignificant in comparison with the overall pattern that they form. What *is* significant in the end,

Nietzsche emphasizes, is that "the constraint of a single taste" has formed everything. As a result, self-poeticization calls for a great deal of discipline and stylistic restraint, which is why it can only be attempted through "long practice and daily work at it." This is one reason Nietzsche maintains that it is only the strong who "enjoy their finest gaiety in such constraint and perfection under a law of their own" (1882, p. 232). The noble man, Nietzsche suggests, honors in himself not only "the man of power," but also "the man who has power over himself" (1886, p. 196).

THE DOER BEHIND THE DEED

Bracketing for a moment the fact that Nietzschean self-mythologization seems to assume the kind of mastery over the self that contemporary theory has taught us is impossible—and overlooking for the time being the fact that it advances an explicitly elitist vision of existential nobility—it is clear that it seeks to promote those parts of life that remain alive and capable of transformation. Nietzsche invites us to consider the fact that myths are con-stitutive of our reality in two very different ways. On the one hand, we remain inextricably enmeshed in collective mythologies that predate our existence, organize our sense of selfhood, and quite often entrap us in destructive patterns of behavior. On the other hand, myths enable us to access an imaginative world that empowers us to construct alternatives to the social fictions that are handed down to us at birth. By this I do not mean that we are free to imagine our lives as we please, for there is, strictly speaking, no such thing as a purely personal mythology. If poststructuralism has taught us anything, it is that our private stories are always inevitably embedded within the stories of the collectivity. This imbrication of our private narratives in their larger context is, moreover, what in large mea-sure accounts for their oppressiveness; it is because our personal processes of making sense of the world are never entirely separate from normative paradigms of meaning-making that we frequently become implicated in meanings that undermine our psychic well-being. As a result, it would be counterproductive to try to conceive of a mythological realm that would somehow remain wholly uncontaminated by regulatory power.

At the same time, I would argue that our inability to distinguish be-tween myths that harm us and others that enrich us leads us to view the world too negatively—as an adversary rather than as a chance to mobilize the innovative resources that we all possess by virtue of being human. As Nietzsche proposes, it is not our ability to bypass fictions that makes us strong but rather our capacity to creatively manipulate the fictionality of our multiple "realities." This implies that it may be much more productive to enter deeper into the process of myth-making than to dwell on the impossibility of escaping collective mythologies. Mythologies allow us to constitute a sense of who we are, as well as to contemplate the contours of what we would like to become. As a result, it is only by actively engaging with the mythological possibilities of the world—by acknowledging that the fictions we weave can and do make a difference in the world—that we can begin to transform it.

The Nietzschean subject aspires to fully live out the potentialities of its particular existential mythology. Nietzsche's notion of living one's life as poetry is significant precisely because it encourages us to think about agency as a matter of self-mythologization. Indeed, if posthumanist theory has frequently found it difficult to reconcile the collapse of metaphysical models of selfhood with the ideal of agency, Nietzsche admits no contradiction between the constructed subject and self-authorship. Because by necessity we operate within the realm of language, our understanding of the self can never be anything but metaphoric—we can, in other words, never know the "truth" of ourselves or of our meanings—yet this lack of ontological justification, far from disenfranchising us, is what allows us to experience ourselves as beings of potentiality, to treat our existence as an open-ended narrative rather than as a teleologically motivated search for definitive existential foundations. In this manner, Nietzsche offers us a model of subjectivity that is at once constructivist and strongly agentic.

But if the self does not possess a metaphysical core of autonomy, where does its power come from? To put the matter differently, how are we ever to reconcile Nietzsche's ideal of the self-poeticizing subject who is capable of disciplining the various components of its being into an artistic plan of great stylistic coherence with his well-known assertion, in *On the Genealogy of Morals* (1887), that there is no doer behind the deed? In a passage that has been famously adapted by Butler, Nietzsche maintains that it is only the language of cause and effect that seduces us to divorce the "subject" from its "actions." In the same way that we separate lightning from its flash, and regard the latter as an action caused by the former, we tend to separate the doer from its deeds. We, for instance, separate strength from the expression of strength, "as if there were a neutral substratum behind the strong man, which was *free* to express strength or not to do so." However, Nietzsche insists, "there is no such substratum; there is no 'being' behind doing, effecting, becoming; 'the doer' is merely a fiction added to the deed—the deed is everything" (1887, p. 45).

Butler correctly reads Nietzsche's statement as a denial of the possibility of subjectivity apart from performativity (Butler 1990, p. 33). Since there is no essential self behind its performances, it is the repeated performance of one's identity that produces the psychologically as well as socioculturally compelling metaphorics of interiority. In this sense, Nietzsche anticipates much of contemporary performance theory in refusing to distinguish between essence and appearance, core and surface, self and performance; for Nietzsche, as for Butler, the self *is* the performance. So far so good. However, the trouble starts when Butler takes Nietzsche's statement to mean that Nietzsche refuses the possibility that the human subject could be the "agent" of its own actions. I think that to read Nietzsche as a theorist of performativity without at the same time acknowledging his relentless emphasis on the subject's creative capacity—on its capacity not only to fashion itself but to actively intervene in the surrounding world—is to erase what is most empowering and hopeful about his philosophy.

For Nietzsche, there is no doer behind the deed . . . except that there always is. I think it would be very difficult to argue in any unqualified manner that Nietzsche conjures away the doer from behind its deeds. If anything—as I have already implied—it would be possible to accuse Nietzsche of vastly overestimating the extent to which the subject possesses agency over its actions. The Nietzschean noble is a self who masters the art of "watching" itself from a distance so as to be able to manipulate the outlines of its existence (Nietzsche 1882, p. 133). In this sense, its "performativity" remains deliberate and keenly self-aware. Indeed, the wakeful attentiveness of the performer—like the dreamer's ability to recognize the dream—is indispensable, for without the performer's consciousness of its performance as a performance, the performativity of the noble would scarcely be different from the rote performativity of the herd.

Self-stylization endeavors to enhance the subject's sense of agency. Yet it obviously also presumes such agency. Although this may seem like a frustrating paradox, I find it to be an enormously productive point of tension, for if we are able to figure out how Nietzsche can have it both ways—how he can retain the ideal of an agentic doer without upholding a metaphysical notion of foundational subjectivity—we will have discovered a way of conceptualizing agency in the constructivist context. This in turn might help us work our way through the deadlock of thinking about posthumanist subjectivity through the disabling lenses of subjection and hegemonic power. It might enable us to open a space for imaginative agency at the very heart of anti-humanist theory.

The solution to the paradox can be found in what I have already out-lined, namely the power of metaphors to mold our existence. I would like to propose that for Nietzsche the doer behind the deed—the performer behind the performance—is one important locus in which metaphors manage to congeal into the kinds of "truths" that wield a tremendous power over the subject's existence. This is to say that the process of naturaliza-tion, described above in the context of the fossilization of collective fic-tions, functions equally efficiently on the level of the individual, producing a psychologically convincing inner "reality" that the subject comes to live as its self. This means that there is a self behind its actions, even if it is not an ontologically secure self. This self arises from a temporary crys-tallization of metaphors that are able to exercise a high degree of agency when they are fully operative in the subject's psychic life. The Nietzschean self is never stable, for Nietzsche recognizes that each of its momentary incarnations is bound to be supplanted by new incarnations that are nec-essarily always already in the process of solidification; each transitory version of the self will in the end succumb to a more recent version—to a more recent set of metaphors. Yet this does not in the least lessen the power of these metaphors at the moment when they have seized hold of the individual's psyche.

This insight allows us to envision a sedimented sort of subjectivity where those layers of metaphoric meaning that have already solidified into "truths"—that are already established enough in the individual's psychic landscape to appear intrinsic—exert a creative power over more recent layers that are still in the process of being formed. In this model, the longer-standing layers of meaning are able to determine the shape and content of the more recent layers; the self acquires depth and imaginative agency not from any human essence, but from the gradual accumulation of meanings, all equally metaphoric, yet also at the same time entirely convincing (at least for the time being). The self behind the performance therefore func-tions as a layered depository of former performances, and the self-stylizing subject emerges as an endless process of revitalization in which the form of the newly constituted self is conditioned by the character of earlier per-formances. The fact that the older self is no more ontologically real than the emerging one in no way diminishes its supremacy over the latter for, as we have seen, fossilized fictions can be compelling, even tyrannical. Yet this "tyranny" of the old self must always in the end yield to a new birth. The rejuvenating impulse of the Nietzschean self can therefore only be understood in terms of its suicidal impulse.

The problem of course remains that the initial layers of metaphoric meaning that establish us as creative and agentic subjects *do* originate in the external world. None of us arrives in the world with a fully developed set of internal metaphors securely in place. As a result, the account that I have given may seem to merely reinforce the idea that subjectivity cannot be meaningfully distinguished from processes of social subjection. The fact that the metaphors that inhabit our psyches in the manner that I have described undoubtedly arise from outside of us implies that our psychic structures come into being exactly through the kind of Althusserian interpellation that Butler analyzes. Yet I would argue that while socio-cultural interpellation may initiate us into hegemonic systems of power, it simultaneously contributes to the solidification of our psychic structures in ways that over time grant us the capacity for both action and discernment. Though we may be subjected to power, we are also given the power to contemplate our lives, including the capacity to think critically about the power structures that surround us. In other words, once the initial layers of metaphoric meaning have been laid down, they can help us make decisions about subsequent layers and screen out at least some of the unwanted elements of social power. As adult subjects —as subjects with well-established psychic lives—we do have a fair amount of choice about which meanings we invite into our inner world. This choice is obviously far from infallible, for the defenses that we set up against unsolicited cultural inscriptions are not always strong enough. Moreover, a substantial part of socio-symbolic acculturation takes place on a wholly unconscious level, which means that we cannot always circumvent it. But even so, I think it would be incorrect, not to mention dangerous, to posit that we do not have any control over the form or direction of our psychic lives. Is not one of the privileges of adulthood that we are not entirely defenseless against the cultural chatter that surrounds us?

My disagreement with Butler may be largely a matter of emphasis— of seeing not only what is disempowering but also what is potentially empowering. I do not deny that the social world conditions us. But does this mean that we are always and forever subjected? It seems unnecessarily defeatist to read the social world as inherently disabling when it is in fact a complex network of meanings that offers us endless opportunities for innovative self-enactments.[7] Given that subjectivity is intrinsically so-

---

7. Butler's theory of performative subjectivity of course recognizes this, which is why it is more agentic than her later theory of social subjection. However, as I will argue below, even performance theory does not offer us a strong enough account of creative agency.

cial, claiming that sociality is the cause of all evil—and that it is only capable of evil—immobilizes us in a theoretical framework that does not leave
a whole lot of wiggle-room. The more interesting question for me is the
extent to which we possess the capacity to retroactively reconfigure our
earliest interpellations—the foundational layers of metaphoric meaning that
constitute us as subjects. If early layers of metaphoric meaning exert a creative power over later layers of the psyche, is the reverse also the case? Can
we use fresh metaphors to alter the structure of our most entrenched and
firmly internalized psychic meanings? Nietzsche implies that we can. And
as we will see in the second half of this book, psychoanalysis is premised
on the idea that we can.

For the time being, it is important to recognize that reading Nietzsche
in the manner that I have done allows us to conceive of agency in the context of a fundamentally anti-essentialist view of subjectivity. The Nietzschean
self is strong not in spite of, but rather because of, its constructed character.
Nietzsche reveals that while metaphors can certainly induce us into states of
subjection and complacency, they can also sustain us in our quest for creative agency. Moreover, Nietzsche's multilayered model shows that it would
be misleading to assume that the performatively constituted self is automatically a superficial one, readily readable on the level of its discursive inscriptions. Nietzsche in fact suggests that the performative self is capable of the
same kind of feeling, sensibility, and inner intensity as the so-called humanist self. It is also as vulnerable to psychic injury, as fragile and woundable,
and consequently as desperately in need of strategies of living, as any more
metaphysical self. Nietzsche is notorious for being able to skid the surface of
life without losing sight of its depths. It may be for this reason that he manages to theorize a self that is constructed without being one-dimensional, a
self whose performativity builds layer upon layer of psychic meaning and
complexity.

FOUCAULT'S CARE OF THE SELF

If Nietzsche's empowering vision of creative agency has for the most part
been neglected by contemporary theories of performativity, it is because
the Nietzschean strain tends to be undercut by a Foucaultian insistence on
the omnipresence of power. Foucault explains that power infiltrates all of
our social relationships—that it is ubiquitous yet diffuse—which means
that there can be no outside of power, no possibility of placing oneself in

clear opposition to power. Power and resistance are like partners in an eternal dance; the two parties may be dancing to a slightly different tune, yet ultimately they both partake of the same dance. This is a valuable insight, for it allows us to understand how our most taken-for-granted ideas and passions, even those that we take to be original or innovative, can be infused by collective systems of power. Like the Nietzschean processes of socio-cultural fossilization, power in the Foucaultian sense is good at erasing its tracks, which means that we are often not conscious of the manner in which our most basic beliefs and ways of being in the world reflect specific relations of power. We may think that we are doing things of our own volition when we in fact insert ourselves into collective scripts of power. In this sense, it is precisely when we think that we are the farthest from power—when power is the least visible to us—that we are most helplessly wedged in its machinery.

Foucault is obviously a brilliant analyst of social subjection and disciplinary power. But this should not lead us to overlook the fact that he conceptualizes the subject's role in its own self-constitution in ways that follow quite closely in the footsteps of Nietzsche. Here I am not merely referring to the famous Foucaultian assertion that power always produces its own resistances (Foucault 1976, p. 95). Rather, I am talking about the practical consequences of his conviction that power is actively generative rather than merely prohibitory, restrictive, or negating—that it opens the path to the articulation of meanings even as it delimits the field of discursive possibility. Foucault argues that instead of viewing power as something that simply controls and represses us from above, we need to recognize that it causes effects, meanings, and sites of psychic intensity. Power, in other words, is not merely what censors us, but also what mobilizes and motivates us, and what enables us to act in the world. In this manner, Foucault counters the idea that power is primarily a negative force that places the weight of the law upon us. Instead, he views power as a positive energy which, while certainly curtailing the kinds of meanings that are allowed expression, is capable of giving rise to various discourses and self-enactments (see Foucault 1976).

In *The Care of the Self*, Foucault (1984) presents a theory of the "art of living" that shares many similarities with Nietzsche's ideals of self-stylization and living one's life as poetry. Foucault explains that during antiquity, and particularly at the height of the Roman Empire, there was an increasing emphasis placed on the necessity to care for one's self. Although Socrates had already advanced the theme of the care of the self, later philosophers,

such as Seneca, Plutarch, and Epictetus, made it the focus of their doc-
trines, paying particular attention to the various sophisticated techniques
of self-cultivation that could be brought to bear on the individual. This
intensification of the subject's relationship to itself sought to establish the
self as a locus of study, scrutiny, reflection, modification, and transformation. Indeed, the subject was called upon to take itself as the object of the
kind of contemplation and action that would over time lead to self-improvement; the art of living became, among other things, an unending exercise
in self-refinement. The human individual was defined as a special kind of
being whose destiny it was to care for itself. Epictetus, for instance, believed that the care of the self was a "privilege-duty" that ensured the
subject's freedom while demanding it to take a diligent interest in itself
(Foucault 1984, p. 47).

Epictetus's formulation prefigures those later philosophies, among
which we can count Sartrean phenomenology, that define humanness in
terms of self-reflexivity and the subject's absolute duty, obligation, or responsibility to itself. Foucault remarks, however, that what is distinctive
about the care of the self in the context of antiquity is that far from being
a purely individualistic endeavor, it gave rise to a whole variety of social
practices, ranging from intimate interpersonal confidences, communications, and exchanges to highly institutionalized modes of knowledge production. One engaged in the care of the self when one sought or gave advice
as much as when one turned inward in contemplative moments of self-
questioning. The care of the self was thus not merely "an exercise in solitude, but a true social practice" (p. 51). In this manner, the care of the self
engendered intricate social networks, of which the practice of philosophy,
and the attendant conventions of discussion and debate, were among the
most important. Philosophy was in fact considered a quasi-spiritual practice that was designed to impact people's lives on a very concrete level.

The fact that the care of the self entailed a social dimension did not,
however, mean that it encouraged the individual's indiscrimate immersion
in the concerns of the world. Quite the contrary, the care of the self asked
the subject to withdraw from those of its worldly preoccupations that kept it
from cultivating its soul. Such cultivation of the soul, Foucault maintains,
was not simply a matter of a general or diffuse attitude, but called for practical exercises—such as reading, writing, meditation, and introspection—
that were designed to allow the subject to "return" to itself. The purpose of
these exercises was to place the whole of one's life before one's eyes so as to
become better acquainted with oneself (pp. 50–51). As Foucault asserts, the

cultivation of the soul was "not a rest cure" (p. 51), but a form of disciplined self-examination that was intended to distill the individual's existence to its essentials. Energy was not to be squandered in "an idle curiosity" regarding either one's own everyday agitations or the anxieties and ambitions of others. Rather, the goal was to acquire a high degree of mastery over the movements of one's interiority. By escaping the enticements of the outside world, one became capable of a pleasant kind of tranquility that allowed one to live "like a harbor sheltered from the tempests or a citadel protected by its ramparts" (p. 65). As the philosopher Demetrius explains, the soul that has abandoned its dependence on external things stands on "unassailable grounds" in the sense that it is no longer subject to the unpredictable whims of fortune; since fortune "can seize none except him that clings to her," the individual who recoils from the external world ensures that every weapon that is hurled from this world "falls short of the mark" (quoted in Foucault 1984, p. 65).

The emphasis on self-mastery as a means of protecting oneself from an unreliable world was of course far from new. Many of the pre-Socratic schools of thought, including the Stoics, the Epicureans, and the Cynics, had already underscored the idea that since an excessive attachment to the concerns of the world causes suffering, the subject who wishes to shield itself from pain needs to find a means of tempering its passions. The Stoics, for instance, held the passions to be the cause of vice insofar as they possess the power to engulf the individual in irrational and uncontainable emotionality. Similarly, the Epicureans, while promoting pleasure as the supreme goal of life, nevertheless advocated the necessity of a simple, at times almost ascetic lifestyle, for they recognized that the immoderate pursuit of pleasure only enlarges the subject's desires and leaves it vulnerable to the waywardness of the world. The Cynics in turn advised the subject to minimize its needs so as to guarantee its sovereignty. What these ancient philosophies share is the conviction that existential composure can only be attained when one restricts one's desires and reduces one's wants to what can actually be attained; only those who have eliminated their longing for external gratification possess the capacity to live calmly, liberated from the exigencies of passion.

The composure that the subject sought through the care of the self was therefore not a matter of practicing renunciation for its own sake, but rather a carefully elaborated means of declaring one's independence from the external world. It was a way of asserting that one was "answerable only to oneself" in the sense of exercising over oneself an authority that nothing could erode or disturb (p. 65). The quiet satisfaction that the subject was able to take in itself followed Seneca's injunction that one should seek to find the sources of one's pleasure within oneself, to "rejoice only in that which comes from [one's] own store" (quoted in Foucault 1984, p. 67). Seneca contrasts this serene type of pleasure with *voluptas*—with pleasure that originates from outside the self—and posits that while *voluptas* might be more acutely felt, it is always tinged with the fear of loss and uncertainly and, as such, is inferior to the pure and reliable sort of pleasure that the subject is able to generate from within its own being. Because *voluptas* is inherently conditional in that it involves external objects that the subject can neither possess nor control, it always carries the risk of disappointment. As a result, it should only be indulged in sparingly.

The care of the self thus gave rise to an "ethics of pleasure" (p. 67) that elevated the subject's pleasure in itself over the kinds of pleasures that it might derive from external objects. Although this ethics was characterized by exercises of abstinence and self-limitation, Foucault stresses that it was not necessarily a matter of heightened prohibitions as much as of an art of existence that revolved around the ideal of self-possession. The exercises of self-control that constituted such an important part of this ethics were thought to provide the conditions for an enjoyment that was impervious to external disturbances. As a result, if sexuality became increasingly viewed as dangerous, it was not always because of a moral judgment against sexual pleasure per se, but rather because such pleasure seemed capable of compromising the self's supremacy over itself (pp. 238–239). From this perspective, the more restrictive outlook on pleasure that came into being during the Roman Empire was not necessarily rooted in an increase of austerity, but merely in the wish to ensure the subject's autonomy as well as its access to what was considered a far superior sort of pleasure.

The self-mastery that Foucault describes as emblematic of ancient attempts to care for the self is problematic for all the same reasons as the mastery of the Nietzschean noble. The Freudian discovery of the unconscious alone makes it impossible to concede that the self could ever possess unconditional mastery over itself. However, as is the case with Nietzsche's notion of self-fashioning, Foucault is not necessarily depicting mastery as something that has been—or ever could be—achieved but merely the subject's struggle to approximate the ideal of such mastery. The fact that the subject can never master itself does not mean that it cannot profitably engage in the task of self-improvement. Moreover, there is something quite convincing about the idea that pleasure is often most intensely felt when it takes place in the context of restriction and delimitation. As Jeanette Winterson once put it, passion is "sweeter split strand by strand. Divided and re-divided like mercury then gathered up only at the last moment" (1987, p. 59). Similarly, the ancient art of cultivating the soul was, in the tradition of Epicurus, a matter of showing how in the satisfaction of the most elementary needs "one could find a fuller, purer, more stable pleasure than in the delight one might take in all that is superfluous": by dispensing with everything that habit, fear of the future, concern for reputation, or taste for ostentation had taught one to revere and pursue, one was believed to attain a more unadulterated pleasure (Foucault 1984, p. 59). The mastery that the individual sought through the practice of self-discipline was therefore not solely a matter of a rule exercised over disorderly desires, but also a means of engendering new forms of enjoyment. The ethics of pleasure, and the care of the self that this ethics served, was in this sense not merely a question of limitation but also of augmentation. It was self-affirming as well as restrictive, productive as well as constraining.

STYLE AND *ASKESIS*: AGENCY IN THE CONTEXT OF CONSTRAINT

What interests me about Foucault's care of the self is that Foucault presents a subject who is not merely passively molded by power, but able to dynamically participate in the fashioning of its own subjectivity.[8] Foucault may have less faith in the individual's capacity for agency than Nietzsche, but he is still keenly interested in questions of psychic resourcefulness. By this I do not mean that Foucault abandons the idea that subjectivity is discursively constituted within socio-historical conditions of power. But it is clear that these socio-historical conditions are not, in *The Care of the Self*, merely limiting, but rather facilitate the emergence of a certain type of subjectivity and mode of inhabiting the world. In the words of Arnold

---

8. The reflections that follow have profited from my exchanges with David Plunkett. David urged me to reread *The Care of the Self* in search of an alternative to the subjection model, and he also directed me to the work of Arnold Davidson. The idea that Foucault, while emphasizing the ways in which the subject remains embedded within socio-historical and discursive structures of power, is nevertheless profoundly interested in the subject's capacity to actively participate in the fashioning of its existence arises directly from my conversations with David.

Davidson (2001), they constitute the "conditions of possibility" for specific processes, practices, systems of knowledge, and ways of talking about the self.

The Foucault of *The Care of the Self* is at least as much—if not more—interested in the conditions of possibility for specific discourses about the self as he is in the ways in which the individual is restricted or dominated by power. Indeed, Foucault's objective is to uncover the socio-historically and discursively specific operations of knowledge that created a conceptual opening for the kind of subject that was preoccupied with the task of caring for itself. This is not to say that the subject that Foucault portrays in *The Care of the Self* is free or original in any metaphysical sense. It is still an embodiment of a particular set of dominant socio-discursive conventions—conventions that give rise to and legitimate certain meanings, values, and behaviors while curbing others—and its capacity for agency and self-fashioning is consequently not by any stretch of the imagination absolute. Yet Foucault also foregrounds the productive role that the self takes in its own formation. The self may be an effect of discourse, but it is also quite explicitly a self that takes an active interest in the shaping of this discourse. Like the Nietzschean ideals of self-stylization and living one's life as poetry, Foucault's care of the self calls for the subject's conscious manipulation of the conditions of its existence—of its "art of living." This is not a form of unconditional or unqualified agency, yet it suggests that the subject does possess a degree of creative leeway over the direction of its life.

I would like to suggest that Foucault is as much a theorist of potentiality as he is of subjection and hegemonic power. The same way that the Nietzschean noble engages in the "long practice and daily work" that is required by the stylistic constitution of the self, the Foucaultian subject employs the various techniques, exercises, and self-limitations that I have outlined to promote the potentialities of its being. Indeed, as we have seen, the two visions have a great deal in common in that both seem to demand a rather astonishing degree of inner resoluteness on the part of the subject. Whereas the Nietzschean self submits to the firm constraints of style in order to secure a degree of creativity agency, the Foucaultian subject follows the stern demands of *askesis* and self-discipline so as to adequately care for itself. While Nietzsche is forceful in his insistence that poetic self-fashioning can only be undertaken by strong and noble spirits, the Foucaultian subject similarly displays the kind of single-minded concentration that implies a remarkably high degree of commitment.

It is difficult to reconcile the inner resoluteness of the Nietzschean and Foucaultian subject with contemporary notions of psychic life. As I have already implied, I think that these discourses of self-fashioning and care of the self only make sense in the constructivist context if we read them as being indicative of the subject's open-ended attempt to make sense of its life rather than of self-mastery as an attainable goal. At the same time, I am interested in the idea—foregrounded by both Nietzsche and Foucault— that the subject's self-constraint can give rise to creativity and artistic possibility. Nietzsche and Foucault in fact invite us to reconsider the relationship between constraint and agency. While contemporary theory tends to envision constraint as what diminishes the individual's agency, both Nietzsche and Foucault present agency as something that emerges in the context of constraint. Nietzsche maintains that the noble appreciates stylistic constraint because it knows that such constraint opens the path to beauty, pleasure, and inspiration (thus it is the strong "who enjoy their finest gaiety in such constraint"); the Foucaultian care of the self similarly suggests that the constraints the subject places upon itself engender a refined kind of contentment. This makes it difficult to think about agency as something that we only gain at moments when we are able to break out of the various collective structures of sociality and meaning-making that constrain us. Rather, we are led to consider the manner in which it might be possible to forge agency from *within* constraint—out of conditions of necessity.

Nietzsche in fact points out that although we are prone to consider necessity as a state of painful conformity and unfreedom, the creative spirit knows that is it precisely when it begins to do everything out of necessity that its sense of imaginative power, subtlety, and sensitivity attains its height; from the perspective of the artist, necessity and freedom amount to the same thing in that it is only when the artist obeys a strictly and precisely articulated set of rules that he manages to give birth to a work of art (1886, p. 145). The artist knows, Nietzsche explains, that the embers of creative genius only glow in an atmosphere of restraint, and that his "natural" condition consequently has little to do with the "feeling of letting himself go" (p. 111). Creativity, Nietzsche thus insists, is a matter of cultivating "a proper mastery" over oneself, for it is only when one has learned the difficult art of "self-outwitting" that one can become one of those marvelously enigmatic spirits who are "predestined for victory and the seduction of others" (p. 122). The subject who has profitably internalized this lesson, Nietzsche concludes, knows that it has received something in return for its efforts—that it has surrendered one piece of itself to gain access to another, infinitely more precious, facet of its being (p. 150).

Nietzsche thus recognizes that creativity is not a function of freedom, but rather of learning how to make the most of constraint. This should allow us to think about agency in terms other than unbounded freedom. If we are willing to entertain the idea that the subject attains creativity precisely when it places limits on itself, then might it not be possible to understand agency as something that is facilitated by the socio-historical and discursive conventions within which it unfolds? By this I do not mean to imply that social relations of power do not restrict our actions in the world. And I also do not mean to say that such power does not frequently take insidious forms that can be hurtful and oppressive. But the idea that agency is best attained by evading collective systems of meaning-making only keeps us from being able to think about the possibilities for agency that exist all around us. The same way that the artist's work is enriched by the artistic traditions, techniques, and conventions within which she operates, our capacity for meaning and self-definition can be enhanced by the larger structures of meaning-production that surround us. At the very least, these structures can spare us the effort of having to reinvent the wheel over and over again.

The fact that not all meanings and self-definitions are possible at any given point in time should not lead us to think that agency is therefore unachievable. Post-Foucaultian theories of performative reiteration and ironic repetition of course recognize this, which is why they emphasize that agency is something that arises from the manipulation and reenactment of already existing meanings. But I would go further and argue that insofar as our capacity for meaning-making is dependent on our participation in collective structures of sociality and meaning-production, agency, rather than being merely a matter of subversive reenactments, is made possible precisely by the fact that subjectivity takes shape within discursive conventions. Agency, in other words, is not merely reactive. Rather, it seeks to actively engage the enabling dimensions of collective systems of meaning-production.

Contemporary theories of performativity in many ways share the Nietzschean insight that the destabilization of collective mythologies calls for the creation of counter-mythologies. However, they tend to divest this insight of its more affirmative energies by insisting that such counter-mythologies are always mere citations of already existing mythologies. All other words, the performative gesture tends to be reiterative rather than genuinely innovative. As a result, it dilutes our understanding of creative agency by implying that the subversive repetition of cultural norms is the only form of agency that the subject possesses. While Nietzsche—and to a lesser extent, Foucault as well—suggests that human beings have imaginative capacities that empower them to become dynamic creators of new mythologies of being, the subject of performance theory remains imitative at best.

The purpose of theories of performativity is to catch the signifier at its own game so as to alter its trajectory. In the next chapter, I will address the ways in which this is an important endeavor in that it undermines the dominant order's ability to stabilize cultural meanings. At the same time, the fact that theories of performativity are conceptually reliant on normative conventions as the point of reference that (alone) makes subversive acts readable as such—that makes them recognizable as resistant—implies that they are better at criticizing, ironizing, and mocking than at inventing and imagining; they are defensive rather than forward-looking.

I would like to suggest that agency entails the capacity to make good use of the inherently social (and therefore dependent) nature of subjectivity. By this I do not want to fall into the sentimental pitfall of claiming that our dependence on others is always a wondrous and empowering thing. Above I pointed out that many ancient philosophers emphasized the dangers of seeking our happiness in external objects over which we have little control. I find this longstanding bit of wisdom so compelling that I will propose, in Chapters 3 and 5, that one of Lacan's best insights is to give it a psychoanalytic rendering. Moreover, I will argue in the next chapter that it is possible to go too far in valorizing the enabling promise of intersubjective dependence. I do not then wish to counter the Butlerian subjection model by resorting to an overly romanticized account of human sociality. Yet I do not think that our dependence on others should be regarded primarily as a form of painful subordination either. I imagine dependence to be a state of affairs that possesses the potential for both subordination and enablement—that at times victimizes us, yet at other times sustains us in brave and miraculous ways. Butler seems to insist that there is no dependence without subordination. But is this in fact the case? Can we not at times depend on the external world in empowering ways? Are there not benevolent and genuinely productive forms of dependence? Forms of dependence—such as our dependence on our closest social and interpersonal networks—that enrich rather than erode us?[9]

I like to think of agency as the subject's ability to forge a special kind of relationship to the discourses and social structures that surround it—a relationship that manages to activate the enabling potentialities of these discourses

---

9. Many psychoanalytically minded thinkers, among them Lynne Layton (1998) and Kelly Oliver (2001), have criticized Butler's theory of social subjection along similar lines.

and social structures without getting caught in their more oppressive elements. From this point of view, collective social systems are not exclusively what impede our agency, but also what provide us with the raw materials—the conditions of possibility—for such agency. Each of us possesses the potential for a whole range of subjective enactments, and the question of which of these enactments materializes as our "self" is to a large extent a function of our socio-discursive circumstances. That is, the constitution of selfhood is always a matter of negotiating the often quite incompatible and conflicting possibilities that encircle us at any given time. But negotiating the parameters of one's existence is not necessarily the same thing as being socio-symbolically subjected. It can be an important site of creativity and innovative energy, not to mention a source of considerable pleasure. Moreover, though it is possible for the self to shift considerably over time, as a result of larger transformations in the discursive fields it inhabits, these shifts do not take place without its active participation. If discourses constitute our psychic and social realities, they also allow us to give meaning to and transform these realities. Being forced to negotiate does not mean that one always loses.

MYTHS OF EXISTENTIAL METAMORPHOSIS

Nietzsche and Foucault give us an initial understanding of the ways in which creative agency can arise from within the socio-discursive structures of the world. In Chapter 3, we will discover that Lacan follows a similar line of reasoning by revealing creativity to be a question of the subject's capacity to take advantage of its status as a symbolic being. What we have learned thus far is that agency calls for a continuous balancing act between engagement and disengagement. On the one hand, self-constitution cannot take place entirely independently of collective systems of sociality and meaning-making. On the other hand, agency demands the subject's ability to dissociate itself from those elements of its social world that are complacent or outrightly hurtful. The challenge then is to learn to partake in the cultural world without becoming subsumed by it. Or, to turn the matter around, agency is a function of being able to take a degree of distance from the world without at the same time ceasing to participate in the rhythm of its unfolding.

This manner of formulating the issue explains in part why Western philosophy has been so perennially obsessed with the question of how the individual might be able gain a measure of "autonomy" from the world. I know that the very mention of autonomy all too easily conjures up images of a ruthless desire to rule the world and its creatures. And indeed, there is no doubt that the pursuit of autonomy has often been driven by less than noble motives of conquest, and that it has frequently led to the denigration of others so that the self could thrive. But self-authorship is not always about ruling the world or belittling others. It can also be a matter of protecting the self's vitality, creativity, and sense of potentiality, as well as of taking advantage of the opportunities for growth and development encountered in the world. If Nietzsche is so vehement in his opposition to the processes of naturalization that conceal the metaphoricity of collective meanings, if Foucault is so invested in the art of living, and if so many Western philosophers have historically focused on how the human being can exist in the world in innovative ways, it is at least in part because they recognize that the subject's capacity to actively participate in the production of its meanings and values is of paramount importance for the viability of its inner life.

Though both Nietzsche and Foucault are aesthetically minded in that their accounts of self-mythologization draw heavily on artistic metaphors, their theories also probe the intricacies of human interiority. As a consequence, these theories are highly compatible with the psychoanalytic models that I will discuss later in this book. Psychoanalysis does not aim at self-mastery in the Nietzschean or Foucaultian sense; it engages in practices of subjective self-fashioning. I would therefore like to illustrate that just as Nietzsche views stylistic self-constitution as a means of enhancing the subject's creativity, and Foucault regards *askesis* as a specific way of caring for the self, psychoanalysis promotes the kind of imaginative flexibility that opens up the possibility of empowering existential mythologies. Indeed, psychoanalysis as a clinical practice is explicitly interested in the individual's ability to construct a viable psychic space—to craft a soul of sorts—so as to accede to a sense of inner possibility. Such inner possibility, I believe, is what Nietzsche and Foucault also aspire to cultivate, which is why I have attempted to read them in ways that provide an alternative to the subjection model that is so prevalent in contemporary critical theory. In endeavoring to make sense of agency without a stable notion of subjectivity, I have begun to suggest that rethinking interiority in the posthumanist era would entail, among other things, highlighting the psychic processes that enable the subject to come to terms with the ambiguity and fragmentation of its existence without losing its capacity for transformation.

Sometimes agency is nothing more than the subject's ability to survive its positioning in the world. Other times, it is an opening to something extraordinary. Insofar as posthumanist theory has to a large extent exhausted the critical gains to be reaped from the demythologization of humanist notions of interiority, it seems to me that we are desperately in need of new and enriching myths of existential metamorphosis. Late twentieth-century analyses of subjectivity were tremendously effective in revealing the mechanisms by which we become mesmerized by collective metaphors—by which we get hopelessly entangled in, and imprisoned by, the web of dominant socio-cultural mythologies. What has been less consistently explored, however, is the transformative potential of myth-making.

Why should the collapse of metaphysical models of identity result in the destruction, rather than the reconfiguration, of existential mythologies? Should not the posthumanist insight into the constructed nature of reality by definition free us to explore the enabling potentialities of myth-making rather than lead us to reiterate, over and over again, our hopeless entrapment in hegemonic collective mythologies? As essential as it is to explore the roots of subjection, it seems equally vital to nurture our confidence to combat and conquer what restricts our lives. Indeed, as long as we fail to embark upon an investigation of the more empowering dimensions of psychic life, we risk perpetuating a reactionary return to a reified past—a past which, however chimerically, promises exactly the kind of existential plenitude that late twentieth-century discourses appear to denigrate. That this promise may be illusory, that this state of plenitude may represent a purely imaginary state of inner abundance, does not in any way diminish its seductiveness, and it is precisely our inability to constructively address the sources of this seductiveness that urges us to rethink our critical paradigms. If we cannot figure out why constructivist theories of subjectivity and psychic life so often remain relatively powerless against the allure of humanistic models, it will be difficult for us to reverse the tide of conservatism that threatens to drown the progressive voice in the American academy—not to mention in society at large. This is one reason that it is important for us to talk about psychic potentiality and self-actualization—about the things that bring fullness to human existence rather than merely about the things that rob and deprive us.

If subjectivity as such represents a kind of mythology of being, a sedimented and multilayered site of psychic meanings, why should concerns over inner potentiality and self-actualization—not to mention soulfulness

—not comprise an essential part of that mythology? While we do not want to underestimate the tenacity of disciplinary power, we also do not want to lose our ability to dream—to devise the kinds of mythologies of psychic life that not only help us cope with our present hardships but also allow us to envision a more promising future. The utopias of yesterday do at times turn out to be the realities of today. It would be a shame, then, to forget to think in visionary terms.

2

Soul

On we go, the blurring body and the cheated soul. Why did no-one
tell me to provide for it? Everything I have has been the outward
show. Everything I have belongs to Time. Art? Don't be silly. The
contemplative life? Where can I get one? What then for my soul as
Time pulls me on. What then for my soul?

Jeanette Winterson, *Art and Lies*

"THE CHEATED SOUL"

I have talked in this book about the soul in terms of psychic agility, resilience, and resourcefulness, creative and imaginative capacity, as well as
the subject's ability to connect with others in meaningful and rewarding
ways. One of the most persistently recurring themes of twentieth-century
theory—taken up by thinkers as varied as Heidegger (1927), Horkheimer
and Adorno (1944), Marcuse (1955, 1964), Kristeva (1993), and Teresa
Brennan (2000)—is the idea that there is something about the assaultive,
fragmenting, and numbing quality of life in post-industrial Western societies that devastates human interiority in a manner that leaves us psychically crippled—that "cheats" us of soul. Horkheimer and Adorno, for
instance, maintain that the mass-produced "culture industry"—which includes the various messages disseminated by radio, television, the movies,
magazines, advertising (and these days, the Web)—leaves the subject nomi-
nally free (in the liberal capitalist sense) while directing "its attack on the
soul" (1944, p. 133). The culture industry ensures not only that the messages of the economically powerful become dominant, but also that these
messages are internalized and obeyed by the rest of us without question. It

targets consumers at different price ranges—offering a whole array of products and services in varying qualities—but this merely perpetuates the illusion of choice while simultaneously ensuring that no one escapes the system. The system, moreover, encourages "individuality" in its most superficial forms—welcoming calculated distinctions in hair styles, clothing, and status symbols, for instance—only to better impose its uniform stamp on everything that actually matters. The system is in fact so seamless that even deviations from the norm in the end serve to solidify the power of the norm in the sense that we recognize them as deviations only to the extent that we are intimately familiar with the norm.

One does not have to endorse Horkheimer and Adorno's pessimistic vision in its entirety to know that it represents an accurate depiction of many aspects of contemporary society. Indeed, the emergence of postmodern culture has only accelerated the immersion of individuals in a system that sanctions and proliferates surface-level differences while at the same time leveling genuine distinctions. As Lynne Lu (1997) has argued, the contemporary culture industry even manages to market ethnic "difference" as a commodity while diverting attention from the often harsh everyday experiences of minoritarian subjects. Only the "exotic" surface of international cosmopolitism and multiculturalism, rather than the deeper realities of ethnic identities, enters into the dominant culture's collective consciousness. Postmodern forms of multiculturalism, in this sense, have merely introduced "new opportunities for appropriation, exploitation, and commodification" (p. 18), making ethnic images readily available to any use. As a result, ethnic difference frequently becomes simply another fashion, style, or cuisine catering to the dominant culture's "desire to incorporate the essence of the other without being transformed" (p. 23).

How are we to reconcile this demoralizing picture of dominant culture with the argument that I made in the previous chapter regarding the empowering dimensions of collective structures of sociality and meaning-production? How do we discriminate between forms of sociality that sustain the soul and others that attack it? I propose a two-pronged approach. First, it is necessary to differentiate more rigorously between loving and harmful types of sociality. Second, it is essential to distinguish the creative dimensions of sociality from what Foucault means by hegemonic power. In this chapter, I will proceed with the first of these endeavors insofar as I will concentrate on aspects of collective life that drain the individual of psychic multidimensionality, as well as on recent efforts by feminist philosophers to envision modes of sociality and intersubjectivity that counter these debilitating forms of collective life. The second endeavor will have to wait until Chapter 3 where I argue that Lacan theorizes the symbolic order as a potentially enabling site of significatory and psychic possibility that should not be conflated with Foucault's analysis of regulatory power. The arc of the argument that I began in Chapter 1 will therefore not be completed until the end of Chapter 3.

In this chapter, I connect the soul to Freud's theory of psychic energy, outlining some of the ways in which contemporary life can immobilize our psychic lives in rigid and incapacitating patterns. I then consider Kelly Oliver's theory of intersubjectivity and "witnessing" as a means of repairing the psychic damage caused by oppressive social structures. I also compare Oliver's analysis of the transformative working-through of trauma with Butler's model of performative subjectivity to better understand why progressive debates about agency and psychic life are often so charged. Toward the end of the chapter, I contrast Cynthia Willett's theory of "social eros" with Audre Lorde's celebration of everyday eroticism to arrive at a definition of the soul that recognizes the importance of the subject's social aspirations without at the same time marginalizing its more "autonomous" or "solitary" pursuits. My objective is to show that distinguishing between loving and harmful forms of sociality is vital for our ability to develop a sophisticated appreciation for the complex relationship between intersubjectivity and autonomy.

Willett links psychic richness to the subject's capacity to fully realize itself as a social entity; I propose that it is equally important to explore those aspects of identity that thrive at a distance from sociality, that tend toward the contemplative rather than toward the company of others. This is because one of the unfortunate effects of contemporary culture is that it all too easily turns our lives into an "outward show"—to borrow from Winterson—in the sense that we are not always taught how to provide for the more introverted dimensions of our being. Because post-industrial society defines "success" primarily in terms of public displays of prowess and popularity, it can be difficult to take genuine pleasure in more solitary pursuits. It can in fact be quite challenging to even slow down to a rhythm that would be conducive to such pursuits. As a result, I would like to conceptualize soulfulness as a psychic state that requires both the support of loving intersubjective ties and the ability to carve out a refuge of introspection.

FIXED AND MOBILE FORMS OF PSYCHIC ENERGY

If we think of soullessness as an expression of contemporary cultural pathology, a good place to begin is Freud's notion of libidinal energy. One of Freud's most far-reaching (if contested) discoveries was to recognize that all of us possess a degree of energy that seeks an outlet in our daily activities, and that our well-being depends on our ability to productively release or cathect this energy. In practice, this means that the energy that circulates in our bodies and psyches needs a means of binding itself to some object, idea, or activity. We can, for instance, apply it to an important intellectual project, invest it in a person we love, or translate it into a beautiful work of art. We can also expend it in physical or sexual activity, direct it into ideological, political, or communal commitments, or attach it to our favorite television show. The process of socialization is in many ways one of learning how to cathect our energies in ways that are culturally intelligible. In this sense, our cathexes—the countless psychic investments that we make throughout our lives—give structure and consistency to our existence; without the channeling of energy into more or less predictable patterns of discharge, our egos would lack coherence, and we would not be able to function in society.

A certain degree of fixity in psychic investments is therefore necessary for the development and stability of the self. Yet Freud makes it abundantly clear that psychic energy can become fixed in excessively inflexible ways. Such inner rigidity is often caused by specific traumatic experiences that test the limits of what we find psychically tolerable. Whenever we experience something so devastating or disappointing that we are not able to cope with it fully or immediately, we tend to form defensive adaptations that ensure our inner survival but do not directly confront the core of what is causing our distress. Such adaptations can be a response to either physical or mental suffering, and they can develop quickly or over long periods of time, depending on the nature of the traumatic stimulus. These defensive adaptations can then become entrenched in our bodies and minds in ways that block the fluid circulation of energy and erect barriers to our ability to adequately process and integrate our diverse life experiences.

The challenge that we as social beings face is to learn to walk the tightrope of life in such a way that we internalize enough of what society deems proper to be able to participate in the life of the collectivity without at the same time losing our capacity for transformation. But this is more easily said than done. What Freud reveals is that the process of learning how to channel psychic energies into culturally condoned pathways entails a massive amount of familial and socio-cultural disciplining. The specific ways we are taught to desire, for instance, foreclose a whole host of other possibilities, which is why Freud frequently remarks that we tend to experience "civilization" as a source of deeply felt frustration and discontentment; the pervasiveness of psychic pathologies indicates that the repressive elements of socialization are at times too ruthlessly imposed, encumbering our ability to meet the curve balls of life in open and innovative ways.

Psychic energy can thus be mobile or immobile, nimble-footed or heavy-hearted. Psychoanalysis regards immobile energy as an impediment to creativity and the expansion of the subject's psychic potentialities, which is why it seeks to dissolve impasses of energy by allowing the hidden and buried residue of the individual's psychic history to surface on the level of consciousness. Indeed, the idea that energy can become frozen in stubborn patterns that resist our every effort to reroute them into more productive endeavors resides at the very root of Freud's concept of symptomatic behavior. While our capacity to establish inner pathways along which energy flows in familiar ways is what offers us the comforting illusion of a cohesive personality, Freud shows that it is all too common for energy to become trapped or otherwise misdirected in ways that make certain types of psychic investments seem inevitable even when they are clearly wounding.

In one of his most memorable similes, Freud likens the neurotic to a Londoner who, instead of going about her daily business, pauses in deep melancholy before the monument at Charing Cross that commemorates the death of Queen Eleanor. Freud maintains that like this distraught Londoner, the neurotic not only remembers painful experiences that took place in the remote past, but clings to these experiences emotionally in ways that prevent her from getting on with the real and immediate concerns of her life. This inability to liberate oneself from the pain of the past points to a fixation of inner energy—to what Freud describes as a kind of "strangulation" of affects (1910, p. 15). The neurotic symptom arises because the free circulation of energy is prohibited due to repression, and the individual's psychic life is immobilized around a conflict that remains unconscious. In this sense, the symptom lends angry expression to energy that cannot attain a proper outlet, and that consequently seeks satisfaction in pathological formations that cause discomfort yet simultaneously provide a space for the articulation of what otherwise remains inarticulable. The clinical task of analysis is then to find a means of accessing this unconscious conflict so as to release the affects that have gotten trapped in this tormenting manner and, in this fashion, to enable the subject to consciously mourn or otherwise confront what it has hitherto only been able to approach through the indirect means of a symptom. In this sense, psychoanalysis could be argued to assist the subject in remobilizing the current of energy that sustains human existence.[1]

For some time now, clinical psychoanalysts have been suggesting that there is something about contemporary life that, quite independently of the classically Freudian understanding of repression, produces the kind of "strangulation" of affects that Freud associates with symptomatic behavior. It seems that the present-day subject, less troubled by sexual inhibitions than by an overwhelming sense of inner emptiness, often finds it impossible to articulate the meaning and value of its life; instead of possessing a multidimensional psychic space, the subject experiences itself as internally impoverished. These new disorders—what Judith Feher-Gurewich (Feher-Gurewich and Tort 1996) has described as the "new disorders of the unconscious" and Kristeva (1993) has called the "new maladies of the soul"— lend expression to a drastic hollowing out of the individual's psychic structures (see also Green 1986, Lasch 1984, Modell 1993). The frenzied pace of contemporary life means that the subject has no time or conceptual space to cultivate its psychic life, and this lack of care for the psyche gives rise to an inner desolation that limits the subject's capacity to live its life dynamically. Individuals in this predicament often describe themselves as psychically dead, as if suffering from a profound deficiency of desire that prevents them from feeling fully engaged in their daily activities. It is then these lifeless individuals who enter into analysis in a desperate effort to free themselves from the sense of meaninglessness that makes it difficult for them to relate to their emotional states in any authentic manner.

The contemporary subject could thus be said to suffer from a profoundly melancholy yearning for genuine experience that would allow for a deeper connection to self, others, and the world in general. That such a connection is missing—that the psyche is experienced as flat and barren— seems related to a crisis of symbolization that prevents the subject from effectively expressing its innermost yearnings, longings, and desires; what ails the subject is that discourse has become severed from affect—that lan-

---

1. Anna O appropriately describes analysis as a form of "chimney sweeping"—as a cathartic device that dislodges unconscious matter from its resting place and allows it to find release through channels of narrativization (Freud 1910, p. 8).

guage has become uncoupled from emotion—in ways that complicate its ability to make sense of its existence (see Kristeva 1993, Chapter 1). The subject has, in other words, lost its capacity to represent its experiences in imaginatively empowered ways, with the result that it finds it increasingly challenging to conceive of itself as a possessor of psychic agency.

What is more, this constriction of psychic life—this loss of soul—causes an inner paralysis that propels the subject to seek solace in the proliferation of mass-produced images that allow it to undergo vicariously, at a safe distance as it were, the emotional intensities that it finds impossible to experience in its own being; the fear, anxiety, sadness, desire, and pleasure that the subject is incapable of accessing in its own psyche find expression on the television screen, producing a momentary catharsis that consumes its affective resources yet simultaneously leaves behind a residue of inner malaise. No longer able to infuse its existence with meaning and value, the subject pours its energies into projects and preoccupations that offer distraction but no real satisfaction. In this manner, the subject extinguishes the spark that animates its existence. As Kristeva explains, in stark contrast to the traditional maladies of the soul that preoccupied the doctors and philosophers of antiquity and that usually had to do with an excess of passion—with outbursts of joy, sadness, or delirium, for instance—the "new" maladies of contemporary Western culture seem symptomatic of the subject's inability to feel passionate about its life (1993, p. 3).

Clinical accounts thus suggest that it is the sense of having been cheated out of something existentially fundamental that resides at the heart of the contemporary subject's unease. Although ours is clearly an overwhelmingly individualistic era, it appears that the subject often finds it difficult to assert its individuality in meaningful ways. Its sensibilities effectively eroded by the incessant demands of a harried, over-stimulating, and staunchly utilitarian culture, it is forced to trade its passions for habits, and to allow routine to stifle its most cherished aspirations. Yet it mourns the poetry that should have been; it regrets the collapse of its psychic space, grieves the loss of inspiration, and shudders at the shortage of spirit. Even a cursory glance at contemporary pathologies reveals a strong yearning for an existential basis that would alleviate the anxieties of trying to make sense of an increasingly erratic, perfunctory, and impersonal world—a world that provides no reassuring sites of conviction, no calming bedrocks of certainty, and where even the most carefully crafted designs frequently fall apart. It reveals a pursuit of personal profundity, of the kind of inner expansiveness that would dispel the banality of everyday existence and reactivate the more mysterious recesses of the psyche. And it reveals a search for "soul," for a more full-bodied sense of inner vitality and imaginative capacity.

The tough question facing constructivist thinkers within the academy is the following: If the erosion of the post-industrial subject's psychic resources has been so extensively discussed by philosophers and clinical psychoanalysts alike, why has it had so little impact on how those of us working with Lacanian and poststructuralist paradigms characterize the self? Although there are certainly constructivist thinkers—among them Kristeva, Brennan, and Oliver (all of whom are discussed below)—who have taken an interest in this aspect of psychic life, constructivist criticism as a field seems much more interested in socio-cultural "subversion" than in questions of psychic well-being. Why is this? What are the conceptual "strangulations" that might make it difficult for constructivist criticism to overcome the dichotomies—between, say, lack and potentiality, alienation and self-actualization, or performativity and experience—that tend to organize its paradigms despite its valiant efforts to overcome the reductive logic of binary categories?[2] To what extent do the discourses of lack, alienation, and performative playfulness merely mime the contemporary subject's soullessness instead of offering solutions? Or is this soullessness simply not "our" problem?

---

2. One pertinent example of such a "strangulation" might be the fact that the firm dichotomy between discourse and affect that I characterized above as the contemporary subject's lot is often quite faithfully reproduced on the level of post-Lacanian theory in that this theory tends to envision discourse in opposition to affect, and to insist that since Lacanian psychoanalysis is centered on discourse, it by definition excludes considerations of affect (see Feher-Gurewich and Tort 1996, pp. 248–249). The origins of the anti-emotionality of Lacanian theory are of course understandable in the sense that Lacan's critique of American ego-psychology was aimed at the utilization of affect to produce a "well-adjusted" subject whose inner coherence depended on its unwillingness to confront the veil of illusions and misrecognitions that shrouded its existence. Yet so much has changed in Anglo-American psychoanalysis in recent decades that the divide between Lacanian and other psychoanalytic approaches at times seems based on nothing more substantial than the stubborn tendency to worship—in a manner reminiscent of Freud's Londoner—the monuments of the past. Moreover, the post-Lacanian denial of the importance of affects seems to carry an immense affective charge; there is, in other words, nothing unemotional about the Lacanian belittling of the emotions.

OPPRESSION AND INNER IMPOVERISHMENT

One reason the problem is "ours" as much as anyone else's is that the erosion and impoverishment of psychic resources is quite obviously linked to questions of power. Brennan argues forcefully that oppressive social conditions can actively conspire against our ability to lead elastic and empowered lives. She elaborates on Freud's insights on psychic energy by pointing out that our ability to invest energy in socially sustainable directions is a double-edged sword in that the very pathways of energy that we lay down as we establish a secure sense of self make us less able to adapt to new developments—to what she, following Freud, calls the "movement of life" (Brennan 1992, p. 235). From this perspective, what our egos gain in strength and consistency, they at the same time lose in versatility, elasticity, and capacity to grow. Indeed, we tend to experience discomfort whenever our familiar energy circuits are jeopardized, for these circuits are what make us feel like "ourselves"—what give us our established sense of social subjectivity. Yet if these circuits are never questioned, we risk getting stuck in stiff and uncompromising patterns of behavior. In Brennan's words, "As time passes, as experiences multiply, ever more fixed pathways for dealing with 'life's exigencies' are established. Identity, accordingly, becomes stronger but less plastic" (p. 235).

Because our psyches are caught in intersubjective circuits of energy—because they are fundamentally social rather than self-contained—the external world exerts an enormous amount of influence over our inner states. Brennan in fact proposes that the poststructuralist critique of the autonomous subject that has been so successful on the level of language and culture needs to be extended to encompass the intangible flows of energy that connect individuals to their environment. We know that certain people consistently lift our spirits and infuse us with energy while others deplete it. Similarly, we know that various types of economic or socio-cultural exploitation can exhaust our inner resources. Even our physical or natural environment can have a tremendous impact on our psychic states. There are certain environments that tire us while others replenish our senses; the experience of rushing through a busy city street can be so fundamentally different from hiking up a calm mountain trail that our entire sense of self shifts. In this manner, we are highly responsive to changes that take place around us.

For Brennan, the fact that individuals are energetically connected to others and to their larger social and physical environment provides the basis for an intensely politicized account of psychic life that explains exploitation in terms of a transfer of energy from the exploited to the ones who exploit. As she states, "In personal life, the wrong sex can assign one to a draining emotional tie, and an inexplicable fixity or inertia. In social interaction, this exploitation may be brief or glancing, but it is pervasive: the wrong accent, the wrong colour, the wrong sexuality can lead to a thousand slights in brief encounters, all of which give a temporary leverage to the subjects on the other side of them." In this manner, interpersonal benefits accrue to subjects "in the same ways as economic benefits" (Brennan 1993, p. 185). Oppression—understood here not only as what takes place between individuals, but also on the level of institutionalized inequality, the global economy, and environmental degradation—is linked to the relentless march of global capitalism that appropriates the individual's creativity only to fix it in commodities. This type of existence—which consumes the subject's energies without providing any genuine rest—causes a profound sense of exhaustion, a sensation of running hard to stay afloat in an increasingly accelerating world (Brennan 2000, pp. 11–13).

If the subject is capable of effective action in the world only when it possesses a rich and versatile psychic life, then the erosion of its sense of existential potential under conditions of oppression can exacerbate its powerlessness. Kelly Oliver maintains that oppressive social conditions, such as racism, impinge upon the subject's psychic space, draining its energies and constricting its capacity to name itself and its world. Moreover, because oppression forces its victims to internalize the ideals of the dominant group, it denies them access to an empowering social space that would allow them to represent themselves independently of the hegemonic systems that distort their existence; the oppressed are asked to accept the dominant culture's representation of themselves as inferior and incapable of full membership in the social order, with the result that it is difficult for them to retain a strong sense of psychic agency. In this fashion, oppression renders its victims "speechless" (2001, p. 95), and destroys the collective space of meaning-making that under more favorable circumstances supports the individual's processes of self-representation; since the subject's understanding of itself is dependent on the surrounding environment, the contamination of this environment can be experienced as a form of psychic death. In this manner, oppression shatters the communal mirror that reflects back to the subject a positive image of itself, robbing it of the capacity for self-love. The fracturing of the individual ego here echoes the fracturing of the social ego.

Oliver argues that the subject's sense of dignity and inner possibility depends on its ability to interpret its experiences from within an imaginative framework that enables it to defend itself against the structures of power that seek to annihilate its voice and perspective. Oliver moreover proposes that the subject's capacity to meaningfully bear witness to and interpret its experiences (its "inner witness") is produced in dialogic relation to loving external witnesses who, through their caring response, create the conditions for viable subject positions. She explains:

> Our lives have meaning for us—we have a sense of ourselves—through the narratives that we prepare to tell others about our experience. Even if we do not tell our stories, we live our experience through the stories that we construct in order to "tell ourselves" to another, a loved one. As we wander through our days, an event takes on its significance in the narrative that we construct for an imaginary conversation with a loved one as we are living it. [2001, p. 220]

It is therefore the other who fosters our capacity to generate personal meaning and to fashion a multifaceted sense of self. Moreover, it is the other's enabling response that provides an intersubjective space into which we can pour our stories of abjection, thereby allowing us to assert our right to represent our experiences. The effect of extreme forms of oppression, Oliver maintains, is to crush our capacity for self-representation by depriving us of external witnesses. In this manner, oppression destroys our inner vitality by short-circuiting the compassionate social energies that replenish such vitality.

Above I talked about the crisis of self-representation that makes it difficult for individuals to find meaning and value in their lives. Oliver's examination of the devastating effects of oppression points to the specific ways that this crisis can be hegemonically enforced through a repressive monitoring of which life narratives count and which do not. Agency in this sense is a question of socio-symbolic legitimation—of who gets to speak and whose stories and narratives come to be regarded as normative and prescriptive.

The subject's capacity to create meaning for itself is essential for its ability to survive the forces of dehumanization that seek to undermine its self-respect. Oliver suggests that the subject's inner victimization is best remedied by restoring its capacity for witnessing—and this not only in the sense of being able to bear witness to its own life, but also in the sense of being able to respond to and take responsibility for the experiences of others. This is to say that if oppression threatens the individual's capacity to maintain a strong sense of specificity, and therefore to adequately care for the self, the cure must actively endeavor to rebuild what has been so forcefully obliterated. For Oliver, the cure reinstitutes the subject's ability to testify to its experiences so as to allow for a transformative working-through of the trauma of oppression; by being able to reclaim its voice, the subject is able to break the repetitive logic of victimization and to forge a discursive space for reinterpretation and inner revitalization. Oliver's cure is therefore classically Freudian in that it moves from repetition to interpretation and working-through. While repetition entails the subject's tendency to act out its past traumas in painful and self-undermining ways, interpretation provides the possibility for the kind of insight that potentially dissolves trauma; while acting-out merely displaces psychic tensions along an endless chain of repetition, working-through changes the internal conditions that gave rise to such tensions to begin with, thereby ending the cycle of repetition. As Oliver puts it, through interpretation, "repetition is transformed from compulsory behavior into more open possibilities" (2001, p. 78).

Oliver draws on Kristeva's suggestion that the imagination is a means of promoting a form of subjectivity that is not completely seamlessly interpellated into the dominant order. From her early work on the revolutionary potential of poetic language (Kristeva 1974) to her later, more psychoanalytic writings (Kristeva 1983, 1987, 1993, 1996), Kristeva's vast theoretical apparatus has been designed to elucidate how individuals come to generate meanings that in one way or another challenge the dominant socio-symbolic repertoire—meanings that are "revolutionary" precisely because they seek to transfigure the very parameters of this repertoire. Imaginative forms of interpretation and working-through, Kristeva contends, facilitate processes of inner renewal because they allow the individual to create meanings that in one way or another exceed the discursive conventions of the dominant order. In this sense, the imagination provides a potent "antidote" (1983, p. 381) to the subject's psychic abjection. It can in fact be seen as a form of psychic "revolt" that allows the individual to resist the cultural pressure to conform to predetermined identity categories (see Kristeva 1996). Moreover, in allowing the individual to symbolize its unavowable losses, the imaginative working-through of trauma provides a vocabulary with which to address the sense of injury that results from these losses.

Kristeva thus emphasizes that the working-through of trauma relates to the power of naming. Oliver in turn maintains that this power of naming can be effectively mobilized only through the individual's relationships with others. Indeed, Oliver explicitly extends Kristeva's analysis to a more social and overtly political direction by asserting that working-through requires a sustaining communal space within which affects and experiences can safely be recuperated. Like Kristeva, Oliver emphasizes that working-through demands the individual's capacity to capture affects in words, but she goes further than Kristeva in stressing that such symbolization can only be successful in a social context that supports alternative narratives.

Affects, Oliver argues, can be "deadly" without a collectively sanctioned setting for their expression (2001, p. 111). This is because the ability to speak to one's victimization is far from self-evident. Not only is it difficult to testify to one's oppression, but the very act of bearing witness to one's subordination in many ways repeats and reenacts the experience of this very subordination. Oliver explains that testimonies of oppression often reinscribe the survivor as a victim and worthless object even when the act of testifying is meant to reinstitute her as a subject (p. 98). Bearing witness to one's own oppression therefore places the individual in a paradoxical situation in that it recalls the memory of lost humanity at the very moment that it seeks to restore this humanity. Since the right to speak is granted only to those who have been accredited as legitimate subjects, to testify from the position of the oppressed necessarily "flies in the face of a culture that silences people by making them the other and reducing them to inarticulate objects" (p. 100). In this manner, the act of testifying to one's victimization can place subjectivity on trial in that dominant culture judges and quite often questions the credibility of one's narratives.

Oliver's analysis reveals how very important it is for those who are struggling to translate their psychic realities of marginalization into livable spaces of hope and agency to have access to an enabling social context that sustains their imaginative ability to both envision alternatives to their current repressive conditions and to enact an empowering working-through of past experiences of psychic wounding. Such imaginative agency can obviously never replace the tangible benefits that would result from the eradication of inequalitarian social structures, but in circumstances where such an eradication does not yet appear on the subject's immediate horizon, its capacity to own, reclaim, and rewrite its experiences remains crucial for its ability to retain a sense of inner possibility; although nothing can compensate for the concrete gains that would result from a realignment of economic and socio-symbolic power, the subject who, in the here and now, is called upon to face the hardships of oppression cannot easily relinquish the consolation of being able to tell its story in ways that grant it a sense of personal integrity.

Constructivist criticism tends to be suspicious of identitarian attempts to forge a legitimate voice, either on the personal or collective level. Yet such attempts make a great deal of sense for those who are forced to continually negotiate their relationship to power structures that are at best indifferent, and at worst hostile, to their interests. When individuals burdened in this manner are given the opportunity to transmit their stories and narratives in the context of an enabling social network, they may be able to evoke meanings, connotations, and communications that resonate productively and affirmatively with the surrounding world. The transformative power of this should not be underestimated. From this viewpoint, the subject's capacity to exchange stories with others, as well as to construct, in conjunction with like-minded individuals, the kinds of collective narratives that provide a basis for a shared sense of kinship and belonging, serves as the foundation of both private and public regeneration.

The imaginative working-through of trauma therefore not only facilitates the subject's private processes of healing, but allows collectivities to voice their concerns as well. Indeed, if working-through on the individual level can alleviate the subject's sense of inner malaise, then collective acts of working-through can potentially restore a community's confidence in itself. This explains in part why the desire to translate collective grief into political vocabulary has historically resided at the very heart of identity politics. From the Civil Rights movement of the 1960s to contemporary AIDS activism, the objective of consciousness-raising has been not only to provide individuals with the means of signifying their pain, but also to forge a public outlet for that pain; though it would be possible to argue that the kinds of imaginative resources I have connected to psychic empowerment are in principle unavailable to those most in need of such empowerment, in seems clear that, in terms of collective action, it is precisely the ability to draw on such resources that has enabled those under duress to mobilize against their oppression. This is to say that, politically speaking, it has been essential for subjugated groups to retain their ability to creatively construct meaning in the face of the dominant order's attempt to fix the limits of acceptable meaning. Such marshaling of shared resources has allowed collectivities to unleash the power of concealed affects, and therefore to turn the silences of oppression into the vocalized demands of political resistance. It is for this reason that, as Oliver implies, the notion of working-through applies to collective as well as individual realities, for it supplies collectivities and individuals alike with a narrative space in which to retell their stories.

REPETITION VS. TRANSFORMATION

Oliver presents her theory of witnessing as an essential component of a larger project of developing an intersubjective understanding of identity that takes as its starting point the individual's fundamental connectedness with others. Oliver criticizes contemporary neo-Hegelian paradigms of subjectivity—such as Butler's theory of subjection—for portraying the self as a site of perpetual intersubjective strife, conflict, and antagonism. She points out that although these neo-Hegelian approaches may explain the prevalence of war and violence, they are wholly inadequate when it comes to envisioning the possibility of peaceful relationships with others across differences. This is because they tend to equate the dynamic of oppression (which is based on strife, conflict, and antagonism) with the dynamic of subjectivity as such. Oliver's alternative notion of witnessing, on the other hand, does not require the individual to abject or exclude others so as to attain a sense of self, but rather endeavors to honor the profoundly inter-dependent nature of subjective realities. Such a vision of subjectivity, rather than regarding the other as an alien and potentially hostile entity, recognizes that the self's agency and well-being depend on its sustaining relationships with others (2001, pp. 10–11).

Oliver specifies that one of the main problems with the neo-Hegelian paradigm is that it renders the subject's sense of its own humanity conditional in that it forces it to seek recognition of this humanity from those more powerful than itself. Witnessing, in contrast, takes the humanity of both self and other for granted, and moreover demands the individual's capacity to respond to the other's "pathos" beyond mere recognition (p. 8). Indeed, Oliver regards this willingness to respond to the deep well of the other's pathos as an ethical obligation that founds subjectivity as such. The Hegelian recognition model, Oliver contends, is faulty because it all too easily casts the oppressed into the desperate double bind of having to ask recognition of their worth from those who are least likely to acknowledge them as subjects in their own right, namely their oppressors. This obviously only perpetuates their victimization, for the experience of consistently falling short of the dominant ideal drives them deeper into the spiral of self-denigration. From this point of view, the subject's striving for recognition is "a symptom of the pathology of oppression" rather than its solution (p. 29).

In teasing out the distinction between recognition and witnessing, Oliver contrasts Butler's theory of performative subjectivity with Kristeva's delineation of the transformative potential of the imagination, arguing that while Kristeva's account opens up the possibility of working-through, Butler's analysis, driven as it is by the logic of repetition, cannot ultimately escape the narrow parameters of acting-out. Oliver maintains that the Butlerian subject, who comes into being through, and can only exist within, the operations of normative power, is condemned forever to repeat the original trauma that it has suffered at the hands of others; because Butler can only conceive of subjectivity as a function of subjection and subordination, her subject can only sustain itself through the repetition of the very conditions of power that produced it in the first place. This in turn means that it can only conceive of sociality as a space of hostility and hegemonic power (see Oliver 2001, pp. 74–77).

Oliver thus implies that Butler's model of subjectivity does not allow for any real opportunity for the working-through of trauma, but instead holds the subject caught in the hurtful cycle of acting-out, therefore barring the possibility of any genuine transformation. I already made it clear in the previous chapter that, like Oliver, I take issue with Butler's tendency to conflate subjectivity with subjection. I also agree with Oliver that Butler's analysis of performativity is not a convincing model of working-through in the psychoanalytic sense. Moreover, as I tried to show through my reading of Nietzsche and Foucault, it is not a strong enough example of creative agency. However, I am a little reluctant to reduce Butler's theory to a mere repetitive form of acting-out. I would be willing to concede that Butler's performative model *can* function as a theory of transformation. How we understand the matter depends on what we mean by transformation, and who we are talking about.

The personal and political stakes of performance theory within the queer community have been high precisely because many members of this community have experienced Butler's theory as genuinely transformative—as an opening to a fresh way of "doing" both gender and sexuality. In the context of a normative order that casts heterosexuality as the only valid and desirable form of sexuality, the idea that gender and sexuality are performativity constituted, open to parodic appropriation, reiteration, and reconfiguration, as well as playfully fluid and transgressive, has obvious merits. Whereas the psychoanalytic notion of working-through reaches into the deepest layers of psychic trauma, theories of performativity reconstitute what takes place on the surface, which means that they can help us understand the very real risks that pertain to visibility and alternative embodiment. For those who live gender and sexuality in non-normative ways, risk is quite often a function of having to inhabit the world in "over-visible" ways. Against this backdrop, performance theory can bring about transformation in that it exposes the performative conventions of normative gender and sexuality, and in so doing redistributes the stigma of visibility so that hegemonic heterosexuality becomes as detectable (and open to ridicule) as queer sexuality; by reallocating the burden of visibility, performance theory can carve out an invaluable space for alternative renderings of gender and sexuality. The effect may not (yet) infiltrate culture at large, but its benefits in sexual subcultures can be considerable.

It may seem that I am trying here to have my cake and eat it too in that I wish to honor both Butler's model of performativity and Oliver's insights about the very real limitations of performance theory. And indeed, this is exactly what I am trying to do (sometimes stuffing one's face with cake is the only sensible thing to do). One reason for wishing to have it both ways is that I would like to hold onto my determination to remain cognizant of the uselessness of drawing categorical battle lines. The fact that I disagree with Butler's subjection model does not mean that I therefore find her theory of performativity to be wholly without merit as well.[3] The complexities of the world always exceed the neatness of our interpretative grids, and while I certainly agree with many of Oliver's criticisms of performance theory, I would hate to lose sight of the fact that Butler's theory presents a courageous revision of the ways in which gender and sexuality signify in our culture.

Finding the appropriate theoretical toolbox is highly context-specific. It occurs to me, for instance, that when Oliver accuses Butler of not having developed a strong enough theory of transformation, the disagreement may in part stem from the fact that Butler's performative project is centered around gender and sexuality, whereas Oliver is (in this particular instance)

---

3. Indeed, my disagreement with Butler arises from the fact that she consistently undercuts the creative dimensions of her performance theory by an excessive emphasis on hegemonic power (on the ways in which subjectivity equals subjection). I realize that this may be an unfair criticism insofar as Butler seems to have shifted to the subjection model in part as a response to critical attacks of her earlier more agentic account of performative self-constitution.

more interested in the traumatic effects of racial oppression. Along closely related lines, my own dissatisfaction with poststructuralist theories of psychic life initially arose from the fact that the discourse of fluid and ever-mobile subjective realities made little sense in the context of my effort to understand the psychic legacies of socio-economic privation. I remember that by the late 1990s, when I first started to think about this book, I had grown more than a little frustrated by the fact that virtually every progressive poststructuralist text I read prescribed "subversion" as the all-purpose solution to our ills. I had also reached the point where the idea that parody and irony—so powerfully destabilizing in the context of normative configurations of gender and sexuality—represent a universally valid form of resistance rang quite hollow. A parodic and flamboyant performance of gender norms might be a potentially effective means of denaturalizing gender and sexuality. But how does one flamboyantly perform poverty?

The performative response to this question might well be that it is not the performance of "poverty" that is subversive, but rather the performance of "wealth," provided that it is undertaken by the poor (as in the oft-analyzed film *Paris Is Burning*). The idea here is that if the poor can enact wealth, then there is nothing real, essential, or authentic about class divisions (which in turn opens these divisions to "subversion"). However, I have never found this reasoning particularly persuasive for the simple reason that the distinction between the poor and the wealthy is predicated on the kinds of concrete material realities that cannot be conjured away by a mere performative wave of the conjurer's wand. The performance of wealth may provide a momentary pleasure (of playfulness, of spectacle, of the fantasy of belonging), but at the end of the day, one still needs food on the table and a safe place to sleep. This is to say that the performative "solution" to the predicament of poverty may offer a momentary release from the grim realities of the everyday, but ultimately it is an empty solution. One could even argue that in the long run it is a harmful solution in the sense that it only perpetuates the yearning for what remains out of reach, thereby feeding the subject's sense of falling short of an impossible ideal and deepening the ever-expanding spiral of abjection. Although theories of performativity are adept at disclosing the various ruses of power that naturalize social constructs, I would say that the idea that class is constructed actually plays into the logic of power rather than subverting it. In the context of the American reification of upward mobility—the myth that anyone can make it in this society—to claim that class is fluid in the constructivist sense is to fall for a ruse of power hook, line, and sinker.

What I am saying is that the strategies that performance theory has devised to subvert dominant systems of power—such as parody and misrepetition, the valorization of fluidity, mobility, and surface effects, as well as the foregrounding of the theatrical dimensions of identity—may be quite productive in the realm of gender and sexuality, but less convincing in other registers of human experience. Moreover, even within the realm of gender and sexuality, theories of performativity fail to be universally useful. The recent clashes in sexuality theory regarding the complexities of transgenderism (see, for instance, Prosser 1998 and Halberstam 1998) have made it clear that performative fluidity is not the ideal for everyone in the realm of gender and sexuality either. The issue is in fact highly charged in that arguments that promote the need for psychic and bodily security are all too readily read as conformist and essentializing scions of heteronormativity, whereas arguments that promote fluidity are all too easily seen to perpetuate a shallow form of postmodern flippancy.

I think that what makes debates regarding performance theory so touchy is that this theory tends to "derealize" trauma (here Oliver is entirely correct). There is obviously a great deal to be said for the pleasure and subversive potential that adhere to the performative notion that identities remain open to reconfiguration because they are never entirely "real" to begin with. However, the problem begins when this "unrealness" of identities translates—however implicitly—to the idea that the trauma of subjectivity is *also* somehow not "real." More specifically, the problem begins when the statement "I take pleasure in the fact that I am not 'real' in any essential sense" translates to something like: "if you do not want to perpetuate the normative order, you'd better realize that *you* (and thus your trauma?) are not 'real' either."

While the belittling of trauma may not be at all the objective of performance theory, it is not difficult to see how the call for subjective "inauthenticity" is unpalatable to those who live trauma as an everyday reality, for there is rarely anything about trauma that feels "inauthentic." This is why I have sought in this book to stress that the fact that something is socio-culturally constructed does not mean it is not lived as a life-determining reality. The fact that gender is a cultural construct—as I believe it to be—does not in any way change the fact that being (or not being) gendered in particular ways can bring a considerable degree of pain and suffering. It also does not change the fact that many individuals live their gender as a concrete bodily reality (which often clashes quite radically with their "fantasy" of gender). Similarly, the fact that class divisions are not rooted in any essential distinction between individuals does not alter the painful material realities of these distinctions.

Life is rarely either/or (Kierkegaard notwithstanding). This is one reason that I do not find the dichotomies between fluidity and fixity, movement and stability, or performativity and experience the least bit useful. While I value fluidity in the context of gender and sexuality, I recognize at least some of the reasons why others might feel differently. Moreover, although gender fluidity is dear to me, the immigrant in me yearns for permanence (of legal status, among other things) for the simple reason that incessant flux and boundary crossing in this context is exhausting and paralyzing. Similarly, my longing for economic security consistently trumps the poststructuralist disdain for stability. This blurring of the binary—the fact that I find stability utterly unbearable in certain circumstances, yet experience it as a matter of psychic survival in others—has taught me to respect the manner in which life-worlds remain resistant to theoretical purity; the better we are able to deal with the messiness of identities, the more convincingly we will be able to address the lived parameters of subjective realities.

More generally speaking, it seems to me that the various ways that contemporary theory has chosen to characterize identities—as either fluid or fixed, for instance—are, on a very fundamental level, statements about the nature of human potentiality. Posthumanist theory may implicitly (and sometimes even explicitly) eschew questions of self-actualization, but I would contend that it is actually deeply invested in these questions. Is it not the case that those of us who value fluidity do so in part because we believe it to be the best expression of our humanness—because we think that it is what will enable us to lead lives that feel fulfilling and meaningful to us? Similarly, are debates about the nature of identity, gender, and sexuality not on a rather basic level debates about the best way to live? About what makes us happy, what is fair, and what we want the future to look like?

It may well be that disagreements about the nature of subjectivity and psychic life are so contentious precisely because they are at bottom disagreements about self-actualization. After all, what constitutes self-actualization remains an open question, and the stakes of being able to take stabs at a definition can seem terribly high. Consider, for instance, the heated disagreements between poststructuralism and identitarian movements. Whereas supporters of identity politics have historically been interested in restorative approaches to subjectivity, poststructuralist thinkers have tended to be dismissive of such initiatives, at times accusing them of advancing an essentialized notion of subjectivity. David Eng remarks that in the deeply polarized debate between poststructuralism and ethnic studies, for instance, it is often assumed that thinkers in ethnic studies seek to recuperate a naïve notion of identity whereas poststructuralist theorists have transcended such naïveté by dismantling the very possibility of a coherent identity. In this manner, poststructuralism manages to posit itself as a sophisticated discourse capable of interrogating the most basic parameters of human existence, while ethnic studies appears to perpetuate a much more transparent notion of experience. Another way of conceptualizing the matter is to say that whereas poststructuralism has over the years sought to problematize the ideal of an autonomous and self-willed subject, the identity politics of race and ethnicity has historically been centered around the question of autonomy and self-will (Eng 2001, pp. 25–26). That is, where identitarian movements have traditionally focused on the strategies by which it might be possible to gain agency in the socio-cultural arena, the goal of poststructuralist theory has been to destabilize subjectivity in ways that make such agency a very difficult, if not an impossible, proposition.

Eng challenges this simplistic distinction, arguing that the dialectical tension between the poststructuralist questioning of subjectivity on the one hand, and identitarian demands for agency on the other, can open up new avenues for theorizing subjectivity and agency alike. Eng points out that poststructuralist theory need not diminish, but can in fact enrich and strengthen, the claims of identity-based movements. The poststructuralist understanding of the decentered subject can, for instance, enable identitarian discourses to question their tendency to resort to highly exclusionary models of identity in order to advance their political agendas (p. 27).

Eng provides the example of Asian-American cultural nationalism which, in its 1970s version, sought to counter the denigration of Asian-American identity by constructing a strict and inflexible definition of what Asian Americans—particularly Asian-American men—should aspire to be. Threatened by the mainstream characterization of Asian-American men as passive, feminized, and homosexual, the cultural nationalist movement focused on "the recuperation of a strident Asian-American masculinity and a 'pure,' heroic, Asian martial tradition." In so doing, Asian-American cultural nationalism not only advanced a constrictive model of Asian-American masculinity, but "reinscribed a dominant system of compulsory heterosexuality with all its attendant misogyny and homophobia" (p. 210). Similar charges could be leveled against certain forms of feminism that define their constituency in such narrow terms that they effectively exclude men, lesbians, and transsexuals, as well as against those forms of gay and lesbian activism which, in the name of gender authenticity, shun transgendered individuals and transsexuals. All of these political constituencies would profit from a deeper understanding of the ways in which identities can never be straightforward or straightforwardly authentic.

I take it for granted that identitarian movements would benefit from the poststructuralist understanding of subjectivity as fractured and unstable— as always haunted by the multiple and unpredictable discourses of the other. At the same time, I believe that the identitarian emphasis on agency, healing, and restoration, when placed in a more constructivist context, can energize poststructuralist theory by directing it toward the kinds of more existential considerations that it has for the most part disregarded— considerations that have to do with inner potentiality and self-actualization, for instance. I also believe that poststructuralist criticism would benefit from taking more seriously the idea that active meaning-making and self-definition are necessary for overcoming the psychic imprint of oppression. I agree with Oliver that the capacity to fashion meaning for oneself is essential for agency, even if this meaning cannot aspire to any permanent or transcendent status.

It may well be that we have in many ways reached a post-identitarian age in that our current theoretical understanding of subjectivity makes it difficult to build a political program on the basis of identity categories. Indeed, it is apparent that such categories can never provide the desired political stability for the simple reason that identities themselves are never fixed, unambiguous, or transparently available as sites of identification. The intersectionality of race, class, gender, and sexuality, for instance, is one important axis along which subjectivity must always be understood to be in turmoil. Such axes of differentiation and self-division abound in the lives of all of us, making it impossible to construct either a theory of interiority or a politics of liberation on any uncomplicated notion of unitary identity. However, it is still the case that economically and socio-symbolically marked bodies remain under attack as a result of their hegemonically assigned placement in specific identity groupings. From this perspective, the group-based demand for voice—for a validation of a common experience of past and present concerns—can be interpreted as a valid strategy of combating an externally imposed sense of collective impoverishment. The problem with such identitarian claims—as Eng's critique of Asian-American nationalism suggests—only emerges when the "voice" that is being sought is not recognized for what it is, namely a particular and necessarily partial manner of representing experience, but is instead regarded as an essential reflection of some pure or exclusive identity. When such a miscalculation takes place, communal narratives become totalitarian rather than enabling, sorting individuals into normative categories. What gets lost at such moments is the fact that the capacity for meaningful self-representation is not the same thing as a stable identity.

EROS AND SELF-ACTUALIZATION

Another problem that weakens identitarian approaches is that they tend to valorize the empowering dimensions of intersubjectivity without always distinguishing between loving and harmful forms of sociality. By this I obviously do not mean that identitarian approaches fail to differentiate between oppressive dominant culture on the one hand and enabling communities on the other, but merely that they tend to view communities as invariably loving even when they are not. In their attempt to find a remedy for the alienating effects of dominant culture, they all too easily resort to an over-idealized vision of what it means to participate in communal life, with the result that "intersubjectivity" becomes a blanket solution not only to oppression but to the ills of Enlightenment liberalism as well. Consider, for instance, Willett's attempt, in *The Soul of Justice*, to replace traditional Western notions of individuation, freedom, and self-actualization with a more communal model of subjectivity. Willett's argument shares many similarities with the anti-Hegelian conception of intersubjective ethics that Oliver builds around the notion of witnessing. Willett contends that traditional accounts of agency and autonomous self-constitution neglect "the deeper meaning of freedom" (2001, p. 22) that emerges from the loving social bonds that connect individuals and communities alike. Commenting specifically on Kierkegaard's (1843b) famous rendering of the story of Abraham and Isaac in *Fear and Trembling*, Willett questions the fact that Kierkegaard portrays existential freedom as a matter of a painful and potentially traumatizing "rite of passage" (Willett 2001, p. 233) that demands the subject to break all social bonds so as to be able to resurrect itself as a sovereign entity. Willett explains that in setting out on his journey to sacrifice Isaac, Abraham does not listen to his family or to his community, but rather chooses to face the question of mortality, of nothingness, and of the "wholly other," alone. This emphasis on separation and detachment, this denigration of human sociality and intersubjectivity, Willett maintains, creates unnecessary anguish that leaves "scars on the individual soul" (p. 234). More generally speaking, the traditional Western view of self-constitution errs by consistently privileging autonomy over sociality, with the result that self-actualization is conceptualized as a function of "stoic rituals of separation" (p. 186) that mark us as "true individuals" but simultaneously place us in an antagonistic position in relation to our communities (p. 230).

Kierkegaard's version of the story of Abraham may not be the best example of the kind of "rigorous discipline of radical self-choice" (Willett 2001, p. 232) that Willett wishes to criticize. While it may well be that Kierkegaard does in many ways seek, as Willett believes, to induce the subject to take full responsibility for the singularity of its existential path, it should not be overlooked that his retelling of this biblical narrative also opens to a whole other realm of Western thinking about self-actualization. Although autonomy and individuation obviously play a major role in traditional accounts of self-realization, transcendence has also frequently been theorized in terms of the individual's absolute surrender to a higher principle, such as the "Species," "Absolute Spirit," or—as in Kierkegaard's parable—"God."[4] Such absolute surrender implies a radical dissolution of the subject's rational boundaries and therefore explicitly undermines the ideal of autonomy and individuation.[5]

---

4. Schiller, for instance, describes self-actualization as an expansion of being whereby "all barriers disappear," and "we are no longer individuals, but species" (1795, p. 67). Along related lines, Hegel's (1807) dialectical project aims at the translation of material realities into Absolute Spirit in ways that imply that it is by losing himself in the divine that the individual attains a state of grace. Moreover, Christian visions of self-overcoming—and Hegel's analysis of the spirit's ascension is explicitly Christian—are frequently centered around the idea that it is the subject's mortifying self-negation that most convincingly affirms its transcendent status. This self-renunciatory impulse is most readily discernible in the mystic's yearning to annihilate the self so as to make space for the fullness of God. As Bataille puts it, mystical passion is driven by the mystic's "desire to die to himself" (1957, p. 230).

5. Whereas Willett's critique of Kierkegaard focuses on Abraham's renunciation of his community to meet the abyss and agony of existential freedom alone, it should not be forgotten that Kierkegaard presents Abraham as someone who makes a leap of faith in the face of the absurd, and who, in being willing to sacrifice Isaac, acts in accordance with principles that are both rationally inexplicable and ethically unjustifiable (Kierkegaard 1843b, p. 65). While such extreme anti-rationality and anti-morality may be a good example of the kind of anti-communitarian spirit that Willett criticizes, it seems to me that

The fact that Kierkegaard's story of Abraham does not necessarily best exemplify the kind of narrative of "loneliness and alienation" (Willett 2001, p. 234) that Willett finds paradigmatic of Western accounts of self-actualization does not invalidate her overall critique. It is certainly true that traditional depictions of self-actualization frequently define freedom in terms of the subject's ability to separate itself from its social ties and obligations, and that the existentialist tradition—to which Kierkegaard undoubtedly in many ways contributed—has been particularly prone to rely on an unnecessarily individualistic understanding of both freedom and responsibility. This is to say that I appreciate Willett's attempt to envision "a more amorous path for the existential spirit" (p. 234)—a path that would respect the individual's social capacity "to flourish with others in history, culture, and a work-based community" (p. 4).

Willett builds upon the African-American critical tradition of positing love as a basis of justice and freedom (see, for instance, Hill Collins 1991, hooks 1994, and West 1993) to develop a conception of ethics that shies away from heroic feats of autonomous self-constitution and endeavors instead to foster the individual's ability to form and maintain meaningful social relationships.[6] Willett explains that for African Americans who retain the memory of the Middle Passage and the horrors of slavery—particularly the way in which slave owners habitually split families and communities with little regard for the integrity of shared lives—separation connotes traumatic loss and social death rather than freedom (pp. 211, 235).

Willett's community-based ethics is centered around her notion of the "erotic soul" as a force that enables individuals to lead "a fully human existence" (p. 187). Willett maintains that while oppressive social conditions such as racism are an assault on the soul in that they drain both individuals and communities of their strength, eros is a "healing art" that is capable of replenishing this strength; if the subject is diminished by the various crimes of arrogance that impoverish its ability to cultivate nurturing

---

Abraham exiles himself from the domain of collective discourse not so much in order to constitute himself as an autonomous and fully individuated subject, but because for him faith constitutes a realm of experience that cannot be resisted—that in fact leaves no room for "self-choice." In this sense, Abraham abandons his community less because he wishes to assert his freedom than because such freedom is no longer a possibility for him.

6. Cornell West, for instance, explains that racism is a "disease of the soul" that can only be "tamed by love and care" (1993, p. 29). Along related lines, bell hooks (1994) regards love as a practice of freedom that possesses the power to liberate both self and other.

social connections, eros works to "regenerate the soul by mending the bonds that hubris tears apart" (pp. 178, 215).[7] As a result, a system of justice needs not only to protect the subject's rights, but also to enhance its capacity for communal relationships and social transformation. It needs to facilitate the power of eros to reconnect individuals with their communities. In this sense, Willett's definition of justice revolves around the subject's capacity to fully realize itself as a social entity.

There is much about Willett's analysis of psychic and social rejuvenation that I appreciate. Her community-centered approach may, for instance, be an accurate depiction of the kinds of social networks that have sustained the African-American community—as well as other marginalized communities—in the face of tremendous external pressure and exploitation. Yet I would posit that this is unfortunately not a universal characteristic of communities as such. Again, the matter is highly context-specific. I agree that there are situations when membership in a close-knit community is essential to the individual's inner viability, but we cannot ignore the fact that communities (not unlike dominant culture) are frequently also a source of considerable psychic wounding. Willett's analysis is founded on the assumption that communities are uniformly empowering and compassionate. But this is far from being the case: communities can often be a source of enormous anxiety and ambivalence. Consider, for instance, the immigrant woman who finds herself torn between her native community's views on the appropriate role of women and the views held by her adopted country (cf. Das Dasgupta and DasGupta 1997). Consider also the fact that multiple oppressions easily create networks of exclusion that make it impossible for certain subjects to find a loving community—that banish them into a state of (metaphoric or literal) homelessness. There are individuals who have no easy recourse to community—who are, say, shunned in gay, lesbian, and queer communities because of race while at the same time excluded from communities of color because of sexual orientation. Finally, consider the possibility that the "community" into which one is born holds the kinds of reprehensible views that one does not wish to promote. What if one's "community" happens to be that of the slave owners rather than of the slaves?

Clearly the solution in instances when one's community is a source of internal strife rather than of comfort is to find oneself a more welcom-

---

7. Willett uses the term "hubris" in the Ancient Greek sense of designating a crime of arrogance that violates another person's sense of honor and integrity.

ing venue for the cultivation of social bonds. This often calls for the willingness to form uneasy alliances—alliances that are not necessarily built on love but rather on shared need. Moreover, the ability to accomplish such new alliances sometimes requires one to separate oneself from one's original community—requires, in other words, precisely the kind of "autonomous" inner resourcefulness that has been celebrated by traditional Western accounts of self-actualization. Detaching oneself from one's community of origin—as many immigrants do, for instance—can be psychically quite demanding. Ideally, one does not need to tackle this challenge alone. However, there are times when there is literally no place to turn—when the world withdraws or retreats in the face of one's appeal. At such times, being able to draw upon one's strength as an independent entity may be the only thing that shields one from inner disintegration, as well as rescues one from becoming a powerless supplicant vis-à-vis an indifferent world. Being able to turn to others when misfortune strikes is a wonderful thing. But not everyone is so lucky. And most of us are not so lucky all of the time.

To put the matter succinctly: whereas Willett starts from the premise of an enabling community, more individualistic thinkers recognize that communities are often ethically and existentially complacent; whereas Willett views community as a source of psychic energy, other thinkers concentrate on those aspects of communities that exhaust the subject's inner resources; whereas Willett finds in communal attachments the seeds of resistance and transformation, others—and not just canonical thinkers—have found communities to be a site of regulatory power (and as such, not very different from hegemonic dominant culture). Neither of these perspectives is wrong, strictly speaking, for each is obviously valid with regard to some communities and invalid with regard to others. My point is that although Willett is entirely correct in highlighting the social dimensions of self-actualization, more traditional thinkers are not necessarily *always* mistaken either when they emphasize that existential freedom arises from the subject's ability to distinguish itself from its community.

The solution to the impasse between Willett and more traditional philosophers is to distinguish more carefully between loving communities on the one hand and oppressive forms of sociality on the other. Obviously Willett and other community-minded philosophers are seeking a means for marginalized individuals and social groups to find love and value in a world in which they are despised and atomized. The search for a loving community that will hold and protect one against the violence of hegemonic culture is not only psychically and socially necessary but also—and here I agree with Willett—potentially a powerful foundation for an alternative vision of ethics. However, when traditional Western philosophers promote the ideal of "autonomy," they are usually not pitting individuals against loving communities but rather against types of hegemonic sociality—mass culture and collective complacency, for instance—that can curb the richness of subjective potential by erasing distinctions between individuals. Similarly, twentieth-century thought from Althusser, Lacan, and Foucault to poststructuralist feminist theory has focused on how social power can trap individuals in hegemonic patterns of thought and behavior. While I have tried to show in this book that the contemporary critical emphasis on disciplinary power tends to overstate the degree to which individuals are held hostage by social collectivities, I would be equally reluctant to endorse the idea that sociality is invariably a seat of transformative social energy. If questions of autonomy and individuation have played such a prominent role in Western philosophy, it is because the capacity to set oneself apart from the conventions of one's society—and sometimes even of one's community—is in many instances crucial not only for self-actualization, but also for ethical and political effectiveness.

Another way of approaching the matter is to better distinguish between traumatic separation and necessary individuation, for these are far from being identical. The dominant order's power to divide and conquer marginalized communities is trauma-inducing. But the individual's ability to gain distance from a suffocating community is a matter of necessary individuation. There are at times excellent reasons for resisting the strong tug of societies and communities alike. As Durkheim (1915) recognized long ago, communities can induce individuals to participate in violent, irrational, and destructive behavior—a fact brought home every day by current events, such as ethnic cleansings around the globe. Although it is true, as Willett points out, that communities can enhance the subject's ability to find a voice, they often also seek to repress that voice. To argue that communities are not uniformly enabling is therefore not to refuse the possibility of loving social space, but merely to distinguish between forms of sociality that protect the subject's well-being and others that fail to respect its basic humanity. Sociality obviously sustains us as human beings. However, neither societies nor communities always fulfill this promise of sociality but rather contribute to our further abjection. Moreover, there is a big difference between empowering sociality on the one hand, and the (arguably "social") experience of being elbowed in the subway during rush hour on the other. If the former mends the soul, the latter quite effectively tears it apart.

BEYOND AUTONOMY VS. SOCIALITY:
EXISTENTIAL INTENSITY

I would like to suggest that self-actualization in the end has less to do with the choice between autonomy and sociality than with the intensity with which we are able to experience the various dimensions of our lives—the autonomous and the social alike. By "intensity" I do not necessarily mean to evoke things like force, tension, alacrity, or momentum—rest and contemplative stillness can be intense in their own way—but rather the acuteness with which we are able to encounter the world. Audre Lorde, writing in 1978, placed eros at the center of the individual's ability to lead a fulfilled and empowered existence. In this regard, her argument is not unlike that of Willett. However, in contrast to Willett, Lorde does not seek to determine the relative value of autonomous and social endeavors, but rather conceptualizes self-actualization as a matter of existential intensity—as a matter not only of what we do, but of how "fully we can feel in the doing" (Lorde 1984, p. 54). More specifically, Lorde concentrates on the power of eros to intensify all of our experiences. As she puts it, eros is the "kernel within" that colors life with an energy that "heightens and sensitizes and strengthens" everything that we do (p. 57).

Lorde thus conceptualizes eros as a source of energy that permeates our entire existence. While eros is clearly a way of connecting with others— of sharing a physical, emotional, or intellectual connection with loved ones—Lorde envisions it more broadly, as a dynamic and responsive manner of interacting with the world in general. Lorde stresses that many of the things that make up our everyday realities—from dancing to building a bookcase to examining an idea to writing a beautiful poem (pp. 56–57)— can potentially take on an erotic quality if we allow ourselves to approach them with the kind of keen and impassioned attitude that they deserve. And though there is a hierarchy between such activities—though there is a qualitative difference, for instance, between painting a fence and writing a poem—there is for Lorde no difference between writing a really good poem on the one hand and "moving into sunlight against the body of a woman" on the other (p. 58).

While it would obviously be possible to criticize Lorde for eradicating the distinction between sex and the rest of life in ways that take the passion out of sex, I think her objective is merely to point out that we are capable of finding pleasure in a much wider range of erotically rewarding sensations than we tend to realize. Lorde is, in other words, asking us to reconnect erotically with those dimensions of our existence that we have been culturally conditioned to approach in purely instrumental or rational ways. Every level upon which we sense and experience the world potentially "opens to the erotically satisfying experience," Lorde explains, for eros is, generally speaking, the "open and fearless underlining" of our capacity for joy (p. 56).

Lorde maintains that once we have fully experienced the power of eros—once we know what we are capable of and what we can aspire to—we can no longer, if we are at all honest with ourselves, expect any less of ourselves. Lorde therefore views eros as a kind of measuring stick that we can use to evaluate the rest of our lives so as to make sure that we are living all aspects of our existence to the fullest of our capacity; eros for Lorde is the lens through which we scrutinize our lives in an attempt to ensure that we do not settle for the merely conventional or convenient, but rather pursue those activities and modes of being that give us the kind of satisfaction that only an erotic attitude toward life can offer. When we are in touch with the erotic, Lorde maintains, we become less willing to accept states of despair, resignation, and powerlessness, and begin instead to take responsibility for ourselves and our actions in the world. This is because eros allows us to live "from within ourselves" rather than by external directives that guide us into normative psychic and social arrangement (p. 58). In this manner, eros is what allows us to look at the world from a fresh perspective, and what thus also allows us to be surprised by the obvious.

Lorde's expansive conception of eros offers a useful contrast to Willett's social eros in that it does not seek to privilege the individual's social tendencies over her private aspirations. Like Willett, Lorde recognizes the social dimensions of eros, arguing that eros represents an important reservoir of communal energy, and that the suppression of this energy among the oppressed consequently perpetuates a social system that "defines the good in terms of profit rather than in terms of human need" (p. 55). However, Lorde's analysis of the social importance of eros does not lead her to devalue its more artistic or contemplative potentialities. One of the main problems with Willett's argument is that it consistently does exactly this—that in seeking to discredit conceptions of self-actualization that overemphasize the value of autonomy and individuation, Willett veers in the opposite direction of burying the individual under the social in ways that obscure all solitary or asocial sources of erotic pleasure.

An excellent example of this is Willett's critique of Marcuse's analysis of the sense of emptiness that characterizes the modern "one-dimensional" man whose erotic energy is drained by the capitalist "performance principle" that defines his existence (Marcuse 1955, 1964). Modern society, Marcuse argues, drives the individual to excessive rates of productivity by narrowing his self-definition in such a way that cycles of production and consumption take precedence over other more amorphous desires— such as the desire for peace and quiet, the desire for artistic and intellectual play, and the desire for contemplative pleasure. What this means is that the modern subject is often unable to complete its process of individuation, and ends up developing its potentialities in a one-sided, unbalanced, and disconnected manner. Marcuse's solution to the problem resides in the subject's renewed ability to foster its creative capacities through artistic and introspective endeavors. Willett, while agreeing with the main outlines of Marcuse's critique of modern society, takes issue with his solution, labeling it individualistic, narcissistic, and aristocratic (see Willett 2001, pp. 112–122). There may well be something about the manner in which Marcuse presents his views—such as his emphasis on high art and the kinds of creative pursuits that require a great deal of leisure time—that justifies Willett's assessment. Yet I find Willett's predominantly social solution to the individual's existential malaise equally limited. It may well be that writing poetry is a narcissistic enterprise. But does this mean that we want to discourage people from writing poetry?

To be fair to Willett, we should note that her criticism of Marcuse is staged in the context of an analysis of the various forms of arrogance that poison intersubjective, social, and even global relationships. Willett rejects Marcuse's aestheticist utopia in part because she recognizes that the individual's ability to effectively mobilize her creative capacities is in many instances directly dependent on the sustaining labor of others—that the ability to write poetry is often purchased at the price of denying others the same privilege. Yet I would insist that the problem resides not with the act of writing poetry, and even less with the erotic pleasure that inheres to this activity, but rather with the economic and socio-political forces that make it impossible for everyone (who so wishes) to lead the kind of life that would allow for artistic pleasure—as well as for play and contemplation—along with material survival. Lorde argues that eros supplies us with the inner spark that enables us to approach our lives with both ardor and dedication. There is no doubt that unequal social arrangements frequently destroy our ability to access this spark. But this does not mean that the spark itself is not worthy of our respect.

What I am saying is that the resurrection of the social power of eros does not have to take place at the expense of the individual's more private preoccupations. The "totality" of character that Marcuse endorses has less to do with the kind of totalitarian exclusion of alterity that characterizes metaphysical notions of unitary subjectivity than with the idea that a full life does not exclude parts of the self, but rather aspires to find a way for the disparate components of the individual's being to co-exist in a meaningful manner. We are all composed of multiple desires, some of which lean toward connection, others toward separation. The way in which the currents of sociality and autonomy intermingle within an individual—determining whether the individual is more inclined toward the collective or the contemplative—depends in large part on the particulars of that individual's psychic history, but we know that it is when the balance between the social and the private is disturbed that the individual experiences symptoms of malaise: those whose existence is consumed by the demands of sociality may find themselves yearning for privacy, whereas those who experience long periods of solitude may yearn for the company of others.

Ideally, our private time feeds our social capacities, and our social existence enriches our privacy, but when the demands of one sphere are sacrificed for the exigencies of the other, it is difficult to feel well-rounded and at ease with oneself. The fact that traditional Western notions of self-actualization were often centered on private acts of creativity and fulfillment does not mean that we should now categorically condemn all such acts; the solution to the historical overvaluation of the private over the social lies not in reversing the tide by subsuming the private under the social, but rather in honoring both of these components of human experience. I agree that sustaining social bonds can go a long way in making us feel healthy and empowered. But they alone do not satisfy all of our existential yearnings. Moreover, I would say that the ideal of the creative and polyvalent psyche that Marcuse promotes is actually highly compatible with the ethos of intersubjectivity that Willett advances, for it is those individuals who possess a multifaceted inner life who are best able to cultivate the kinds of loving and responsible relationships that Willett sanctions. Psychic versatility does not in any way compromise, but rather enhances, the individual's ability to respond to the needs of others; in Oliver's terms, such versatility makes us better witnesses, enabling us to fulfill our ethical obligation to those around us.

I would say that it is when we are able to cultivate meaningful social and communal ties without losing our sense of being rooted in our own "being" that we approach the soul—that we approach a way of inhabiting the world that remains open to it without being overly dependent on it. To argue that sociality does not fulfill all of our needs is therefore not to denigrate intersubjectivity, but merely to recognize that our psychic lives are too complex to be satisfied with either/or solutions. As we have seen, the fast pace and multiple demands of contemporary life—not to mention oppressive social circumstances—frequently deprive us of much needed contemplative space, which is why I think that it is necessary to defend solitude along with forms of loving sociality. Solitude, in muting the immediacy of life's multiple demands, can give the subject a glimpse of psychic domains rarely visited or apprehended, asking it to confront those aspects of its existence that under normal circumstances remain banished to the remote corners of its consciousness. This distillation of inner resources can contribute to the enrichment of the soul, and it in no way forecloses the possibility of loving interpersonal connections.

While Willett appears to presume that the only options available to us are the traditional narcissistic and autonomous subject on the one hand, and the fully socialized individual on the other, it seems to me that the individual is always inevitably autonomous and social at once. Narcissism is, moreover, a tricky concept, for even if we were to allow that the attempt to bolster the individual's private aspirations is a narcissistic endeavor—which I do not think it always is—there are situations in which such narcissistic support is highly necessary. Indeed, when it comes to socially inflicted psychic injury—the kind of injury that Willett's own notion of social eros is meant to redress—what are we dealing with if not a form of narcissistic wounding that erodes the individual's sense of self-esteem? As Lynne Layton maintains, even if those outside of dominant culture possess a critical perspective on this culture in that they are able to see through its hegemonic codes and conventions, they may not always be able to escape the "narcissistic injuries" imposed upon them by this culture (1998, p. 36). As a result, although our ultimate objective should be to contest narcissistic constellations of identity (see Layton 1998, Chapter 2)—for it is true that these constellations in the long run limit our existential options as well as our ability to interact with others in non-repressive and constructive ways—the problem is not always, as Willett seems to assume, an excess of narcissism. At times, it is the absence of such narcissism that marks the experience of psychic abjection.

RISKING LOVE, RISKING ONESELF

Willett's notion of eros is also somewhat problematic in that it is based on the relationship between mother and child. Although Willett acknowledges the existence of various forms of erotic attachment, she argues that it is in the bond between mother and child "that we find an origin of human eros and a source of a most basic conception of justice" (2001, p. 216). Echoing Jessica Benjamin's (1988) earlier critique of the Freudian argument that fusion-love is a regressive force that obstructs processes of differentiation and individuation, Willett criticizes those psychoanalytic theories of subjectivity that locate maturity in the child's capacity to separate from its mother. She then proceeds to reroot subjectivity in the child's erotic attachment to its mother by theorizing mothering as the foundation of both agency and ethics (cf. Oliver 1997, Willett 1995). Though Willett does an admirable job of trying to sidestep the essentializing tendencies of this approach—insisting, for instance, that the mother–child relation is a cultural rather than a biological nexus of "eros, economic labor, and social force" (2001, p. 34)[8]—her analysis suffers from the same blind spot as her analysis of community, namely the assumption that all mothers are good mothers and that the child's relationship to its mother is always a rewarding one.[9]

It is, moreover, very difficult to ground ethics in the mother–child bond without heterosexualizing subjectivity and ethics alike. Willett makes a valiant effort to avoid this—providing, for instance, an incisive critique of the heterosexism of Irigaray's analysis of motherhood (Willett 2001, p. 151)—yet her discussion does not fully manage to displace the hetero-

---

8. Particularly interesting in this context is Willett's discussion of caregiving as skilled labor, as well as her analysis of the economic and socio-cultural implications of paid domestic labor. On this, see Chapter 4 of *The Soul of Justice*.

9. Willett states: "The paradigmatic case of carework is the preservative love that children reserve from their mothers. While the liberal model takes either the self-interested agent of the marketplace or the disinterested rational thinker as paradigmatic of the moral subject, care ethics emphasizes the nurturing and altruistic qualities of caregivers" (2001, p. 24).

sexual mother from the throne of the primary caregiver. Indeed, although Willett certainly emphasizes the importance of alternative caregivers, it is difficult to read her text without getting the impression that what is most powerful about eros—namely its infinite versatility and unpredictability— has been domesticated into the gentle touch of the (invariably) loving mother. Willett's notion of social eros, perhaps precisely because it cannot fully avoid the essentializing, idealizing, and heterosexualizing currents that almost inevitably undermine theories that seek in motherhood the remedy for the failings of individualistic accounts of self-actualization, offers a remarkably docile image of eros. Willett's eros is caring, giving, and infinitely faithful. Yet one does not have to be Georges Bataille to know that while eros often mends the rifts that separate us from one another, it also holds the potential to throw us into tumultuous states of internal disarray, and to destroy our sense of security and social belonging.

Bataille posits that the destruction of sociality is the whole point of eros in its more passionate manifestations. He describes eros as a yearning to fall, to lose one's balance, and to relinquish self-control precisely so as to attain a taste of what resides beyond the social. While we are "discontinuous" beings who live in a state of radical separation from each other, Bataille explains, we yearn to experience ourselves as continuous with others. By this Bataille does not mean that we wish to form loving social relationships in the sense that Willett is talking about, but rather that we suffer from a deeply nostalgic yearning for a state of originary continuity that predates the rules and regulations that uphold us as social beings.[10] As a result, we are driven by a primordial temptation to annihilate ourselves as distinctive identities so as to achieve a state of absolute (and entirely asocial) union with others. Eros, insofar as it explicitly challenges the boundaries that separate the self from the other, offers one of the most direct means of pursuing this state of unconditional continuity. As Bataille puts it, the purpose of eros is to test and defy "the self-contained character of the participators as they are in their normal lives"; because eros strikes at "the inmost core of the living being, so that the heart stands still," it can bring about the momentary dissolution of the individual as she exists in the realm of culture and everyday reality (1957, p. 17).

---

10. Bataille's conception of eros shares a great deal with that of Lacan for, like Lacan, he believes that human beings suffer from a sense of discontinuity—from a sense of having been severed from an originary state of continuity (cf. the Lacanian imaginary)—and that they are consequently driven by a powerful primordial urge to merge with others.

Passionate eros, by temporarily suspending the social structures that hold the self apart from others, provides a glimpse of the kind of experiential reality that is in many ways the very antithesis of sociality. By this I do not mean to counter Willett's notion of a healing and restorative eros with one that is wholly disruptive, but merely to add another dimension to the story. While Willett views eros primarily as the social glue that strengthens interpersonal relationships and communities, eros can also challenge the individual's social integrity in a rather fundamental manner. Eros tempts the individual to invite the other to dwell within, and in some ways to take possession of, the self. In Kristeva's words, "in the rapture of love, the limits of one's own identity vanish"; "in love 'I' has been an *other*" (1983, pp. 2, 4). In this sense, the blurring of the distinction between self and other that eros entails can bring about a state of radical instability. This is what gives passionate eros its power to thrill. But it is also what grants it the potential to cause intense suffering. In risking oneself in love, one always risks oneself as a subject as well.

Yet if eros represents a risk, it often seems like a risk well worth taking. One reason for this is that eros possesses the power to confer upon the individual the ardent and much-coveted sense of feeling fully alive. As Kristeva puts it, the subject in love "has the impression of speaking at last, for the first time, for real" (p. 3). In the *Phaedrus*, Plato tells us that the sight of the beloved being causes the feathers of the lover's soul to grow so that it can soar to the heights (370 B.C., p. 58). This image vividly evokes the sense of inner renewal and self-awakening that can accompany erotic experience. Precisely because passionate eros implies the incorporation of the other within the self, it allows the self to overstep its normal boundaries, and to access facets and potentialities of its being that ordinarily remain hidden or inactive. The instability of eros can therefore be lived as deeply transformative in that it enables the subject to arrive at a new understanding of itself. Simone de Beauvoir once stated that love "is the developer that brings out in clear, positive detail the dim negative, otherwise as useless as a blank exposure" (1949, p. 647).[11] Along related lines, Kristeva remarks that passionate love is "the time and space in which 'I' assumes

---

11. De Beauvoir makes this statement in the context of her critique of the manner in which socio-cultural expectations encourage women to seek self-actualization through romantic love. De Beauvoir's point is therefore not to argue that love gives meaning to our lives, but merely that it possesses the power to mislead us into thinking that this is the case (cf. my comments on Lacan below and in Chapter 3).

the right to be extraordinary"; "I am, in love, at the zenith of subjectivity" (1983, p. 5). Eros can thus give rise to an unparalled expansion of the self, creating a living, breathing, and uniquely inspired entity. At least for the time being.

The dynamic of risk and rebirth that eros entails implies that it is when the subject surrenders its social boundaries that it attains the sought-after experience of rejuvenation. Emmanuel Ghent (1990) defines such self-surrender as follows: "The meaning that I will give to the term 'surrender' has nothing to do with hoisting a white flag; in fact, rather than carrying a connotation of defeat, the term will convey a quality of liberation and expansion of the self as a corollary to the letting down of defensive barriers" (p. 108). In Ghent's view, the subject's longing to surrender, to give itself over to the other in the sense that Bataille describes, arises primarily from a wish to be reached, known, and acknowledged in some profound manner. That is, rather than expressing a masochistic or self-undermining need to submit, the impulse to surrender speaks to a yearning for some dead, buried, or repressed part of the self to be dug up and resurrected. The self-shattering that takes place in surrender, Ghent proposes, works to renegotiate and reorganize the self's contours in that it allows the self to momentarily "lose" itself so as to be able to resurface transformed, with its limits reconfigured. From this perspective, the longing to surrender emerges "as a special detail in a more inclusive picture: growth and the restitution of impeded growth, healing" (p. 132).[12] This is one reason that the undoing of the self that eros brings about is also the zenith of subjectivity. Surrender can be conceived of as a particular way of giving life to the self and, as such, as a form of self-actualization.

Ghent's notion of surrender is conceptually connected to Oliver's account of witnessing in that both require the support of a loving other who is willing and able to facilitate the subject's quest for self-discovery. The task of the facilitating other is to enable the subject to access (and perhaps, after the fact, even to articulate) a part of its being that it would not be able to access on its own. Ghent explains that, unlike submission,

---

12. There are components of Ghent's argument—such as his usage of Winnicott's distinction between a "true" and "false" self, as well as his vocabulary of authenticity, completeness, and psychic integration—that are difficult to navigate in the posthumanist context. However, I think that there is no need to equate "authenticity" in the Ghentian sense with any notion of essential subjectivity. Rather, authenticity for Ghent is simply a marker of a creative, vibrant, and versatile psyche.

surrender cannot in any way be induced, forced, or compelled. As he observes, "One may surrender 'in the presence of another,' not 'to another' as in the case of submission" (p. 111). Moreover, because surrender conveys the subject so perilously close to self-annihilation, it calls for the presence of someone reassuring enough to make it possible for the subject to "take a chance on surrendering" (p. 112). Bataille already notes that while passionate eros encourages the subject to surrender, this surrender needs to take place within a larger structure of constraint so that the subject is able to lose its footing "without falling irrevocably" (1957, p. 244). Eros, in other words, demands a safety net that guarantees that when the structures of the self crumble, the structures of the other remain solid enough to provide the necessary support. For Bataille, the disorder of eros can in fact only be exciting within the context of order; a permanent state of disorder would quickly lose its attraction, turning lack of control into a constant state with neither savor nor interest. Ghent in turn emphasizes that surrender without a strong "ally" is impossible for the simple reason that it is too frightening (1990, p. 112).

For Ghent, the other serves as a transitional object that facilitates the subject's psychic unveiling without in any way contributing to the content of this unveiling. What is required of this other is the ability to vacate the intersubjective space in such a way as to make room for the subject's surrender. By this I obviously do not mean the kind of vacating that would provoke a sense of emptiness or abandonment, but rather the kind of enabling presence that affirms without making a demand. The position of the facilitating other is therefore rather demanding in that while the other needs to be careful not to intrude on the subject's experience, it is at the same time asked to project an illusion of strength. There are some individuals in the presence of whom it is easy to surrender, who in fact seem to spontaneously *solicit* such surrender, and who know how to respond to the other's unraveling in productive ways. Such people are good witnesses. Others, such as analysts, may train themselves in the art of witnessing.[13]

The shattering of the self in passionate eros transports the subject to an alternative realm of consciousness, and consequently speaks to those aspects of its life that aspire to stretch the limits of the possible. In this

---

13. Self-surrender can obviously take place outside of passionate eros as well. In the present context, it is interesting to contemplate the similarities between Ghent's understanding of the facilitating other on the one hand and Lacan's notion of the analyst as the *sujet-supposé-à-savoir* on the other.

sense, eros offers the subject a rather singular experience of existential intensity. Indeed, insofar as eros is undertaken with the whole of one's being,
it is one way to attain the kind of acuteness of experience Lorde talks
about (and Willett for the most part ignores). While eros appears to reach
beyond the world in that it tends toward the transcendent, from another
perspective it is merely a mode of experiencing the world in the most
piercing manner possible. After all, fully experiencing the world does not
necessarily mean that one has to remain in the realm of the ordinary, predictable, and everyday. At times it implies being able to access what is
exceptional about the world. Because eros possesses the power to rupture
the monotony of our daily lives, it can provide us with a new and powerful lens through which to view the world. Whereas passion can blind us in
astonishing ways, it can also offer us a sharper intuitive vision of those
hopes, dreams, wishes, and desires that cannot find an outlet in ordinary
life—that normally remain masked under the morass of our mundane preoccupations. In this manner, eros confers an epic quality upon the everyday. While eros makes us wholly unreliable judges of most aspects of our
lives, it gives us a "higher" form of insight into what might satisfy the less
rational aspects of these lives.

There are ways in which passionate eros is, quite literally, not of this
world. This explains the impulse toward mythologization that so often
enters into our attempts to make sense of the immensity of sentiment that
seizes us in passionate encounters. This process of mythologization is what
transforms our loves into legends, lending them an otherworldly aura and
significance; it is through love that we most easily and consistently enter
the realm of the mythological, constructing the kinds of tales or tapestries
of extraordinariness that transcend time, space, and reality. Whether or
not our myths are true in any conventional sense is much less important
than their ability to speak evocatively about the power of eros to give rise
to inspiration and inner revitalization.

In the chapters that follow, I will talk about why Lacan views this kind
of passion with a great deal of suspicion, arguing that the subject's longing
for fusion-love leads it to look for self-actualization in all the wrong places.
In the previous chapter, I emphasized the inherently mythological nature
of identities, and suggested that psychoanalysis, like Nietzschean self-
stylization and Foucault's care of the self, is one possible technique through
which the subject can seek to refashion the various myths that govern its
existence. For Lacan, passionate eros is one of the greatest obstacles to the
subject's ability to undertake this task of remythologization because such

eros possesses its *own* mythological power that matches—or even exceeds—that of psychoanalysis. Passionate eros, in other words, wields a mythological power that is strong enough to successfully compete with whatever similar power analysis might possess. However, Lacan argues, it is always a misplaced attempt at self-constitution. Indeed, Lacan implies that when the subject experiences eros as its (mythological) destiny, this is simply an indication that it has been hard-wired, on the level of unconscious desire, to seek its happiness in objects of a particular kind; the "otherworldly" power of eros expresses the fact that it is driven by unconscious desire that exceeds the subject's rational comprehension. This is why, among the different forms of self-mythologization available to the subject, eros is the one that most consistently and painfully deceives the subject.

Though I for the most part agree with Lacan's analysis, it is important to note two ways in which passionate eros might be considered a valid site of self-mythologization (and thus of self-actualization). The first is that the very essence of passion is to break out of conventional and well-established modes of behavior, which implies that it is potentially innovative. Eros has no patience with rigidity: it moves and forces us to move with it; it may be transient, but it renders us forever altered; it leaves behind a lasting imprint, a trace of the other within the self. When this type of passion ends, it is difficult to say categorically that we have made a mistake, for even the suffering that eros brings can initiate and enlighten. As I will argue in Chapter 5, getting things right is not always the best thing that can happen to us, for our mistakes—perhaps more than our successes—force us to evolve in new and unforeseeable directions.

Second, passionate eros offers us a vision of self-actualization that is in many ways the very antithesis of the traits that we are culturally taught to esteem, such as coherence, mastery, self-possession, and critical insight. Above I mentioned that traditional Western philosophies sometimes conceptualize transcendence as a matter of the individual's absolute surrender to a higher principle. This strain of thought has been all but lost in contemporary discussions of subjectivity, whether humanist or posthumanist. Yet it is potentially quite valuable, for it not only provides an incisive critique of the rationalist self of humanist philosophy, but it puts the body and its delights into play in ways that remind us that existential intensity is a matter of sensory experience as much as of psychic or affective experience. Moreover, to the extent that passionate eros highlights the psyche's permeability, it underscores the self's dependence on others in ways that contradict the socio-culturally sanctioned ideal of subjectivity as a site of sovereign self-constitution. As such, it complements Willett's critique of traditional Western conceptions of autonomous subjectivity without losing sight of the more disorderly side of eros. Neither Willett's model of social eros, nor the discussion of self-surrender that I have presented here, in itself provides a sufficient account of self-actualization; placed together, however, they bring us closer to an understanding of how the loss of autonomy does not necessarily translate to the impossibility of self-actualization.

What connotes self-actualization for a particular person may connote the very opposite for another person in a different context. And what self-actualization signifies for a particular individual across time is also a matter of constant negotiation. In this book, my hypothesis has been that psychic vitality and multidimensionality are important features of self-actualization, and that the enrichment of the subject's inner potentialities demands its capacity to participate, in however partial a manner, in the making of its own meanings. I have in fact suggested that creative agency calls for the subject's ability to generate new forms of meaning without full faithfulness to preexisting conventions of meaning-production. I have also assumed that psychic resilience—the ability to turn obstacles into a site of possibility—is a valuable asset. The purpose of this chapter has been to highlight the context-specific nature of the theoretical tools that we possess to discuss agency and self-actualization, and to shift us away from the ultimately futile quest to determine the relative value of social and private endeavors. In emphasizing the distinction between loving and harmful forms of sociality, I have tried to provide a multifaceted rendering of what it means for the individual to relate to collective structures. My discussion thus far suggests that the soul is best cultivated by protecting its aptitude for transformation. The final three chapters of this book will focus on the insights that psychoanalysis (with some help from Nietzsche) can offer us about psychic transformation.

3

Lack

The psychoanalytic experience . . . manipulates the poetic function of language to give to [man's] desire its symbolic mediation. May that experience enable you to understand at last that it is in the gift of speech that all the reality of its effects resides; for it is by way of this gift that all reality has come to man and it is by his continued act that he maintains it.

Jacques Lacan, *Écrits*

LACAN'S GIFT OF SPEECH

I have chosen in this book to honor the posthumanist insight that at the core of human subjectivity there is no enduring substance, but rather a lack or nothingness. I have done so not only because I think that it would be a mistake to revert to a reassuring notion of inner totality, but also because the idea of constitutive lack provides a means of positing a certain kind of profundity at the very inception of psychic life. It is, after all, difficult to envision psychic wounding as purely a surface phenomenon; the very idea of a wound steers us toward a vertical rather than a horizontal model of subjective reality. At the same time, it must be recognized that placing lack at the center of subjectivity all too easily conjures up images of abjection and disempowerment. It is in part for this reason—to resist the intuitive alignment of lack with a paucity of psychic resources—that I have begun to suggest that the subject's lack-in-being should not be read exclusively as a site of alienation. The loss of secure existential foundations may be an indispensable dimension of posthumanist thought, yet this decentering of the self should not be equated with the impossibility of honoring the creative capabilities of the psyche.

In this chapter, I would like to take a closer look at the Lacanian notion of lack in an attempt to discover how we might be able to read lack affirmatively, as what gives rise to the subject's innovative capacities, and what consequently allows it to actualize itself as a being of psychic potentiality. What Lacan understood so well is that it is only as a creature of lack that the subject possesses the power to generate meaning. In Chapter 1, I argued that Foucault envisions power as that which enables the subject to produce new discourses about the self even as it limits the terrain of discursive possibility. Similarly, Lacan shows us that the signifier bestows upon the subject the gift of meaning even as it renders it alienated by drawing it into a symbolic system that it cannot control. Indeed, if my search for a restorative theory of psychic life—for a compelling means of capturing the elusive contours of the posthumanist soul, if you will—draws on Lacanian theory, it is because Lacan is so centrally interested in the signifier's ability to grant meaning even as it dispossesses the subject of its fantasies of omnipotence and ontological wholeness.

The purpose of this chapter is twofold. First, I would like to show that if we are able to extract from Lacanian psychoanalysis a theory of creativity, we can arrive at a more tangible and psychically informed understanding of what it means for the individual to exist as a being of potentiality. We will gain a better sense of how to talk about self-actualization in the constructivist context. And we will discover that although Lacan is frequently accused of denigrating love, he in fact offers us a remarkably generous account of love. Second, I would like to consider what Lacan might still be able to contribute to progressive critical discourses, particularly feminist and queer theory. I will argue that reading Lacan as a clinician will give us access to the kinds of insights about gender and sexuality that highlight the generative—as opposed to merely the hegemonic—dimensions of the symbolic order.

While much of Lacanian criticism has recoiled from the very idea that Lacan might be interested in the innovative potentialities of the psyche, I would like to suggest that Lacan is in fact intensely invested in the individual's psychic viability. By this I do not mean to imply that Lacan presents a fully articulated theory of psychic potentiality—for this is far from being the case—but merely that his work can be read in ways that take us a long way toward such a theory. To follow this path, however, we must be willing to engage in a paradigm shift that draws out the clinical aspects of Lacanian thought. I believe that if contemporary criticism has tended to neglect the more imaginative dimensions of Lacanian theory, it is in part because Lacanian analysis in the United States has for the most part been filtered through academic discourses that entirely neglect its clinical aspirations. Academic Lacanians—of whom I am one—often talk about Lacanian theory as if it had nothing to do with clinical concerns, with the result that everything "therapeutic" becomes associated with relational or other Anglo-American schools of analytic practice. This in turn leads to an unnecessarily reductive notion not only of what it means to read Lacan, but also what it means to be a clinician.

I would like to suggest that it may in fact be quite useful to read Lacan as a clinician, as someone who takes seriously the fact that psychoanalysis at its Freudian inception was centered around the impetus to alleviate the analysand's psychic pain. Indeed, although Lacanian theory is often presented in ways that might lead one to believe that it is wholly divorced from ideals of psychic well-being, I like to remind myself that whatever else Lacan was, he was always a faithful interpreter of Freud and, as such, could not possibly be wholly unconcerned with the recuperative goals of analysis. The fact that Lacanian approaches are not compatible with the ideal of a coherent self does not mean that they cannot help the subject live its life in rewarding ways. Lacan may not have been in the least interested in the notion of a secure ego but, as I hope to illustrate, he was quite strongly invested in the kind of resilient subjectivity that is able to constructively inhabit a highly contradictory space of existential instability and irresoluteness.

There is of course no doubt that the Lacanian subject is irrevocably split by discourse. I agree with other Lacanian thinkers that the subject emerges as a being of lack when it enters the realm of signification. The condition of the speaking subject is therefore inherently tragic in that alienation is the price it pays for social intelligibility. Lacan consistently emphasizes the power of the signifier to undermine the autonomy of the self, explaining that it is not only the subject who speaks but rather the "passion" of the signifier that speaks through the subject (1966, p. 284). This is Lacan's way of reminding us that the subject's unconscious "speaks" a language that originates in the realm of the symbolic Other—the collective realm of language, culture, and sociality into which every individual is interpellated through a complex system of kinship and prohibition. The signifier carries the trace of the desire imprinted in the subject's psyche by this process of interpellation, which means that whenever the subject speaks, it is at least in part its unconscious desire that is uttered. In this sense, the signifier is, quite literally, what transports the subject's passion.

Another way of stating the matter is to say that the Lacanian subject is always born out of the loss of love. The transition from the imaginary to the symbolic[1]—a transition that is mediated by the castration complex and that gives rise to the unconscious—is marked by loss on two different levels in that the signifier not only fractures the beauty and coherence of the emerging ego of the mirror stage, but also demands a renunciation of those preverbal cathexes which, even if in their preoedipal form they cannot yet be categorized as "love," come—retroactively, as a result of their loss—to be experienced as such. To the extent that the subject comes into being by submitting to the law of the signifier, what gets sacrificed, what undergoes a repression, an existential elision, is the unnameable, unrepresentable, and unsymbolizable "nonobject" of desire that Lacan (1986) calls *das Ding*, and that for the subject commemorates the loss of imaginary wholeness.

The signifier's intrusion into the infant's imaginary space therefore not only results in a narcissistic wound (the shattering of the mirror stage), but also gives rise to an archaic lack (the loss of *das Ding*) that remains beyond the subject's conceptual and significatory capacities, but that nevertheless continues to disseminate its effects throughout its unconscious psychic states. In this manner, it is the subject's encounter with the signifier that teaches it to desire, and that propels it on an interminable quest to recover, repossess, and reactivate the "love" whose loss haunts the very origins of its being. Subjectivity in this sense is constituted around an existential abyss that separates desire from fulfillment in ways that perpetu-

---

1. Readers unfamiliar with the basics of Lacanian theory are invited to consult one of the following sources: Dor 1997a,b, Feher-Gurewich and Tort 1996, Grosz 1990. Here I would merely like to note that Lacan explains subject formation in terms of the child's transition from the imaginary to the symbolic. The symbolic is quite simply the cultural order into which all of us are socialized as a result of language acquisition. The imaginary, in turn, is the preverbal space of symbiotic attachment to our primary caretakers; it is a space where we do not yet possess any sense of independent selfhood, where there is no separation between the self and the other, and therefore no experience of lack or alienation. Although the relationship between the imaginary and the symbolic is often presented as a developmental, it is important to keep in mind that Lacan emphasizes that we spend our entire lives navigating the terrain between these two registers (as well as the real). Most of our waking hours are spent in the symbolic, which is the social sphere of signification and meaning-production, but there are experiences—such as passionate love—that pull us toward the imaginary, toward the sensation of wholeness and absolute belonging. As we will see below, one reason passionate love is so seductive is that it is driven by the fantasy of accessing a state of being that has not yet been contaminated by lack or alienation.

ate the subject's inexhaustible pursuit of what it perceives as lost. The fact that nothing was lost in reality—that the subject's access to satisfaction is blocked not so much because language bars its return to the lost object but because no such object existed in the first place—does not in any way lessen the subject's determination to find what it thinks it has lost. Yet, because it is this loss that brings into existence the subject's entire psychic life, that initiates its conscious, as well as unconscious, internal processes, it is inherently irredeemable—a constitutive lack without which subjectivity could not exist.

It is thus apparent that the signifier stages for Lacan a scene of separation, alienation, and symbolic castration.[2] Lacan's statements to this effect are in fact so frequent that it would be easy enough to become fixated on the painfulness of this process of acculturation, and to regard subjectivity as a site of the kind of division and disillusionment that can never be overcome. But what if we flip things around, and read the Lacanian notion of lack not as what estranges the subject from being and meaning, but rather as what gives it all the necessary tools for a meaningful kind of being?

Though Lacan certainly emphasizes the alienating dimensions of the subject's interpellation into the symbolic order, he also stresses that this interpellation is what gives the subject access to the signifier as a valuable instrument of meaning-making. The fact that the psyche is inhabited by the signifier may curtail the subject's capacity for autonomous self-authorship, yet it is simultaneously what engenders the possibility of signification in the first place, enabling the subject to constitute itself as a being that possesses the ability to actively reflect on the modalities of its existence. This type of self-constitution remains precarious in that it does not provide any stable subjective reality, yet it is at the same time deeply necessary for the subject's ability to make sense of its life. The inner void instituted by the signifier gives rise to a representational resourcefulness that allows the subject to weave an entire psychic apparatus around its constitutive losses—that, in other words, enables the subject to translate its lack into a livable inner reality. It is for this reason that Lacan tells us that it is only by way of the "gift of speech" (1966, p. 106) that all reality has come to us; if man speaks, Lacan states, it is because "the symbol has made him man" (p. 65). In this manner, Lacan privileges the signifier as the humanizing

---

2. "Symbolic castration" refers to the fact that the signifier divests the subject of its sense of imaginary wholeness. It means that the subject—insofar as it is a subject of the unconscious—is always inevitably traversed by the discourse of the Other.

principle that propels the subject into the realm of sociality and meaning-production.

The Lacanian symbolic could thus be said to render the individual vulnerable and resourceful at once—vulnerable because it causes him to desire, and resourceful because it grants him the ability to construct meaning. Since in Lacanian theory it is most decidedly the signifier that gives meaning to the signified (rather than vice versa), I believe that it would be reductive to focus on the restrictive dimensions of signification without recognizing the manner in which it opens up the wealth and wonder of meaning. Lacan in fact explicitly depicts the signifier as an emblem of a "wholly potential power" (p. 306) that gives birth to possibility. Along similar lines, he describes the symbolic as "the locus of the signifier's treasure" (p. 304), thereby emphasizing the extent to which the human subject benefits from participating in a socio-symbolic system of meaning. The symbolic may place limits on what the subject finds conceptually and representationally possible, yet it simultaneously activates all the creative potentialities of its psychic life. Moreover, the signifier lends much-needed structure to the subject's existence. Without this structure, the subject would not be able to proceed with the task of living in the world, but would instead remain forever caught in the preoedipal network of bodily drives and energies that carry both pleasure and unpleasure but are utterly incapable of generating meaning.

Lacan therefore suggests that it is through the experience of loss that the subject emerges as an imaginatively enabled entity; it is the trace of the absent other—the more or less faint imprint of *das Ding*—that allows the subject to participate in the production of meaning. Lack for Lacan is therefore deeply animated in the sense that it—more than any sense of possession—activates all of the subject's psychic potentialities. As Kaja Silverman has so aptly stated, the Lacanian subject pays the price of loss and alienation in order to gain access to the "world-making capacities" of the signifier (2000, p. 57). The signifier may cause the "death" of being—may introduce a lack within the fullness of being—but this is the kind of death that, rather than extinguishing life, sustains existence.[3]

---

3. Lacan writes: "Being of non-being, that is how *I* as subject comes to the scene, conjugated with the double aporia of a true survival that is abolished by knowledge of itself, and by a discourse in which it is death that sustains existence" (1966, p. 300). Lacan then proceeds to distinguish between the kind of death that ends life (which is death in the sense that we usually understand it) and the kind of death that brings life (which is death in the sense that Lacan is talking about here, i.e., the "death" of the fullness of being).

HEIDEGGER'S POETIC DWELLING

One reason Silverman reads Lacan along the same lines as I have here begun to do is that she connects Lacan's notion of lack to Heidegger's concept of nothingness.[4] Heidegger offers a highly relevant account of what it
means for the human subject to exist as a being of lack and alienation. While
Heidegger does not share Lacan's focus on psychic processes and the unconscious, he, like Lacan, advocates a fundamentally non-essentialist conception of subjectivity. Heidegger calls the human being "Dasein" (literally:
being-there) in order to emphasize its status as an entity that is firmly
implanted in the affairs of the world. For Heidegger, as for Lacan, being
human is a social accomplishment. And living a fully human life entails
coming to terms with sociality.

Heidegger also shares a great deal with Nietzsche (as well as with
Kierkegaard) in that he recognizes that Dasein's immersion in the world
inevitably places it in danger of being engulfed by what is most complacent about collective life. Heidegger labels the collectivity the "they," and
points out that because Dasein is by definition a being who exists among
and alongside other people, objects, and things, it cannot be understood
independently of the "they." At the same time, because Heidegger is deeply
invested in the individual's capacity to find an authentic manner of living
in the world, he endeavors to elucidate the conditions under which it becomes possible for Dasein to resist the appeal of the "they." Whereas the
"they," like the Nietzschean herd, operates under the auspices of conformity, it is Dasein's existential duty—like that of the Nietzschean noble—
to defy the familiarity of the "they" so as to forge its distinctive (and therefore
authentic) path through life.

The challenge that Dasein thus faces is to find a way of participating
in collective life without losing its creativity; although there is no way to
avoid being part of the "they," Dasein's task is to find a mode of existing in
the world that remains acutely conscious of, and resistant to, the power of
the "they" to induce it into states of inertia and inactivity. Heidegger in fact
describes in intricate detail the tension that exists between the everyday "av-
erageness" of the "they" on the one hand and Dasein's dynamic and fully
individualized identity on the other. While Dasein's ability to realize the singularity of its existential promise marks the authentic life, the "inauthentic"

---

4. I will return to Silverman later in this chapter. While my argument was initially
conceived independently of Silverman's *World Spectators* (2000), its final formulation is
deeply indebted to the insights gained from reading Silverman's text.

tendency to "fall" into the "they" is often difficult to withstand for the simple reason that it is by far the less demanding of the two options. Heidegger explains that Dasein, who has been "thrown" into the world without explanation, yields to the lure of the "they" primarily because the sense of uncanniness that arises from having to confront alone the burden of existence is too intense to endure (1927, p. 234). This "levelling down" of subjectivity disburdens Dasein of the necessity to take responsibility for itself, causing it to live "away" from itself, in the shelter of shared norms, judgments, and rationalizations (pp. 164–165). Needless to say, this manner of existing is, in Heidegger's assessment, inherently alienated insofar as it dissolves Dasein's distinctiveness to such an extent that it becomes impossible for it to differentiate its desires from those of the "they," let alone retain its claim on existential resourcefulness.

Heidegger's portrayal of inauthenticity obviously shares a conceptual landscape with what I described in Chapter 2 as the contemporary subject's inability to find meaning and value in its life; the erosion of the individual's inner resources that clinical psychoanalysts connect to existential emptiness in many ways parallels Heidegger's depiction of Dasein's failure to fend off the seductions of the "they." To avoid any misunderstanding regarding Heidegger's account of the "they," I would like to emphasize that it is the homogenizing dimensions of collective life, rather than the reality of intersubjectivity per se, that Heidegger denounces.[5] More than anything, Heidegger's critique of the "levelling down" of subjectivity targets the unbridled consumerism, commercialism, and mass-produced fantasies of satisfaction that characterize the "they." The problem, as Heidegger sees it, is that we tend to get so entirely assimilated into our social context that we lose the ability to ask ourselves how it is that we wish to proceed with our lives. We are, as it were, in a rush to resolve the ambiguities of our existence by identifying too closely with the models of life that we receive from our culture. In this manner, we prematurely fix our identities in a predetermined groove that forecloses any future change or development. Authenticity, in contrast, holds the future open to the proliferation of meaning.

Heidegger's conception of subjectivity, like that of Nietzsche and Kierkegaard, is therefore deeply driven by a sense of possibility. Instead of

---

5. I highlight this point because, as we saw in the previous chapter, Oliver (2001) and Willett (2001) have recently criticized the tendency in Western philosophy to regard the collectivity as a hostile entity the blocks the individual's freedom and potentiality rather than as an empowering source of interpersonal connection.

possessing an innate inner core that would determine its character once and for all, Dasein's being is an ever-evolving entity that is always "beyond" and "ahead" of itself in that it is most interested in what it is "on the way" to realizing. Authenticity, in this sense, is not a matter of revealing a true self that has somehow become obscured by a false or superficial one, but rather of unleashing the self's countless possibilities of becoming (see Cooper 1999, pp. 4, 70, 96). That is, the alienated individual is not estranged from a self that she already possesses but rather from her capacity to actively pursue the opportunities for self-expansion afforded by the fact that she is a creature whose being and potentiality can never be summed up by an exhaustive definition of her "character."

Most importantly for our purposes, Heidegger posits a nothingness at the heart of subjectivity. This nothingness is what gives rise to the sense of primordial uncanniness or anxiety that drives Dasein to the lap of the "they," yet it is also what individualizes it by summoning it to develop an interpretative relationship to its own alienation. Dasein may try to immerse itself in its everyday projects in an attempt to conceal and renounce its nothingness, but anxiety—the moment of acute and uneasy self-observation— brings it face to face with the emptiness that "fills" its being. This anxiety moreover induces Dasein to become cognizant of its status as a "being-towards-death"—as a finite entity who alone bears the responsibility for realizing its existential promise. In this manner, anxiety compels Dasein to acknowledge the dynamic role that it plays in the unfolding of its own destiny. This in turn implies that Dasein can no longer ignore or evade the task of engaging with the world in authentic ways, but must instead embark upon the process of making the most of its capabilities.

The most productive response that Dasein can have to its own nothingness, therefore, is to admit that even if this nothingness causes anxiety, it at the same time allows it to become aware of the various potentialities that comprise its being. From this perspective, nothingness and potentiality are but two sides of the same coin; it is only by accepting the void at the center of being—by recognizing that the lot of the human being is to be inherently lacking—that the phenomenological subject remains a subject of potentiality. Moreover, as Silverman (2000) eloquently argues, it is the void within the self that creates the space for the "presencing" of other people, objects, and things, for without this nothingness—without this "clearing" within the self—the subject would have no means of connecting with its surroundings, and therefore no ability to approach the world with an attitude of care, interest, and solicitude. Without nothingness, the subject would remain uninterested in, and unmoved by, anything beyond its own solipsistic world. The Heideggerian notion of nothingness is thus generative in that it provides the opportunity for the "surfacing" of other entities; it allows other people, objects, and things to materialize as genuinely other.

While Dasein's anxiety tempts it to flee from its nothingness, it can only develop an authentic relationship to the world by keeping its inner clearing open and exposed. Authenticity in this sense is not a matter of finding a shelter for the self but rather of coming to terms with the profound sense of homelessness and lack of shelter that inevitably haunts subjective experience. To turn away from nothingness, Heidegger suggests, means to squander the extensive resources that Dasein possesses for creatively dwelling in the world. It implies Dasein's refusal to heed the call of the unknowns of its future; it closes off the opportunity to allow other people, objects, and things to occupy—and therefore to enrich—its being; and it rejects what is most precious about existence, namely the capacity to actively engage with the possibilities of one's being. In this manner, Heidegger offers us a means of reading nothingness not merely as a site of self-division, but also of potentiality and becoming.

In his later work, Heidegger links human potentiality to poetic language. Like so many other twentieth-century thinkers—Lacan included—Heidegger argues that language speaks man rather than vice versa. As he puts it, "Man acts as though he were the shaper and master of language, while in fact language remains the master of man" (1971, p. 215). In more general terms, language for Heidegger, as for later thinkers, does not express or represent a preexisting reality but rather brings this reality into existence. In this manner, language both shapes human consciousness and conjures the external world into being. In poetry and other poetic usage of language, this creative power of language is particularly apparent because poetry is by definition an imaginative activity that seeks to name the world (or at least a tiny sliver of this world). By bidding a particular image, feeling, or object to appear, poetry gives rise to something new and potentially marvelous. Heidegger's theory of language is therefore in many ways close to that of Lacan (as well as of Nietzsche) in that he believes that even though language speaks man, man in turn possesses the capacity to use language in innovative ways.

What is particularly intriguing about Heidegger's theory of language is that he presents language as a site of creativity that is simultaneously a locus of pure receptivity. To activate the poetic dimensions of language is to listen to the messages of the world—to its appeal to be apprehended in its own terms—with a mindful kind of attentiveness. It is to remain acutely open to the disclosure or unveiling of the world without in any way seeking to control the shape of this disclosure or unveiling. Heidegger maintains that Dasein needs to cultivate an attitude of "letting-be" in relation to the world—needs to adopt a non-domineering outlook which, rather than imposing an interpretation on the world, allows the undertones of the world to emerge without human interference. In this sense, the Heideggerian disclosure of the world entails Dasein's capacity to take a step back so as to create an opening for other entities to come into being and take on meaning.

The attitude of "letting-be" resides at the very heart of Dasein's ability to dwell in the world authentically—what Heidegger describes as a "poetic" type of dwelling. To dwell in the world poetically is to cultivate an open and generous attitude toward the world in the sense of inviting the things of the world to emerge in all of their particularity. Whereas the scientific approach to the world annihilates the world *as* world because it seeks to measure the world according to human standards, dwelling in the world poetically respects the "worldness" of the world—as well as the "thingness" of the things that populate this world—by cultivating a non-appropriative vigilance vis-à-vis the world. As Heidegger states:

> If we think of the thing as thing, then we spare and protect the thing's presence in the region from which it presences. . . . When and in what way do things appear as things? They do not appear *by means of* human making. But neither do they appear without the vigilance of mortals. The first step toward such vigilance is the step back from the thinking that merely represents—that is, explains—to the thinking that responds and recalls. [1971, p. 181]

Human vigilance is necessary for the apprehension of things. However, it does not explain things, but merely responds to their call. It does not clutch or grasp but rather "gathers" the world in a concentrated perception (p. 223); it waits, listens, and takes in without entrapping. Heidegger's ideal of poetically dwelling in the world therefore introduces a wholly different relationship between the individual and the world than that validated by much of posthumanist theory. While poststructuralism has valorized movement, instability, and changeability to the extent that it has become quite difficult for us to envision a more restful mode of encountering the world, Heidegger's ideal of poetic dwelling offers a model for a deliberately watchful stance toward the world.

I hardly mean to propose that we should replace poststructuralist restlessness with Heideggerian restfulness, but merely that we might benefit from a more balanced understanding of the relationship between the two. The idea that meaning could be cultivated in a state of rest is fairly foreign to contemporary thought, which is why I think that we might profit from Heidegger's insight that it is mindful restfulness—the attitude of "letting-be"—that allows the individual to most productively engage with the world. At the same time, because the notion of "letting-be" is conceptually dependent on Dasein's underlying nothingness, it cannot be equated with metaphysical philosophies of ontological serenity. Instead, it gives us an opportunity to begin to theorize creativity in the context of lack. The Heideggerian Dasein is able to translate its inner emptiness into a dwelling-ground for other entities. As Silverman puts it, Dasein "conjures the world out of the void, making something out of nothing" (2000, p. 74).

I would like us to hold onto this idea that Dasein is able to conjure meaning out of a void, for it enables us to think about creative agency from a constructivist perspective—without in any way compromising the notion that the human subject is inherently lacking. Indeed, the fact that Heidegger invites us to conceptualize potentiality as a function of nothingness stands in poignant contrast to the poststructuralist tendency to fixate on how potentiality is always necessarily swallowed up by the subject's lack-in-being. Moreover, although Heidegger, like more recent thinkers, recognizes the difficulty of resisting the hegemonic processes through which subjectivity as a socio-cultural reality articulates itself, his notion of authenticity implies that such resistance is in the end possible. This is to say that Heidegger's insistence on Dasein's capacity for authenticity offers us a way of understanding how the subject can participate in the collective structures and meanings of the world without necessarily surrendering its ability to dwell in this world in a "poetic" fashion.

FROM THE *OBJET A* TO THE SYMBOLIC OTHER

Heidegger thus implies that it is Dasein's inner nothingness (and the anxiety that arises from this nothingness) that compels it to materialize as a creature of potentiality. However, Heidegger does not explain how this nothingness comes into existence. This is where Lacan is more informative, for his theory of language acquisition (and the ensuing sense of primordial loss) provides a sophisticated hypothesis of the manner in which lack emerges as the constitutive lining of subjectivity. Lacan moreover explicitly connects lack to desire, thereby orienting subjectivity around the concept of desire in ways that phenomenological and other philosophical approaches rarely do. Indeed, one of the biggest advantages of combining philosophical investigations of subjectivity with more psychoanalytic perspectives is that this allows us to ask the question of existential potential (How shall I live?) much more concretely, as a matter of the lived experience of desire. While philosophy often talks about inner potentiality without fully acknowledging the psychic forces that are involved in the promotion of this potentiality, psychoanalysis places it in the context of the always highly idiosyncratic specificity of the individual's psychic history.

For Heidegger, it is the seductiveness of the "they" that makes it difficult for Dasein to recognize that nothingness and potentiality are best understood in a productive relationship to each other. Lacan in turn argues that it is because the subject is continually misled by its own desire that it fails to come to terms with the fact that its "being" is always necessarily a function of its "non-being." More specifically, Lacan maintains that it is because the subject fails to appreciate the gift of the signifier as an existential opportunity—because it instead experiences this gift as a wound that gives rise to limitless longing—that it tends to radically misconstrue its life on the level of fantasy, particularly on the level of the imaginary object of desire, the *petit objet a*. Reluctant to accept lack as the precondition of its existence, the subject flees from this lack by recourse to reassuring fantasies of plenitude and belonging. This, Lacan believes, is invariably a mistake because the *objet a* (as an imaginary site of such plenitude and belonging) will never in the end provide the answers that the subject is seeking; the *objet a* will never give the subject the meaning of, or the blueprint for, its existence. Rather, it will consistently lead it along paths that prevent it from realizing the potential that it possesses as a creature of symbolic capacity.

The *objet a* is most powerfully operative in the context of the kind of passionate eros that I discussed at the end of Chapter 2. Because such eros blurs the boundary between the self and the other, it provides the perfect occasion for the subject's fantasies of return and recovery (of primordial plenitude; of lost love) to surface in intense and compelling ways. Indeed, in such instances, the *objet a* is asked to reincarnate *das Ding*, to fill the void which, bottomless and empty, echoes in the innermost recesses of the subject's being. The subject thus behaves remarkably like those unfortunate souls in Plato's *Symposium* who are split in half by Zeus as a punishment for their arrogance, and who consequently spend the rest of their lives in desperate pursuit of their lost halves (Plato 385 B.C., pp. 25–30). Lacan's story of the origins of love is in fact remarkably similar to that of Plato in that it not only hypothesizes a primary arrogance (the mirror stage), but also posits a punishment by splitting (the signifier for Lacan takes the place of Zeus) that not only gives rise to an inconsolable sense of incompleteness, but sends the subject on a wholly fantasmatic quest to overcome this incompleteness through a healing union with a loved other.

Lacan shows us that because subjectivity is based on a sacrificial economy that demands a surrender of primordial "love" in exchange for meaning, the experience of passionate eros later in life all too easily draws the subject into the "mirages" (1966, p. 43) of the imaginary. This means that the subject's pursuit of the *objet a* can ensnare it in fantasy formations that keep it melancholically longing for the type of self-completion that is inherently impossible. The subject therefore remains forever "caught in the rails" (p. 167) of its repetition compulsion, unable to locate the object that would bring an end to its fruitless search and deliver it from the frustrations of its desire. The repetition compulsion, in propelling the subject from one object to the next, reveals that the renunciation of primordial love (*das Ding*) has not been entirely accomplished, and that the unconscious traces of this renunciation retain the power to animate the subject's behavior. Each new object is inserted into the gap left by the original loss in the hope that it will permanently seal this gap. Moreover, the specific character of each new object—the reason that it is chosen for the task at hand—depends on the manner in which the original loss is fixed by the signifier, for this point of fixation is where the ever-fascinating image of the fetish is "petrified" within the subject's psyche (p. 167). As a result, as long as the original lost object keeps displacing itself onto its fetishistic substitutes—as long as the unconscious speaks its desire through the fantasies where the subject's loss is "petrified"—the subject remains entangled in its mirages, and continues to address the question of its existence to objects that are always bound to disappoint its desire in the end.

Passionate eros opens a space for the ecstatic resurgence of the imaginary within the symbolic, thereby posing a direct challenge to the structuring function of the symbolic. What is more, the subject's relationship to the *objet a* is most often enacted through misleading structures of identification and idealization that seek to resuscitate the fully satisfying universe of the mirror stage. In this manner, amorous fantasies serve as a roundabout means of attaining narcissistic gratification in that they allow the subject to endow its object with all the qualities of perfection that it no longer finds in itself. Roland Barthes (1977) captures the dynamic of this type of desire perfectly when he states that the subject in love is like a gambler whose luck cannot fail, for his hand "unfailingly lands on the little piece which immediately completes the puzzle of his desire" (p. 198). Like Lacan, Barthes understands that the object of desire for the subject functions primarily as a figure of fantasy, and that the subject is therefore fascinated by the "image" that best accommodates the specificity of its desire—that most precisely completes the "painting" of its hallucination (p. 198). This in turn explains why desire can be so astonishingly specific:

> It has taken many accidents, many surprising coincidences (and perhaps many efforts), for me to find the Image which, out of a thousand, suits my desire. Herein a great enigma, to which I shall never possess the key: Why is it that I desire So-and-so? Why is it that I desire So-and-so lastingly, longingly? Is it the whole of So-and-so I desire (a silhouette, a shape, a mood)? And, in that case, what is it in this loved body which has the vocation of a fetish for me? What perhaps incredibly tenuous portion—what accident? The way a nail is cut, a tooth broken slightly aslant, a lock of hair, a way of spreading the fingers while talking, while smoking? [p. 20]

> In the fascinating image, what impresses me (like a sensitized paper) is not the accumulation of its details but this or that inflection. What suddenly manages to touch me (ravish me) in the other is the voice, the line of the shoulders, the slenderness of the silhouette, the warmth of the hand, the curve of a smile, etc. [p. 191]

The subject thus walks around with its "nose stuck to the image" (p. 189) that most convincingly corresponds to its fantasy, and that therefore promises the greatest degree of narcissistic satisfaction. As Stendhal once so fittingly stated, "in love only the illusion appeals" (1822, p. 55).

The object that solicits the subject's desire resonates with something quite fundamental about the subject's imaginary world. Put another way, the person who engages the subject's desire is able to provide a satisfactory answer to the question: What am I worth? The problem with this kind of love is obviously that it does not allow the object to exist as an autonomous entity with its own needs, desires, fantasies, and preoccupations. It leaves no space for the beloved other to exist *as other*, but instead encloses it in a hall of mirrors that serves the interests of the loving subject at its expense. As Barthes (1977) explains, the subject caught in the throes of narcissistic desire is always in the final analysis narrow-minded: "[A]s a matter of fact, I admit nothing about the other, I understand nothing. Every-thing about the other which doesn't concern me seems alien, hostile; I then feel toward him a mixture of alarm and severity: I fear and I reprove the loved being, once he no longer 'sticks' to his image" (p. 220). The object's power to entice therefore rests in large part on its capacity to conceal the particularities of its own being so as to be able to provide an entirely lucid and uncluttered surface for the subject's feats of self-specularization. This means that the more accurately the object reflects the subject's desire, the more completely it is erased as a subject in its own right. Within this dy-namic, the object is quite literally the mirror, the fantasy, the projection of the lover. As Kristeva states, "In love I never cease to be mistaken as to reality" (1983, p. 7).

One of the many limitations of this dynamic—as Lacan and Barthes both understood—is that desire dies the moment reality intrudes and the illusion crumbles. Barthes (1977) explains that the death of desire begins the minute the lover perceives in the beloved object a small "speck of corruption"—a minuscule detail that somehow renders the object banal or unoriginal, thereby connecting it to a "commonplace" world. When the image tears, the magic mirror shatters, and the lover finds itself caught in the nightmare of a "counter-rhythm"—something like "the noise of a rip in the smooth envelope of the Image" (p. 25). The other is suddenly em-barrassingly ordinary, a source of shame rather than of narcissistic gratifi-cation. The "bad" image is therefore not a wicked image, but merely a paltry, trivial, or worthless one; it shows the other "caught up in the platitude of the social world" (p. 26). In this sense, it is when the beloved presents a hackneyed image that the structure of fantasy collapses; while the lover ordinarily seeks to protect the sanctity of the beloved being against the assaults of the world, this attitude of devotion falls apart the moment the image alters. The true act of mourning is therefore not to suffer from the loss of the object, but rather "to discern one day, on the skin of the relationship, a certain tiny stain, appearing there as the symptom of a cer-tain death" (p. 108). That is, the true act of mourning is not the loss of love but the realization that the image has been irrevocably marred.

In narcissistic love, the death of desire therefore begins with the death of the ideal. In this scenario, the object retains its value only insofar as it manages to elude; as soon as the subject attains its object, this object loses its charm and the subject's desire either shifts to a new object or finds it-self stifled in boredom. One of Lacan's aims is to teach the subject to listen to its desire in ways that help it circumvent this futile circuit of repetition.

He does this by reorienting the subject's quest for satisfaction from the *objet a* to the less volatile resources for self-constitution contained by the symbolic. As we have seen, Lacan regards the symbolic as an enabling locus of significatory (and therefore psychic) possibility. He consequently wishes to train the subject to distinguish between the *objet a* as a depository of its imaginary fantasies on the one hand and the symbolic Other as a genuinely versatile site of meaning-production on the other.[6]

One reason Lacan shuns the imaginary so much is that the imaginary traps the subject in narcissistic fantasies of love that are ultimately self-defeating, preventing it from accessing its creative potentialities. In this sense, the imaginary represents a formidable obstacle to self-actualization. Because the imaginary represents the realm of the ego, it houses all the grandiose delusions and misconceptions that the subject holds about itself. Indeed, what is sometimes confusing about Lacanian theory—but what is essential to understand if one is to make sense of this theory—is that by the "ego" Lacan does not mean our rational self, but rather the part of us that is most drastically deceived by the imaginary "mirages" of our fantasy world. While in everyday language we sometimes use the term "ego" as a synonym for the self, Lacan implies that the ego is where we are the most disconnected or displaced from our "self" in the sense that we misrecognize ourselves in fantasmatic structures that present an appealing image, but have very little to do with the "reality" of our being. Other forms of psychology sometimes talk about the ego as the locus of the self's strength, but Lacan tells us that this strength is always a narcissistic illusion.

The imaginary realm of the ego is a closed inner world that keeps the subject chasing fantasies, including the fantasy of narcissistic love, rather than facing the tangible demands of its existence. As a consequence, Lacan regards it as his mission to help the subject arrive at a more realistic understanding of what it means to be a human being. Lacan in fact declares as his objective to demystify the subject's existential confusion by dispossessing it of the "certainties" of its psychic life by revealing these certainties to be fantasmatic constructs that consistently entice it to invest its desire in illusory directions. The task of the analyst, Lacan asserts, is "to suspend the subject's certainties until their last mirages have been consumed" (1966,

---

6. Lacan writes: "The aim of my teaching, insofar as it pursues what can be said and enunciated on the basis of analytic discourse, is to dissociate *a* and A by reducing the first to what is related to the imaginary and the other to what is related to the symbolic" (1975, p. 83).

p. 43). This "consumption" of the subject's mirages in turn asks it to acknowledge that its propensity to seek in the *objet a* the guarantee of its existence is an empty endeavor. In this manner, Lacan stresses that it is only when the subject comprehends that the *objet a* will never gratify its quest for self-actualization that it is finally able to direct its demand for meaning to the symbolic Other—to the signifier as a source of psychic possibility. If the *objet a* conspires to preserve the subject's fantasmatic sense of ontological intactness by veiling over the internal rift introduced by the signifier, it is, paradoxically, the Other as a site of symbolic castration that provides an escape from this endless labyrinth of emotional dead ends by offering the subject a means of harnessing the discursive power of the signifier; it is only by accepting lack and castration—the agency of the signifier—as an intrinsic condition of its humanity that the subject manages to gain a degree of existential insight.

What this suggests quite simply is that Lacan asks the subject to live its life—as well as to confront the challenges of this life—within the realm of language rather than within the more precarious space of fusion-love. Readers familiar with Freud's theory of sublimation will see that Lacan is not really saying anything very different from what Freud already posited, namely that sublimation is a far better way of cathecting psychic energies than fantasies of fusion-love. Freud proposed that happiness is a matter of the subject's ability to channel its libidinal energies in ways that maximize its chances for satisfaction (1930, p. 34), and it can be argued that Lacan's wish to reorient the subject's desire from the *objet a* to the significatory promise of the Other is designed to assist the subject's efforts to achieve this goal. Lacan's objective is to enact a psychic reconfiguration whereby the subject's imaginary cathexes get filtered through the signifier, on the level of symbolic structures of meaning-making rather than of harmful patterns of idealization that perpetuate its tendency to repeat its constitutive traumas. Ultimately, what is at stake here is the subject's ability to weave a meaningful account of pleasure and pain, of love and its loss; by building a stronger basis for the subject's relationship to the signifier—by redirecting the subject's desire from the iconography of its imaginary mirages to the creative capacities of the signifier—Lacan aspires to provide it with a more elastic foundation for its self-constitution.

In Chapter 1, I mentioned that many of the philosophers of antiquity already held the opinion that it is more prudent to rely on oneself for one's happiness than it is to search for it outside of oneself. Freud shares this perspective, for he argues that although passionate eros gives us our most intense experience of pleasure, and consequently often motivates our search for happiness, "we are never so defenceless against suffering as when we love, never so helplessly unhappy as when we have lost our loved object or its love" (1930, p. 33). Freud therefore recognizes that while passionate eros quite reliably produces the sense of self-completion that the subject seeks, it also carries a tremendous risk insofar as it makes the subject dependent on another for the validation of its being. Lacan agrees. He believes that imaginary fantasies are self-undermining precisely in that they cause the subject to seek happiness in external objects that possess the power to drive it down an ever-widening spiral of existential blunders. If Freud maintains that sublimatory activities protect the subject from the need for external validation by directing its libidinal energies into endeavors that are inherently satisfying in themselves, the signifier for Lacan fulfills the same function. In this sense, Lacan's endeavor to guide the subject from the fantasmatic fixations of narcissistic fusion-love to the sublimatory potential of the signifier can be understood as an attempt to blunt the knife of desire before it cuts too deep.

Does this mean that Lacan denies the possibility of love? By no means. Rather, Lacan's aim is to enable the subject to realize that its narcissistic fantasies stand in the way of its ability to form meaningful relationships with others. Lacanian analysis is often criticized for its emphasis on separation, and it is true that it tells the subject that there is no lover, no object of desire, who is able to return to it its lost sense of wholeness, and that it is consequently its responsibility to fashion for itself an appropriate metaphorics of existential integrity. However, this should not be confused with the idea that Lacan forecloses the possibility of love or interpersonal relationships. Quite the contrary, as I will try to show below (and continue to argue in Chapter 4), it is merely designed to create the conditions for less narcissistic forms of love. Moreover, it is designed to inaugurate a more realistic—and therefore ultimately more rewarding—notion of self-actualization.

THE RESPONSIBILITIES OF DESIRE

Lacan is notorious for privileging the symbolic over the preverbal imaginary. Insofar as the symbolic is associated with the Law of the Father and the imaginary is aligned with the maternal, this has frequently led critics to accuse Lacan of perpetuating a phallocentric social order. But I hope it is clear by now that the confrontation for Lacan is not necessarily between

the oedipal father and the preoedipal mother, but rather between the signifier and the subject's imaginary fantasies. This of course does not pre-
clude the very real possibility that Lacan's argument is at least in part
motivated by the denigration of femininity, as well as of what has historically been associated with femininity, such as the body and the passions.[7]
However, if we are to give Lacan the benefit of the doubt, I would argue
that what Lacan ultimately wants to accomplish is to impart upon the subject a new appreciation for what it means to love, not to mention to live in
the world as a being of potentiality. He wishes the subject to understand
that because lack is what opens up its psychic life and what enables it to
love others in non-narcissistic ways, its existential task is to learn how to
live creatively with this lack rather than to seek to evade it. What infuri-
ated Lacan about early Anglo-American forms of psychoanalysis, among
other things, was that they tended to view the individual's sense of lack as
debilitating, and consequently sought to heal it. From Lacan's perspective,
the last thing analysis should try to do is to cover over the subject's lack.
Rather, the objective should be to help the subject comprehend that since
alienation is an inherent condition of the human predicament, the best it
can do is to figure out how to live with this alienation without becoming
demoralized.

Above I showed that Heidegger suggests that inhabiting the world
in an authentic manner is not a question of inner totality, but rather of
learning how to productively live with the lack of such totality. This to
me seems to be the gist of the Lacanian teaching as well. Insofar as subjectivity in the Lacanian sense is erected upon an existential abyss, there
is no way to fill this abyss without at the same time annihilating the subject; it is impossible for the subject to ever reach a definitive sense of
psychic or ontological security. It is then the aim of analysis to make this
insecurity—this constitutive alienation—inhabitable in ways that enhance
the subject's well-being.

Like Heidegger, Lacan realizes that encountering lack makes the subject anxious and induces it to pursue satisfaction in external sources. Like
Heidegger, moreover, Lacan believes that it is the subject's responsibility
to work through this anxiety, and to come to terms with the implications
of the fact that existential uncertainty is built right into human subjectivity. Both Heidegger and Lacan acknowledge that this is very difficult to

---

7. This is one reason that I ended Chapter 2 with a discussion of the transformative
potential of passionate eros.

accomplish—that the temptation to flee from one's lack by placing one's fate in the hands of others (the "they" in the case of Heidegger; the *objet a* in the case of Lacan) is often too strong to withstand. Yet both remain firm that it is only by facing up to its lack that the subject can begin to play a meaningful role in the unfurling of its destiny. The paradox of existence, for both Heidegger and Lacan, is that it is only by accepting insecurity that the human being can begin to live in an inspired manner. This is why Lacan would like the subject to understand that the signifier carries the only form of agency that it will ever possess even as it causes the loss of stable existential foundations. He would like the subject to recognize the gift of meaning for what it is—a gift.

This is the general philosophy of life that Lacan bequeaths to us.

Above I mentioned that Heidegger regards Dasein's ability to dwell in the world "poetically" as something that results from its capacity to hold its inner clearing open and receptive to the world (that results, precisely, from its willingness to confront its nothingness without fleeing from it). I think Lacan (1966) is saying something very similar when he argues that the goal of clinical practice is to manipulate the "poetic function" of language so as to give the analysand's desire its "symbolic mediation" (p. 106). The same way as Heidegger links poetry to creativity, the "poetic function" of language for Lacan designates those aspects of language that enable the subject to signify in innovative ways.[8] Not surprisingly, Lacan regards this poetic function as the "privileged field" (p. 106) for the unfolding of analytic discourse. Taking his lead from *Alice in Wonderland*, Lacan playfully asserts that the objective of analysis is restore to the analysand "the sovereign freedom displayed by Humpty Dumpty when he reminds Alice that after all he is the master of the signifier, even if he isn't the master of the signified in which his being took on its form" (p. 81). The poetic function of language therefore allows the subject to understand that even if it can never fully master the signified, it does possess a certain degree of imaginative leeway with respect to the signifier. In situating the subject in the symbolic realm, the poetic function of language enables it (as in Heidegger) to hold open—and even play with—its lack. Lacan in fact maintains that this

---

8. Roman Jakobson also regards the "poetic function" of language as the creative or innovative aspect of language. Jakobson argues that because the poetic function of language focuses on the message itself, it promotes "the palpability of signs" (1987, p. 70). One could argue that this promotion of the "palpability of signs" is exactly the province of psychoanalysis.

emphasis on signification is what distinguishes psychoanalysis from psychology, for while psychology seeks to respond to the subject's yearning for love (and therefore to close its lack), analysis endeavors to empower the subject to meet this yearning on the level of the "poetic" capacities of the signifier.[9]

Lacanian analysis asks the subject to work with its lack. What this means in more concrete terms is that Lacanian clinical practice aims to teach the subject to actively listen to its desire (as an expression of its lack). That is, although Lacan stresses that subjectivity can only be understood as an embodiment of the kind of desire for which no ultimate cure exists, he views the purpose of clinical practice to be to assist the subject to symbolize its desires in ways that allow it to come to terms with the implications of their particularity. Lacan in fact maintains that analysis exploits the creative capacities of the signifier in order to grant the subject access to what he describes as "true" speech—speech that carries the meaning of the subject's desire (p. 95). The same way as Heidegger argues that it is only by poetically dwelling in the world that Dasein manages to facilitate the disclosure or unveiling of this world, Lacan believes that there is something about the poetic function of language that discloses or unveils the "truth" of desire. Indeed, it could be argued that Lacan's understanding of clinical practice shares a great deal with Heidegger's appreciation for the kind of vigilant attentiveness that invites the meanings of the world to step forth instead of imposing an interpretation on the world. The same way as Dasein listens carefully to the call of the world so as to be able to respond, the Lacanian analyst listens to the appeals of the unconscious so as to better respond (or enable the analysand to respond).

Lacan juxtaposes "true" speech with what he calls "false" communication, with the kind of empty speech which, by crowding the subject's interiority with meaningless chatter, allows it to "forget" its subjectivity (and therefore to cover over the "truth" of its desire). False communication is wholly devoid of unconscious meaning, with the result that it leads the subject to misconstrue the parameters of its life to the extent that it—like the Heideggerian subject who finds it difficult to distinguish its desires from the desires of the "they"—comes to drown its specificity in collective fan-

---

9. Another way of stating this is to say that what distinguishes psychoanalysis from psychology is the fact that psychoanalysis recognizes the need for a "scission" between the *objet a* and the Other, whereas psychology perpetuates the subject's propensity to conflate the two (see Lacan 1975, p. 83).

tasies of fulfillment.[10] In contrast, "true" speech—the kind of speech that analysis aims to activate—enables the subject to mobilize its desire in ways that allow it to break out of rigid and lifeless psychic configurations; although there is no way around the fact that the subject is always "spoken" by collective signifiers of cultural meaning, clinical practice aspires to cultivate its capacity to "speak" in existentially rewarding ways.

Psychoanalytic practice is one way of posing the question of what it means to be human. The "truth" of our subjectivity, Lacan implies, resides in the "truth" of our desire, however unstable or convoluted this "truth" might be.[11] This is why Lacan believes that listening to the specificity of our desire allows us to better understand what motivates our behavior in the world. This is not merely a matter of learning how to inhabit the world in more insightful ways, but also of taking responsibility for our desire so as to be able to forge more genuinely generous relationships with others. As I have already emphasized, the fact that Lacan disdains fantasies of fusion-love does not mean that he thinks we are completely incapable of relating to others in loving ways. Quite the contrary, Lacan suggests that because desire is one of our primary means of interacting with the surrounding world, it by necessity forms an integral component of our attempt to fashion an ethical relationship to this world. As Silverman (2000) puts it, "Lacan elaborates an ethics which runs counter to everything that has ever been written about the moral life. He advances the claim that it is through the practice of desire rather than through its renunciation that humans approach what has traditionally been called virtue" (pp. 46–47). This is to say that Lacan recognizes that because desire is what animates the human being and allows this human being to connect with the world, the only way to develop an effective ethics is to work with and through desire rather than trying to repudiate it.

---

10. In this context, Lacan provides a poignantly Heideggerian depiction of the contemporary subject's lot: "He will make an effective contribution to the common task of his daily work and will be able to furnish his leisure time with all the pleasures of a profuse culture which, from detective novels to historical memoirs, from educational lectures to the orthopaedics of group relations, will give him the wherewithal to forget his own experience and death, at the same time to misconstrue (*méconnaître*) the particular meaning of his life in false communication" (1966, p. 70).

11. Foucault (1976) of course criticizes psychoanalysis precisely for the fact that it tends to equate the "truth" of subjectivity with the "truth" of desire. It should be noted, however, that the "truth" of desire—and therefore the "truth" of subjectivity—is for Lacan never stable or absolute.

Silverman argues that if Heidegger regards the subject's inner nothingness as what both generates the preconditions for the surfacing of others and allows the subject to relate to these others, Lacan similarly implies that it is the subject's inner lack that creates the possibility for interpersonal relationships. While the pursuit of the *objet a* aims to close off the subject's inner lack, holding open this lack provides an opportunity—a clearing in the Heideggerian sense—for the other to step forth as a being in its own right. The subject's ability to hold open its lack is therefore important not only because it empowers the subject to access the innovative capacities of the signifier, but also because it enables it to love others without subsuming them into its narcissistic fantasy world. More specifically, Silverman proposes that the Oedipus complex, by obliging us to surrender our original love objects for a series of substitutes, creates room in our psyches for the emergence of others. In this sense, separation (insofar as we are able to live with it without succumbing to the attraction of the *objet a*) does not spell the impossibility of love, but rather functions as the very foundation of our capacity to care for others. Our losses, Silverman thus contends, can paradoxically awaken in us the ability to be concerned with others (p. 15).

Silverman in fact maintains that it is *only* by reincarnating a lost love that another person can ever come to be of value to us. She traces the chain of substitutions all the way back to *das Ding*, positing that we are able to love a new object only insofar as we can somehow make it a representative of what we no longer possess. This is to say that objects do not solicit our desire randomly, but rather according to very particular patterns of desiring that have to do with the way in which we unconsciously relate to the loss of *das Ding*. Although we all enter desire in the same way—through loss—the history of our losses provides us with a unique "grammar" according to which we approach our existence and care for others (pp. 23–24). This implies that each of us is a "speaker" of a very particular language of desire. Moreover, this language of desire is an ever-expanding category in the sense that its contours are renegotiated with each successive loss. Over time, it comes to consist of a multilayered "constellation" of signifiers that provides a record of how we have loved in the past, as well as an indication of how we will be able to love in the future (pp. 39–40).

When we allow other beings to inhabit our lack, Silverman explains, we raise these beings to the "dignity" of *das Ding*, thereby endowing them with "a worth beyond all possibility of reckoning" (p. 46). What this suggests is that each of us, through our particular libidinal history, possesses the power to "ennoble" new people, objects, and things, and to invest these ennobled entities with psychic meaning and value. What enables us to do so are the similarities linking the beings that we have loved in the past to those that offer themselves to us in the present. And though the fact that our present desire in one way or another always refers back to what we have lost in the past carries within itself the danger of exactly the kind of narcissistic identification that Lacan criticizes, Silverman proposes that we can circumvent this danger by allowing others to replicate the past in wholly inaccurate ways (pp. 144–145). The problem with narcissistic fantasies is that the subject of fantasy expects the present to provide an entirely loyal reflection of the past—expects the present to reincarnate the past with picture-perfect accuracy. The subject who has managed to prevail over its imaginary mirages in turn knows that even if its present desire is driven by the losses of the past, the present can never fully redeem the past. It is only when we understand this fundamental fact that we begin to actively speak our desire rather than allowing ourselves to be passively spoken by it (p. 64).

For Silverman, the fact that we possess the capacity to ennoble others in very specific ways implies that our relationship to these others is ethical through and through. Our patterns of desiring either provide or fail to provide an opening within which others can materialize. We, in other words, hold the power to determine which beings will continue to languish in "the darkness of concealment" and which will be allowed to appear (p. 30). The history of our desire in fact situates us in a particular track or destiny that lends expression to an existential debt—to a kind of pressing private responsibility that it is our ethical task to attend. In this context, to "assume" (p. 66)—as Silverman puts it—the language of our desire means not only to affirm our status as subjects of lack but also to become accountable for the particular libidinal choices—the debt of desire—that propel us along the "track" of our lives.[12] This suggests that those of us who wish to begin to actively speak the language of our desire need to understand the precise ways in which our past always inevitably speaks through and shapes our words and actions in the present; since the past cannot help but resurface in the present, the best we can

---

12. Lacan writes: "If analysis has a meaning, desire is nothing other than that which supports an unconscious theme, the very articulation of that which roots us in a particular destiny, and that destiny demands insistently that the debt be paid, and desire keeps coming back, keeps returning, and situates us once again in a given track, the track of something that is specifically our business" (1986, p. 319).

do, ethically speaking, is to remain diligently aware of the manner in which this resurfacing takes place. In this sense, taking responsibility for our desire entails knowing that our capacity to love others is derived from the past even as we cherish the new and multiple forms that this past assumes in the present. It also means to cultivate a "rhetorician's enthusiasm for fresh metaphors and metonymies"—for all the new patterns in which the "impossible nonobject of desire can be miraculously reborn" (p. 50).

Although it may seem like a difficult task to take responsibility for what we can never fully master, Silverman suggests that it is only by paying a great deal of vigilant attention to our desire that we can build an ethical bridge between our past and future desires so as to enter into loving relationships with others. When we fail to do so, when we allow ourselves to be passively manipulated by our desire, we become absorbed in cultural conventions that encourage us to regard other beings through what Silverman describes as the "perceptual coordinates" that are most frequently and forcefully reiterated in our society, and that therefore automatically insert themselves between us and the world (pp. 32–33). At such moments, we are able to perceive the people, objects, and things of the world only through the well-worn and stereotypical parameters that structure our everyday existence. We are, in other words, utterly incapable of respecting the otherness of our others, seeking instead to reduce them to what is familiar and readily accessible to us. In this manner, we not only close off the inner clearing that enables us to love others, but also compromise our ability to love ourselves as living and ever-evolving entities. We allow our desire to be driven not only by the patterns of our own past, but also by the patterns of the collective past that it is the purpose of culture to perpetuate. If the symptom lends expression to a psychic fixation on the level of the individual, the stereotype lends expression to a collective fixation on the level of culture. If fantasy on the personal level keeps the subject stuck in the past in ways that prevent the possibility of new love, fantasy on the collective level keeps cultures and societies enmeshed in the past in ways that make it impossible for them to move forward. As we will see in the next chapter, there are times when it is important for both individuals and collectivities to remain faithful to the past. But if we, as individuals and collectivities, are to retain our imaginative suppleness and capacity to grow, fantasy must in the end relinquish its hold so as to create space for movement.

The Lacanian teaching regarding the subject's relationship to the other is thus actually quite beautiful, for it says: Do not use the other as a means of filling your void. Rather, hold open this void so that the other can enter without having to sacrifice its otherness, without having to mold itself to the shape of your lack. This is difficult, for you have paid the price of lack for your subjectivity, and you have a deeply melancholy attachment to what you think you have lost. You try to plug your void by inserting an object into it. But this is a useless endeavor because the object cannot redeem you, and is thus bound to always disappoint you in the end. Indeed, the object does not have a choice but to disappoint you because you are asking for the impossible. You are asking for the kind of healing that you will never be able to attain. Your task then is nothing less than to change both your way of being in the world and your expectations regarding what it means to be a human being. You need to understand that the void inside you is what makes you human even as it causes you anxiety. It gives you access to meaning by mobilizing all of your creative capacities. And it makes you capable of love. It is consequently your responsibility to learn to live with this void in such a way that these creative and loving capacities do not go to waste.

WHAT CAN LACAN (STILL) OFFER TO FEMINIST AND QUEER THEORY?

Progressive critical theory, particularly feminist and queer theory, has recently fled from Lacanian psychoanalysis because it has deemed it increasingly difficult to distinguish the Lacanian symbolic from the patriarchal and heteronormative conventions that govern our culture. But this reasoning overlooks everything that Lacan has to say about the innovative potentialities of the signifier—about the fact that the symbolic grants us the "gift" of the kind of meaning that can at times take poetic and imaginative forms. As I have tried to show in this chapter, the symbolic is not only, as Judith Butler would have it, what "sets limits" on our efforts to reconfigure existing kinship and social relations (2000, p. 20), but also what in the long run enables and sustains such efforts.

My interpretation of Lacan presupposes that we are able to divorce the poetic potential of the signifier from the normative socio-cultural system within which the signifier operates. It presupposes, in other words, that we are able to separate the signifier from the ways in which social power has historically organized itself. One way to understand the distinction is to emphasize that the Lacanian symbolic cannot be equated with either the Nietzschean "herd" or the Heideggerian "they." The latter two concepts imply a collective space that is by definition complacent (and dominant in its very complacency). The Lacanian symbolic, on the other hand, is a structure that can be filled with any kind of content. While this content can certainly take on dominant and/or complacent forms, Lacan is adamant in his conviction that the symbolic is a space of significatory (and therefore of creative) potential. The Nietzschean "herd" and the Heideggerian "they" stand for what by definition stifles creativity. The Lacanian symbolic, in contrast, is what makes creativity possible. This in turn means that the symbolic should not be confused with what Foucault means by hegemonic power. Although the signifier can obviously be quite easily co-opted by social power, to entirely conflate it with this power makes it impossible to envision forms of meaning-making that resist or exceed the parameters of regulatory power. It makes it impossible to talk about the poetic function of language.

To ignore the fact that Lacan *does* talk about the poetic function of language is to divest his theory of all of its more affirmative aspects, and to place it in the service of a framework that makes an impossibility of the very thing that Lacan places at the heart of his analysis, namely the idea that what makes us human—and what also potentially rescues us from psychic pain—is the fact that we have access to the signifier (and that we consequently possess creative capacity). Just as reading Foucault as a theorist of social subjection without paying attention to the more generative dimensions of his concept of power results in an unnecessarily pessimistic vision of the self's relationship to collective structures of sociality and meaning-production, reading Lacan as a theorist of lack and alienation without paying attention to what he has to say about the creative potentialities of the signifier leads to an excessively disempowered notion of subjectivity and psychic life. There is of course no doubt that psychoanalysis can be put to conservative use, and that Lacanians have been known to uphold normative social structures by recourse to the so-called paternal function and the Name of the Father. Such Lacanians have not, however, understood the basic insight that I have sought to outline in this chapter (and that I take to be the very cornerstone of Lacanian theory), namely that it is only insofar as the subject accepts its status as a subject of lack— and thus as a subject who cannot ever claim empowerment through recourse to phallic signifiers of power—that it exists as a subject of psychic possibility. Any attempt to align itself with phallic power—such as is demonstrated by those Lacanians who wish to perpetuate normative conceptions of patriarchy and heteronormativity—can only distance the subject from its creative capabilities.

It is evident that the current social system is fighting tooth and nail to hold onto the idea that the symbolic is, and always will be, patriarchal and heteronormative—that the subject's desire must always follow the hegemonic understanding of what is desirable. Yet the purpose of the Lacanian symbolic is not to define what is desirable, but merely to bring desire—in whatever form—into being. This is to say that the symbolic establishes subjectivity as a site of constant striving. The fact that this striving often takes normative directions is a function of power rather than of any inherent logic of the signifier. This is proven by the fact that the signifiers of desire that emerge within the clinical experience are frequently deeply at odds with socio-cultural norms. Judith Feher-Gurewich in fact suggests that the analytic encounter discloses that in the realm of erotic strivings, for instance, social discourse and normative gender roles consistently fail to provide "an adequate answer" to the subject's quest, with the result that desire must constantly seek new signifiers for its trajectory (2003, p. 245). These new signifiers in turn only reveal that the question of desire must in the end remain unresolved. In this sense, the analytic situation confirms precisely what Butler, Anne Fausto-Sterling, and others[13] have so persuasively argued, namely that gender and sexuality are always ambiguous, multiple, and open to transformation. If the hegemonic cultural order posits that gender is neatly divided into two categories, and that desire is always heterosexual, the unconscious insists that this is not the case. In this sense, the unconscious is "queer" to the core in that it will always resist any attempt to place limits on the expression of desire. As a result, when Lacan proposes that the clinical encounter exploits the poetic function of language to access the "truth" of the subject's desire, he is very far from upholding a patriarchal and heteronormative structure of desire. Rather, he is acknowledging that, contrary to what the hegemonic system would like us to believe, the truth of the subject's desire is never straightforwardly normative. It is also not in any way stable, permanent, or predetermined.

Clinical practice thus potentially provides the subject with the tools to expose and challenge repressive social configurations. What this implies is that focusing on the clinical aspects of analysis once again establishes psychoanalysis as a useful theory for feminist and queer discourses because it reveals that analysis can go a long way in facilitating the kind

---

13. See, for instance, Bornstein 1994, Butler 1990, 1993, 1997, 2000, de Lauretis 1987, 1994, Eng 2001, Fausto-Sterling 2000, Garber 1992, Halberstam 1998, Haraway 1991, Jardine 1985, Prosser 1998, and Stone 1997.

of reconfiguration and proliferation of gender and sexuality that these discourses have sought to accomplish. This is to say that contemporary critical theory would profit a great deal from paying closer attention to the clinical dimensions of analysis because it is precisely on the clinical level that gender and sexuality manifest themselves in highly subversive ways. It is also on the clinical level that the poststructuralist notion of the fragmented subject becomes a vividly experienced reality. Read in this manner, Lacanian analysis becomes once again an ally rather than an enemy of both feminist and queer theory.

But why does feminist and queer theory need such a troublesome ally? There are at least three powerful reasons that arise from my discussion thus far. The first is what we have just discovered, namely that Lacan shows us that the analytic situation can help the subject identify the signifiers of its desire in ways that outwit hegemonic power. The value of reading Lacan as a clinician resides in part precisely in the fact that it allows us to focus on the manner in which clinical practice empowers the subject to listen to its desire in ways that undermine those cultural conventions that seek to dictate how desire as a lived reality should materialize in the world. We have in fact seen that when the subject fails to do so—when it allows normative definitions to eclipse the "truth" of its desire—it capitulates to the kind of "false" communication that leads to barren and meaningless forms of existence. The subject's ability to protect the particularity of its desire, in contrast, points to one important way in which the subject manages to maintain its status as a being of possibility and becoming—as a being whose future is never foreclosed but open-ended and able to accommodate the unanticipated. In this sense, the "truth" of the subject's desire mirrors the "truth" of its potentiality. This is a psychoanalytic way of understanding what it might mean for the subject to dwell in the world poetically. And it is a wholly constructivist vision of self-actualization.

I believe it is important to examine Lacanian theory from a clinical perspective because a psychoanalytic theory that fixates on alienation without being able to account for the individual's sense of potentiality cannot in the end provide an empowering understanding of psychic life. It is for this reason that I have sought to shift our focus from the wounding effects of the signifier to its more poetic dimensions, for Lacan reveals that clinical practice exploits these poetic dimensions to allow the subject to overcome the obstacles that prevent it from effectively accessing its desire. It is certainly all too easy to place the clinical situation in the service of regulatory power. However, doing so violates the most basic principle of analysis, namely its respect for the chaotic and disruptive messages that emerge from the unconscious. Paying heed to these messages, in contrast, provides a basis for the kind of reconceptualization of desire that can be profoundly transformative not only on the level of individual psychic realities but also— assuming that the individual at times impacts the collective—on the social level as well; because clinical practice changes the manner in which individuals approach their lives, it can over time influence the way in which societies are organized. It seems quite conceivable, for instance, that a greater degree of understanding of, as well as tolerance for, the heterogeneity of one's own desire can lead to a higher level of open-mindedness with respect to the desires of others. Similarly, a tangible awareness of the fluidity of one's own gendered identity can result in a more accommodating attitude regarding how gendered identities, more generally speaking, manifest themselves. Is this not exactly the project of much of feminist and queer theory?

SURFACE PLEASURES, PSYCHIC INSCRIPTIONS

The second reason feminist and queer theory needs Lacanian psychoanalysis is that without a psychoanalytic conception of psychic life, it is all too easy for poststructuralist and other constructivist approaches to conceive of subjectivity in ways that entirely empty the self of interiority and depth. A few years ago, I was intrigued to encounter an argument by Elizabeth Grosz that dismisses psychoanalysis as a workable paradigm for theorizing feminine—particularly lesbian—desire because it is incapable of conceptualizing desire as anything but a function of lack. Since it is Grosz's own *Jacques Lacan: A Feminist Introduction* (1990) that has influenced so many feminist scholars of my generation, I read her argument with particular interest. I immediately found much that I could readily agree with. It is certainly the case—as Grosz explains—that feminine desire has been one of the blind spots of psychoanalytic theory ever since Freud, and that it has been remarkably difficult for analytic thinkers to adequately capture the specificity of lesbian desire.[14] I also found myself quite sympathetic to

---

14. Leaving aside the difficult question of how such desire—desire somehow uniquely applicable and common to all lesbians—could ever be defined, Grosz's dissatisfaction with the psychoanalytic conception of desire as a function of lack is understandable from a feminist and queer studies perspective. As Grosz points out, the relationship

Grosz's suggestion that it is high time for feminist and queer theorists to begin to conceptualize desire more affirmatively than has been customary under the Lacanian model. I was, however, quite astonished to find that instead of trying to unearth the more affirmative dimensions of psychoanalysis, or of trying to combine psychoanalytic insights with other kinds of theories, Grosz replaces the Lacanian paradigm by one that draws heavily on the work of Deleuze and Guattari (1980), as well as Alphonso Lingis (1985). Although I find much that is valuable in the writings of the latter three thinkers, it seems that a wholesale displacement of psychoanalysis by these promoters of "surface effects" creates more problems than it can possibly solve.

Grosz (1995) proposes that instead of viewing desire as something that arises from lack, we should understand it as a "force of positive production" (p. 179)—as a generative form of power rather than as a flaw or imperfection of existence. While Lacan presents desire as a chasm seeking to be filled, and implies that desire can sustain itself only to the extent that it fails to find satisfaction, Grosz regards it as a form of "pure" productivity (p. 179) that is able to maintain itself through and beyond the moment of gratification. Desire, Grosz explains, is a matter of "doing and making" (p. 180)—of continual discovery, invention, experimentation, and transformation—rather than of the kinds of wishes, hopes, aspirations, and psychic histories that psychoanalysis tends to foreground (p. 182). Grosz certainly acknowledges that such wishes, hopes, aspirations, and psychic histories may play a part in desire, but they do not interest her insofar as her objective is to develop a theory of desire that is based on a strongly postmodern celebration of surface intensities, inscriptions, and boundary

---

between women and desire in traditional psychoanalytic discourse is paradoxical insofar as femininity connotes lack yet women are supposed to know nothing of desire. Grosz is also correct in pointing out that psychoanalysis often masculinizes desire, and consequently only recognizes women as objects, rather than as subjects, of desire. She is, moreover, right in calling attention to the fact that the psychoanalytic model of desire tends to heterosexualize and binarize desire, for "it is precisely such a model, where desire lacks, yearns, seeks, but is never capable of finding itself and its equilibrium, that enables the two sexes to be understood as (biological, sexual, social and psychical) complements to each other—each is presumed to complete, to fill up, the lack of the other" (1995, p. 177). Although in principle I agree with Grosz's criticisms, I would at the same time insist that the type of thinking she associates with psychoanalysis—thinking that treats men and women as somehow complementary to each other—is precisely what Lacan seeks to demystify (see, for instance, Lacan 1975).

crossing. Explicitly eschewing notions of interiority and depth, Grosz endeavors to reconfigure desire in terms of fleeting and contiguous encounters between one thing and another—between one part of the body and another, or between a body part and whatever it is that this body part encounters in the world, for instance—that carry no psychic resonance, no genesis, development, or intention, and that leave behind no lasting trace, heritage, or form of knowledge. Desire in this sense is a site of "machinic" connections—of energies, excitations, rhythms, practices, and pulsations—that make various surfaces throb and intensify for their own sake rather than for the sake of some integrated entity or organism (p. 182). Desire is therefore highly nomadic in nature, unfettered by any aim or organizational principle, devoid of lasting allegiances, and wholly divorced from structures of meaning or representation, modes of socialization, or the inculcation of ideas and ideologies. It is a form of production that in the end produces nothing besides "its own augmentation and proliferation" (p. 183).[15]

One of the main problems with Grosz's argument is that it tends to conflate desire (which can be a purely psychic phenomenon) with the way in which eroticism unfolds as a bodily (as well as a psychic) practice. There seems to be for Grosz no difference between erotic experience—what people actually do with each other erotically—and their desires, fantasies, and

---

15. The following passage is representative of Grosz's (1995) new model of desire: "Sexuality and desire, then, are not fantasies, wishes, hopes, aspirations (although no doubt these are some of its components), but are energies, excitations, impulses, actions, movements, practices, moments, pulses of feeling. The sites most intensely invested in desire always occur at a conjunction, an interruption, a point of machinic connection, always surface effects, between one thing and another—between a hand and a breast, a tongue and a cunt, a mouth and food, a nose and a rose. In order to understand this notion, we have to abandon our habitual understanding of entities as the integrated totality, and instead focus on the elements, the parts, outside of their integration or organization, to look beyond the organism to the organs that comprise it. In looking at the interlocking of two such parts—fingers and velvet, toes and sand—there is not, as psychoanalysis suggests, a predesignated erotogenic zone, a site always ready and able to function as erotic: rather, the coming together of two surfaces produces a tracing that imbues eros or libido to both of them, makes bits of bodies, its parts or particular surfaces throb, intensify, for their own sake and not for the benefit of the entity or organism as a whole. They come to have a life of their own, functioning according to their own rhythms, intensities, pulsations, movements. Their value is always provisional and temporary, ephemeral and fleeting: they may fire the organism, infiltrate other zones and surfaces with their intensities but are unsustainable" (p. 182).

anticipations regarding such (possibly future) experience. When Grosz writes that any "attempt to understand female sexual desire on the models provided by male sexuality and pleasure risks producing a new model that is both fundamentally reliant on (heterosexual) norms of sexual complementarity or opposition, and reducing female sexuality and pleasure to models, goals, and orientations appropriate for men and not for women" (p. 188), I question not only her confidently drawn distinction between men and women (since when have we been able to talk about male and female forms of sexuality and pleasure in such a categorical manner?), but also the facile sliding of her rhetoric from "desire" to "sexuality and pleasure." While the two are obviously not unrelated, they are certainly not the same thing. Indeed, Grosz quite consistently equates desire with what she calls "carnal" or "voluptuous" experience (pp. 195–196). This rhetorical move is not coincidental, for it is the only way that Grosz is able to extricate desire from any notion of psychic life. It is only because desire, in Grosz's rendering, takes place within erotic experience itself—in the hand's action of reaching for the breast, for instance—rather than in the psychic anticipation of such experience that it can be theorized apart from the realm of wishes, hopes, aspirations, and psychic histories. Moreover, it is precisely because Grosz does not distinguish between erotic experience and desire, between action and the mind's ability to imagine, prior to its actuality, this action, that there is no more lack or longing—that desire can be conceptualized as a form of "pure" productivity instead.

In discarding the contributions of psychoanalysis, Grosz theorizes away any notion of psychic life. By supplanting the Lacanian conception of desire by a Deleuzian one, Grosz ends up valorizing surface over depth in ways that imply that subjectivity is primarily a matter of bodily effects and intensities. Although I agree with Grosz that there are forms of pleasure that exist for their own sake alone—that seek to reproduce themselves without any reference to meaning or value outside of their own domain—it seems to me that the conceptualization of desire as purely a function of such pleasures leads to a reification of surfaces that cannot in the end be tenable; Grosz's depiction of bodily fragmentation and of disconnected, unstable, and ever-changing intensities may capture a certain dimension of erotic experience, but it cannot possibly convey this experience in its entirety. Indeed, what troubles me is the assumption that when it comes to eroticism and desire, we are somehow compelled to choose between surface and depth (between Deleuze and Lacan)—that eroticism, in other words, is *either* a matter of energies, excitations, rhythms, practices, and pulsations, *or* of wishes, hopes, aspirations, and psychic histories.[16] What is it about depth that prevents us from looking at surfaces as well? Why are wishes, hopes, aspirations, and psychic histories divorced from surface intensities? And why is surface superior to depth in the first place? Why is provisionality and fleetingness always better than having roots and permanence?

I have already made it clear that I have over the years grown more and more apprehensive of the wholesale valorization of flux, chaos, and provisionality that characterizes much of poststructuralist thought. Although I understand the historical motivations for this valorization—that there was a time in critical theory when such a valorization served a highly subversive purpose in that it demolished the ontological integrity of the humanist subject—I feel that it has increasingly become its own form of philosophical complacency: a stale trope that is often mobilized out of habit rather than because it actually serves a substantial critical purpose. I also cannot help but question the denigration of interiority, depth, and affective resonance that it all too frequently implies. Have we not progressed far enough from the moment—already at least four decades in the past—when the attack on the Cartesian self demanded that subjectivity be divorced from notions of depth and substance? Is it not time to try to rethink depth and substance from a more contemporary perspective, not as metaphysical entities that uphold a self-contained and hegemonic kind of subjectivity, but rather as

---

16. I recognize that insofar as I am interested specifically in Grosz's critique of psychoanalysis, I may be drawing this distinction too categorically. After all, in *Volatile Bodies* (1994), Grosz develops a sophisticated analysis, by way of her interpretation of the Möbius strip, of the manner in which the body and the psyche come into being together. As she explains: "Bodies and minds are not two distinct substances or two kinds of attributes of a single substance but somewhere in between these two alternatives. The Möbius strip has the advantage of showing the inflection of mind into body and body into mind, the ways in which, through a kind of twisting or inversion, one side becomes another. This model also provides a way of problematizing and rethinking the relations between the inside and the outside of the subject, its psychic interior and its corporeal exterior, by showing not their fundamental identity or reducibility but the torsion of the one into the other, the passage, vector, or uncontrollable drift of the inside into the outside and the outside into the inside" (p. xii). Clearly, then, Grosz regards the inside and the outside as continuous with each other. My point consequently is not that Grosz misunderstands the relationship between the body and the psyche, but rather that there is something about the attempt to excise psychoanalysis from one's theoretical lexicon—which is in many ways what Grosz is trying to do in her reconceptualization of lesbian desire—that can lead the most careful of critics to (momentarily at least) disregard the psyche.

crucial components of our ability to theorize the self as an infinitely complex site for the enactment of psychic, bodily, and intersubjective realities?

What is the purpose of arguing that desire should be divorced from the concerns of psychic life? And what guarantees that it would in fact ever be possible to accomplish such an artificial separation of spheres? Even if we follow Grosz in conceptualizing eroticism and desire as bodily rather than psychic events—having to do with ways of touching rather than with the meaning of being touched—it seems to me that they cannot in the end be contained by the surface alone: who we touch, how we touch, under what circumstances, in the context of what kinds of power differentials, within what kinds of personal histories, and so on, all have psychic consequences that cannot possibly be discounted without overlooking the intricacies of erotic experience.

Grosz argues that desire leaves no psychic mark that would endure past the momentary eruption of voluptuousness.[17] Yet the idea that desire does not in any way mark the individual's psyche—that erotic encounters do not over time accumulate into deeply sedimented psychic formations—transforms the subject into a perpetual blank slate without any meaningful connection to the experiences of its past. Moreover, if desire held no psychic meaning, contributed to no affective history, and left no permanent mark, it would also not entail any risk whatsoever. If desire and/or erotic experience were always ephemeral in the way that Grosz describes them, there would be no emotional investments, no sense of accountability, loyalty, or love, and there would consequently also be no room for hurt, regret, or bitterness.

It is evident that desire and/or erotic experience often carry a considerable amount of risk, and that in opening ourselves up to the pleasures that they bring, we also frequently invite the possibility of psychic pain. This connection between eroticism and risk is of course not universal—there are forms of eroticism and sexual expression that do not entail such risk—yet because eros is always highly unpredictable in nature, we cannot in the end find any absolute protection against its more volatile manifestations. I am, in other words, not at all convinced that what happens on

---

17. Grosz (1995) cites Alphonso Lingis's claim that voluptuousness "has no tasks and no objectives and leaves no heritage: after the caresses and embraces, the carnal is left intact, virgin territory. . . . It is not the locus from which would emerge the meaning of one's history" (Lingis 1985, p. 67). Grosz (1995) then adds that "desire cannot be recorded or stored, cannot be the site for the production of information or knowledge" (p. 196).

the surface does not mark the psyche in profound ways. Is it not the case that the color, age, and anxieties inscribed on the surface of one's face, for instance, frequently have important psychic consequences? If this is true, then surely what takes place on the surface of the body in erotic experience cannot fail to impact the psyche. What this implies is that a theory of eros—let alone a theory of subjectivity—that does not account for psychic depth, or that does not recognize desire as a site of dense psychic signification, by necessity presents a partial view of what it means for human beings to exist as beings of erotic capacity; whatever our frustrations with psychoanalysis, throwing it out altogether without attempting to replace it with an alternative vision of psychic life results in theoretical deadlocks that diminish our capacity to effectively conceptualize the contours of posthumanist subjectivity.

THE POSTHUMANIST SOUL

The third reason feminist and queer theory needs Lacanian psychoanalysis—and the one that has been my focus in this chapter—is that Lacan allows us to reconfigure lack as generative of meaning. In her rethinking of desire as a matter of surface effects rather than of psychic states, Grosz presents productivity as the opposite of lack, arguing that giving up the notion of lack is what enables us to conceive of desire as a productive force. But this polarization of lack and productivity perpetuates an unnecessarily reductive understanding of what it means for the subject to be lacking. Consequently, while I agree with Grosz that desire can be highly productive, I arrive at this conclusion not by bypassing lack but rather by trying to determine the ways in which productivity arises from lack. This is why I have attempted to demonstrate that whereas the Lacanian "cure" resides in the subject's acceptance of lack as its ontological condition, this acceptance should not be interpreted as a form of capitulation or inner impoverishment but rather as the very basis of the subject's ability to renew its psychic destiny. Indeed, I have suggested that it is in the process of translating lack into meaning that the Lacanian subject experiences something akin to the humanist notion of the imagination.

This manner of reading lack allows us to begin to think about how Lacanian analysis might be mobilized in the service of a more constructive approach to psychic life. The American academic psychoanalytic field has frequently been rather categorically divided between relational approaches where the emphasis lies on psychic agency and well-being on the one hand, and Lacanian approaches that highlight the subject's lack and alienation on the other. These two approaches often find it difficult to relate to each other's languages: whereas the relational focus on core subjectivity seems alien to Lacanians who are invested in the notion of the decentered subject, adherents of the relational school find the Lacanian discourse of alienated subjectivity too universalist to be able to capture the more contingent dimensions of psychic life and intersubjectivity (see Layton 1998). Although it is not my intention to try to reconcile these two rather antithetical approaches, I believe that reading Lacan in the manner that I have begun to do here may allow the two sides of the divide to better speak to each other. It is often assumed that the major distinction between relational and Lacanian approaches is that relational analysis seeks to promote the individual's sense of agency while Lacanian analysis endeavors to demolish it. What I have tried to reveal is that this assumption is wholly unfounded. The difference between relational and Lacanian approaches resides not in the fact that Lacan denies the possibility of agency, but rather in the fact that he theorizes this agency not in relation to enabling others[18] but instead in relation to an enabling (symbolic) Other which, even as it forces the subject to confront its castrated status, opens up all the innovative capacities of its psyche.

Here it is important to emphasize that the fact that the Other provides a basis for the subject's capacity to make meaning does not imply that it is therefore all powerful and holds the key to the subject's destiny. In Chapter 1, I argued that contemporary criticism often talks about the subject's relationship to the symbolic world in ways that acknowledge the subject's lack but fail to acknowledge the lack in the world within which this subject seeks to find its bearings. Yet the relationship of the self to the world is not one that pits the psyche's porosity against the seamlessness of the world. Rather, we must admit that if the self is always decentered, so is the world in the sense that it can never fully "catch up" with "itself."

This is why Lacan emphasizes that there is no Other of the Other— no metalanguage outside the system—that can guarantee the authority of the Other's discourse (1966, pp. 310–311). By this Lacan means that the Other can never offer a definitive answer to the subject's quest for meaning. Nor can it ever fully control this quest, for there will always be times

---

18. The reason Lacan rejects the idea of "enabling others" is that he believes that such others tend to only strengthen the subject's desire to seek satisfaction from the kinds of imaginary and wholly fantasmatic "mirages" that keep it entangled in its repetition compulsion.

when the discourse of the Other falters in ways that provide an opening for the unpredictable to appear. Yet the fact that the Other fails to offer the subject any ultimate existential justification does not in any way lessen its power as long as it continues to grant the subject the possibility of imaginatively utilizing the signifier. The Lacanian "cure," in other words, does not require the subject's access to absolute meaning, but merely implies its ability to galvanize the signifier in generative rather than jaded and lackluster ways. Since meaning is never stable to begin with, the fact that the Other remains eternally elusive is not an impediment to psychic agency but, quite the contrary, its very foundation. The animation of the self and the animation of the world thus both depend on the kind of lack that prevents them from coming to a deadly standstill. Without this lack, there would be no space for movement, and without movement, there would be no space for transformation. There would be no psychic life. And there would be no soul.

Lacanian theory allows us to better understand the distinction between the subject's lack and its psychic life. I have tried to show that the foundational lack that results from the subject's interpellation into the symbolic order is not *equivalent* to its psychic life, but merely the basis for the development of this psychic life; the lack that founds the psyche is not the same thing *as* the psyche but merely its constitutive possibility. This rendering allows us to discern how the psyche can be a site of existential potentiality even when it originates from lack. It offers us one way of comprehending how lack gives rise to productivity. And it makes it possible for us to see that the subject's lack-in-being does not necessarily translate into a lack of agency, but merely invites us to retheorize agency without a stable or reassuring notion of identity.

In Chapter 1, I argued that both Nietzsche and Foucault regard constraint and self-limitation as a potential source of creative agency. What Lacan is saying about lack and meaning-production amounts to something quite similar, namely that being constrained—as the subject inevitably is by the signifier—is not necessarily a bad thing, but rather what makes creativity possible. The same way as Nietzsche regards the constraints of style as a means of poetic self-fashioning, and Foucault recognizes *askesis* as a vital part of the ancient art of caring for the self, Lacan views the limitations imposed by the signifier as a way of propelling the subject into selfhood and meaning-production. Whereas the Deleuzian model of desire that Grosz promotes tends toward the indiscriminate proliferation of pleasures, Lacanian analysis, like Nietzsche's philosophy of the self and the ancient care of the soul, is driven by a certain ethos of austerity that sees value in restraint. As a culture, we are used to thinking about restraint as primarily a negative characteristic because we live in a society dictated by the demands of consumer capitalism—a society that fetishizes abundance and equates freedom with unlimited choice.[19] Indeed, we have so much trouble with restraint that it tends to express itself through pathological formations, such as eating disorders or obsessive compulsive behavior. One of the messages of Lacanian analysis—and perhaps of psychoanalysis at large—is that learning how to place restrictions on oneself without becoming masochistic is one of the keys to psychic well-being.

Lacanian analysis illustrates that psychic well-being is in many ways a function of the subject's capacity to place limits on its pleasure principle (and the repetition compulsion that feeds this pleasure principle). By this I do not mean that Lacanian analysis endorses excessive social restriction. I also do not mean to condone the hegemonic aspects of the symbolic order. And I certainly do not mean to imply that Lacan seeks to kill desire so as to make us happy. The delimitation that I am talking about is not a matter of renouncing desire, but rather of following the thread of one's desire in a more discerning and discriminate manner. Indeed, as we have seen, Lacan regards desire to be foundational not only of our psychic life, but also of our ability to connect with others in ethical ways. Lacanian constraint can therefore not be a matter of destroying desire, but rather of channeling it in directions that are less likely to cause us pain than the gluttonous pursuit of narcissistic and/or primordial pleasure. Undoubtedly a normative judgment of considerable magnitude is being made here. Lacan believes that it is better to train the subject to impose boundaries on its pleasure principle than to feed the inexhaustible and megalomaniac demands of its ego. There may be excellent reasons for disagreeing with Lacan, but I want first to understand what is at stake in his emphasis on constraint (as opposed to fusion-love and the *jouissance* of the body, for instance).

Lacan shows us that while the signifier makes us lacking, this lack in turn transforms us into human beings who possess both creative potential and the ability to love. In Chapter 1, I pointed out that the twentieth century witnessed a radical paradigm shift in which the signifier replaced the humanist soul as the constitutive principle of subjectivity. I hope that it is by now clear that this substitution is, ironically enough, quite appropriate

---

19. The notion of unlimited choice is of course an illusion in the sense that we are for the most part presented with endless versions of the same thing.

in that the signifier is able to furnish the posthumanist subject with many of the same existential resources that the soul historically conferred upon the humanist self. While the signifier is frequently presented as what supplants—or even injures—the soul, my reading of Lacan allows us to consider the ways in which it in fact functions as the posthumanist counterpart to the humanist soul. If the soul, traditionally speaking, was what animated the subject's psychic life and made it innovative, then the Lacanian signifier is a fitting substitute indeed. As we have seen, it is precisely the signifier that breathes life into the subject's psyche. The signifier, unlike the humanist soul, obviously does not grant the subject access to psychic unity and wholeness. Nor does it allow the subject to transcend the realm of the human, but rather anchors it all the more securely in its all-too-human predicament of want and desire. Yet what is the soul if not the ability to read the signifiers of one's desire?

If the humanist soul was in many ways designed to provide an illusion of existential security by covering over the subject's lack and alienation, I would argue that the posthumanist soul has to do with the subject's capacity to come to terms with the fact that existential security is an unattainable dream. As such, the posthumanist soul is linked to the subject's ability to make the most of its fragmented and self-contradictory status. For Lacan, it is the signifier that allows the subject to accomplish this goal. It is in part for this reason that I find the signifier to be such an evocative metaphor for the posthumanist soul.

I have attempted to show that the transition from essentialist to constructivist models of subjectivity should not be conceived as one that annihilates interiority, but rather as one that brings about a different understanding of how psychic interiority as a structure of depth comes about, what it means to possess such a structure, and how this structure relates to the surrounding world. To the extent that inner enablement is linked, on the one hand, to the subject's ability to resist the processes of social subjection that seek to deaden its psychic life and, on the other, to its ability to signify and resignify in ways that permit it to construct psychic meaning and value, it cannot thrive in the world without a strong sense of imaginative capacity. This imaginative capacity—and the attendant sense of psychic potentiality and self-actualization—is what Lacan captures through the notion of the poetic function of language. Lacan in fact teaches us that though much of life makes us feel that we have little control over our meanings, analysis possesses the power to mobilize the poetic potential of language to fashion poets of all of us. What better way to survive loss?

4

Past

The past wasn't past. Just curled up like a prophet in the bosom of time.

Hélène Cixous, *Coming to Writing*

THE AILING SPIRIT

Psychoanalysis shows us that the past is never simply the past—that the past, in the words of Cixous, often resides curled up in the bosom of time, ready to spring upon us when we least expect it. In the same way that nations and other collective entities owe their current shape to complex and at times highly conflicted histories, the lived present of each of us is traversed by a countless number of invisible threads that connect us to our past. We may be largely unaware of these connections. We may also wish to denounce them, attempting to live in the present unencumbered by the specters and recollections of the past. For many of us, such acts of forgetting feel like the only way to proceed with our lives without having the past engulf our present. Psychoanalysis reveals, however, that there are always limits to our capacity to escape the past—that the more we wish to repudiate it on the conscious level, the more insistently it reasserts itself through the unconscious. This is why one of the most important tasks of analysis is to assist the subject to develop an affirmative and imaginatively supple relationship to its own past.

Another way of stating the matter is to say that the objective of analysis is to teach the subject how to productively live its past *in* the present—how, in other words, to enable the subject to regard the losses and impasses of its past as a source of future psychic possibility rather than as what condemns it, past, present, and future, to more of the same. In this chapter, I would like to consider the ways in which this objective entails coming to terms with both the potentialities and limitations of melancholia. I say potentialities *and* limitations because when it comes to understanding the complexities of psychic life, melancholia could be argued to cut both ways. On the one hand, melancholia may be a necessary precondition of the psyche's ability to grow in the sense that a psyche that has never known sadness is not necessarily a well-rounded or fully realized psyche. On the other hand, I would submit that the powers of melancholia remain veiled and unavailable to the subject until it can find a way out of its melancholy entombment.

In the previous chapter, we saw that Lacan's goal is to free the subject from its imaginary fantasies so as to overcome the repetition compulsion and mobilize the creative capacities of the signifier. This ability to detach the signifier from the drive energies of the imaginary is for Lacan the precondition of all the innovative potentialities of the psyche. In this chapter, I revisit the matter by considering the ways in which creativity demands the subject's ability to move from melancholia to meaning. We will discover that insofar as melancholia activates the subject's fantasy of being able to reunite with lost objects, it quite effectively bars the subject's access to the signifier. In this sense, the melancholy subject is by definition a subject of silence. In Lacanian terms, melancholia represents a victory of the subject's fantasmatic fixations over its sublimatory capacity to redirect desire along more rewarding lines. It represents a triumph of the imaginary over the symbolic, of fantasy over the signifier, of sadness over narrativization. And—as I will illustrate toward the end of this chapter—it prevents the subject from developing genuinely loving relationships with others.

In the pages that follow, I will blend Lacanian theory with some of Kristeva's insights regarding melancholia and meaning-production. This is not only because Kristeva has written so extensively on melancholia, but also because I would like to highlight the manner in which Lacan and Kristeva partake of the same psychoanalytic trajectory.[1] Kristeva is often

---

1. Drawing this parallel between Lacan and Kristeva presupposes that one reads Lacan in the manner that I read him in Chapter 3, namely as someone who is interested in the creative capacities of the signifier.

regarded as presenting a critical alternative to Lacan's language-centered theory. And indeed, it is the case that whereas Lacan privileges the symbolic over the imaginary, Kristeva envisions the imaginary—what she often calls the "semiotic"—as a locus of the kinds of preverbal bodily drives and energies that make an invaluable contribution to significatory and imaginative endeavors. Feminist critics in particular have capitalized on this shift from the Law of the Father to the more lawless space of the imaginary because it makes it possible to think about creativity in less phallocentric terms. There is therefore no doubt that Kristeva parts ways with Lacan in her consideration of how that which has been excluded from symbolization nevertheless possesses the power to impact the symbolic realm. Yet I would insist that Kristeva is far more Lacanian than she might first appear, and nowhere more than in her discussion of melancholia. This is because Kristeva, like Lacan, believes in the power of the signifier to rescue the subject from its sadness. And she believes in the capacity of analysis to bring about the necessary transition from melancholia to meaning.

From a classically Freudian perspective, melancholia is the quintessential symptom of an ailing spirit. Although a melancholy attachment is most frequently formed in relation to a person who has been loved and then lost, Freud (1917) acknowledges that it can also arise with respect to revered abstractions such as one's country or ideals (p. 243). Freud defines melancholia by juxtaposing it to what happens in mourning, and explains that while mourning allows the subject to gradually overcome the grief of loss, melancholia ensues from its inability to complete the process of mourning. Mourning for Freud therefore represents a healthy response to loss whereas melancholia suggests a pathological tendency to deny the reality of this loss; mourning entails the progressive severing of affective ties to what has been lost so as to free the subject to direct its love and attention to new objects and endeavors, whereas melancholia signals a resistance to such a separation, and instead clings to the memory of the lost object with the kind of stubborn perseverance that defies the logic of well-being.

Melancholia thus results from the kinds of losses that the subject experiences as unbearable. Freud tells us that the melancholy subject identifies with the lost object in an attempt to circumvent the sad task of giving it up as an object of love. The subject in fact seeks to incorporate the lost object into its own ego so as to be able to hold onto it internally even when it is forced to relinquish it in the external world. As Freud puts it, "By taking flight into the ego love escapes extinction" (p. 257). In this manner, the object's existence is "psychically prolonged" (p. 245), as is the subject's ability to continue loving it. Melancholia therefore provides the subject an indirect means of sheltering objects that it considers so precious that their loss seems inconceivable. Such objects, which often take on a larger-than-life meaning and magnificence, demand the individual's loyalty so intensely that disavowal becomes impossible; if the subject finds it difficult to relinquish its ties to a lost object, it is because psychic energy has been invested in this object so forcefully—with such ferocious fixity—that giving it up seems to threaten the subject's very sense of self.

Freud emphasizes that the subject's melancholy attachment to lost objects is always profoundly ambivalent. This is because the subject's relationships with its intimate others are rarely unequivocally loving, but are frequently tinged with hateful or aggressive impulses that intermingle with its more generous sentiments. In instances where there has been a rupture in the relationship—as a result of death, separation, or disloyalty, for instance—these hostile impulses tend to intensify as the subject blames the other for having abandoned it. However, since melancholia entails the transfer of affects from the lost object to the subject's own ego, the reproaches that the subject initially aims at the object are in the end directed against the self; the anger that the subject feels toward the other is internalized and turned against the ego. More specifically, it is the subject's superego that in melancholia takes the ego as the object of its criticism. The external conflict between the subject and the loved object is, in melancholia, restaged as an internal one between the subject's own superego and ego. It is for this reason that melancholia tends to diminish the subject's self-regard, causing a radical impoverishment of the ego. As Freud famously states, "In mourning it is the world which has become poor and empty; in melancholia it is the ego itself" (p. 246).

Melancholia is a particularly fascinating psychic condition in that it communicates the subject's obstinate propensity to defend desires that are by definition unfulfillable and deeply disappointing. As such, it cannot be divorced from the likelihood that the subject may unconsciously "invite" certain kinds of suffering into its existence. From this perspective, melancholia testifies to an underlying ambivalence that the subject may feel with respect to a successful resolution of its affective knots. Indeed, melancholia reveals the workings of both the repetition compulsion and the death drive in the sense that the subject clings to an object that is already irrevocably lost. As a result, it is emblematic of the hesitation that each of us can feel in the face of change: though our repetition compulsions may harm us, they themselves can be painful to lose.

A LOVE THAT LASTS: MELANCHOLIA'S COMMITMENTS

But what about the possibility that melancholia's faithfulness to lost objects in some circumstances represents an entirely fitting response to loss? David Eng and Shinhee Han (2000) have argued that the subject's refusal to renounce lost objects can at times signify an ethical commitment on the part of the melancholic ego (p. 695). Talking about melancholia as a group phenomenon among Asian Americans, Eng and Han propose that in the context of the kinds of hegemonic realities that impose loss as an inherent condition of minoritarian subjectivities, the subject's refusal to "get over" its losses cannot be regarded exclusively as a pathological response, but must instead be recognized as an attempt to preserve what is most valuable about the past. Group melancholia arises from the loss of ethnic origins and identity that marks the experiences of immigration, assimilation, and racialization, and it consequently necessarily underpins the minoritarian subject's struggle to survive its conflicts with dominant culture (pp. 669–671).[2] Placed in the context of "an ecology of whiteness" that tends toward the obliteration and denigration of minoritarian subjectivities—that in fact seeks to bar the possibility of enabling identifications and affiliations with non-hegemonic cultures, languages, and modes of being—the subject's reluctance to denounce what it is being asked to disparage indicates that it deems certain objects so overwhelmingly important that it is willing to preserve them even at the cost of its own well-being. In this instance, melancholia can be interpreted as an incipient political act aimed at carving a space for disparaged objects within the psychic landscape of those whose identities are under attack and erasure. It consequently becomes a protective gesture that articulates the subject's "militant refusal to allow certain objects to disappear into oblivion" (p. 695).

Insofar as marginalized subjectivities are forcefully robbed of their sense of self-worth, melancholia seems to represent an inevitable consequence of hegemonic power. In this sense, melancholia exemplifies one of the most persistent and poignantly painful conditions of wounded subjectivity. At the same time, Eng and Han suggest that melancholia should also

---

2. Eng and Han also talk about a second form of racial melancholia that can ensue from the marginalized subject's inability to approximate a dominant ideal. In this instance, what is lost is the ideal of functioning as a fully accepted member of society. As a result, minoritarian identities are constituted as a site of melancholic estrangement that delineates racialized subjectivity "as a series of failed and unresolved integrations" (p. 670).

be regarded as a potentially fertile psychic state, as a dormant source of inner resourcefulness as well as of political energy.[3] Indeed, what Eng and Han show is that when it comes to the minoritarian subject's experiences of loss, mourning—which endeavors to open a space for the future by seeking closure vis-à-vis the past—gives up its objects too easily, making it difficult to defend those identities and cultural forms that are the casualties of institutionalized forms of inequality. In this situation, melancholia, in insisting on the continued viability of deprivileged objects, may represent a more ethically appropriate response.

Freud's theory of melancholia is in fact remarkably ambiguous in that while he initially regards melancholia primarily as a pathological formation, over time he comes to acknowledge that a melancholy attachment to lost objects represents a significant dimension of how identities are formed in the first place.[4] This is to say that Freud proposes that the melancholy

---

3. Anne Anlin Cheng similarly proposes that in the context of racialized social realities, melancholia must be understood to be "as much about surviving grief as embodying it" in the sense that it emerges "both as a *sign* of rejection and as a psychic *strategy* in response to that rejection" (2000, p. 20).

4. While the first of these views is foregrounded in the 1917 essay "Mourning and Melancholia," the latter view takes precedence in *The Ego and the Id* (1923). Judith Butler argues that the incorporative logic of melancholia founds the very possibility of psychic life. Moreover, Butler analyzes the manner in which the production of gendered identities—of normative femininity and masculinity—within heterosexual culture depends on the melancholy disavowal of same-sex love. Given Freud's insight into the bisexual nature of infants, how is it that the majority of individuals end up heterosexual? Part of the answer, Butler proposes, is that our culture prohibits homosexual desire at such an early age—before any of us possesses a coherent sense of self—that heterosexual object choice becomes woven into the very process of identity formation. As a consequence, heterosexual love is naturalized while homosexuality comes to function as a site of the kind of loss that eludes conscious recognition. In this sense, heterosexuality rests on a melancholy "taboo against homosexuality" (1990, p. 82)—a taboo that regulates not only who we love but also how we stage and perform our gendered identities. Our society shows little tolerance for ambiguity in gender presentation—often reacting with considerable violence against those who transgress the narrow parameters of culturally sanctioned femininity and masculinity—and heterosexuality operates at least in part to police and perpetuate socially intelligible gender identities. What I find most interesting about Butler's argument is that it suggests that melancholia lends silent expression to an impossible love of which we are not even necessarily aware. Freud already acknowledges that although the cause of melancholia is frequently readily discernible, in some instances "one cannot see clearly what it is that has been lost," and that it is consequently "all the more reasonable to suppose that the patient cannot consciously perceive what he has lost either" (1917, p. 245). Love is lost, in a sense, before we have had a chance to experience it as love. In this context, the least we

incorporation of lost objects is what in the long run determines the "character" of the ego. It is, after all, impossible for the subject to create space within its psyche for newly incorporated objects without renegotiating the contours of its inner world; because lost objects are taken into the self in such a way that they become permanently embedded within—and continue to live on as integral parts of—the ego, melancholia cannot but result in a significant alteration of the subject's psychic economy.

The subject's ego thus comes to house the residue of its accumulated losses.[5] It in fact retains the trace of each successive loss to such an extent that it may be possible to discover, engraved within the folds of its organization, the sedimented history of the subject's past erotic investments. This implies that melancholy attachments possess the power to shape the subject's psychic life in rather fundamental ways. If the subject originally replaces an object-cathexis by a melancholy identification in an effort to shield itself from the painful reality of loss, it is in the end forced to recognize that the "self" that it has tried to protect has in the process undergone a profound realignment.

The ego's ability to accommodate objects from the outside world is a remarkable skill—one that could be argued to contribute to the self's continued aptitude for transformation. Indeed, if I have in previous chapters emphasized that the subject is sustained by loving connections to others, Freud's interpretation of melancholia implies that it may at times also be enriched by the loss of such connections. If it is true, as Freud suggests, that the subject's psyche holds a permanent trace of its past losses—that it is in fact in part through these losses that the subject has become what it is—then the loss of a loved object, though obviously a source of intense

---

can do is to try to understand how the foreclosure of certain kinds of love has contributed to the shape of our identities.

5. Explaining the shift in his thinking since "Mourning and Melancholia," Freud writes: "We succeeded in explaining the painful disorder of melancholia by supposing that [in those suffering from it] an object which was lost has been set up again inside the ego—that is, that an object-cathexis has been replaced by an identification. At that time, however, we did not appreciate the full significance of this process and did not know how common and how typical it is. Since then we have come to understand that this kind of substitution has a great share in determining the form taken by the ego and that it makes an essential contribution towards building up what is called its 'character'. . . . At any rate the process, especially in the early phases of development, is a very frequent one, and it makes it possible to suppose that the character of the ego is a precipitate of abandoned object-cathexes and that it contains the history of those object-cathexes" (1923, pp. 23–24).

suffering, can also, in this highly paradoxical manner, play a role in the regeneration of the self. It is precisely because the subject is unable to discard its lost loves, because it holds onto its most treasured objects with the kind of faithfulness that contradicts reason and logic, that these objects manage to occupy its psyche in ways that provide an avenue for internal change.[6] From this viewpoint, rather than marveling at the counterintuitive persistence of melancholia, it becomes possible to consider the potential value of this persistence. What are the implications of the individual's inability to renounce certain objects? What does it mean for desire to persist beyond the subject's most resolute attempts to extinguish it? What is the significance of the kind of love that refuses to be relinquished?

Melancholia indicates that the individual does not know how to lose gracefully. But it is also conceivable that if certain desires so persistently elude the subject's every effort to surmount them, it is because they in one way or another contribute to the actualization of its psychic potentialities. This is to say that if it proves impossible for the subject to forsake some of its objects, it may well be because these objects carry a vital message about the direction that it needs to pursue in order to cultivate dimensions of its being that remain unnecessarily weak or underdeveloped; if value adheres to particular objects, it may be because the subject's encounter with these objects will on some distant horizon prove indispensable for the cultivation of its inner topography.

An overwhelming sensation of a loving connection to another person, such as is experienced in melancholia, may therefore designate an important facet of the subject's being that has, for one reason or another, been stifled or undervalued. In such instances, the subject is drawn to the beloved person because there is something about this person that promises, in however indirect (or destructive) a manner, to awaken what has been locked away or ignored. Indeed, if the subject experiences passionate love as its "destiny," this is because such love connects with those mythologies of self-actualization that most profoundly resonate with its

---

6. Here I would like to stress that because the object is incorporated into the ego in such a way as to fix it in a "dead" form, there is always a limit to the transformative potential of melancholia. Melancholia changes the ego, but it cannot continue to change it beyond the moment when the object has been fully exhausted of its otherness. Once the incorporation has been completed, the object no longer exists as a separate entity, and thus loses its power to induce change. As I will argue in greater detail below, melancholia is always a self-serving psychic state in that the transformation of the ego that takes place in melancholia can only be accomplished through the destruction of the object.

yearning to be seduced or enchanted in very particular ways. Certain individuals, certain kinds of emotional tones, evoke deep-rooted unconscious longings, and thus prove quite difficult to resist. Nor is there always a reason to resist them, for there may be valuable lessons to be learned by entering deeper into such longings. This may explain in part why some people are so difficult to leave behind or replace while others do not elicit such an attachment.

The objects that the subject has loved the most thus wield an influence over its psychic destiny that far exceeds their actual presence in its life. Indeed, if a particular object continues to live and breathe within the subject after its loss, then loss does not necessarily signify a straightforward annihilation of the prior relationship but merely a significant modification of its form. This idea that the other's impact on the self can outlast the duration of the relationship is in fact one reason that passionate love carries such a strong mythological valence. The subject under the spell of melancholia no longer loves in "real" time but rather embraces a mythical conception of a loving connection that transcends the boundaries of tangible space and experience. In this sense, those that the subject has loved intensely leave behind a lasting legacy, indicative of the power of passion to transform an entire lifetime.

THE CREATIVE POTENTIAL OF MELANCHOLIA

The subject's melancholy refusal to surrender the memory of its loved objects can therefore be a valid means of venerating those who have touched it most profoundly. It is, moreover, important to keep in mind that melancholia has frequently been associated with the imaginative capacities of the psyche. Indeed, there exists a long-standing tendency in Western thought—traceable from Aristotle through the Middle Ages and the Renaissance all the way to nineteenth-century Romanticism—to associate melancholia with inspiration and creative genius (see Eng and Kazanjian 2003, pp. 6–23). The idea that artistic and intellectual extraordinariness arises from the same soil as melancholia's more paralyzing manifestations has generated a powerful mythology that honors sadness as a site of a special kind of truth or knowledge. Melancholia has in fact throughout the ages been understood to play such a fundamental part in creativity that it has often come to be viewed as an intrinsic attribute of the artistic, spiritual, or philosophical character rather than as a deviant or diseased state of mind. And indeed, it is conceivable that melancholia might contain and attempt to communicate forms of meaning that are unattainable through any other means. In contrast to mourning, which seeks to put the past behind once and for all, melancholia dwells in the past in ways that hold this past open and unresolved. This implies that while it is typical to think of mourning as the process that allows the subject to rewrite its past along more constructive lines, it is possible that melancholia facilitates a different type of rewriting—one that does not seek to surmount but merely revisits and reassesses the past. Since melancholia marks a living and ongoing relationship with the past (cf. Eng and Kazanjian, p. 4)—since it retains the past as an active ingredient of the present—it forces the subject to grapple with the losses of its past in ways that reveal, on a highly tangible level, the extent to which the past is never fully the past.

The melancholy subject remains enmeshed in an alternative world—a world that it may in real life have given up, but that keeps resurfacing as a highly charged space of dreams, fantasies, and imaginary constructs. The subject may do its best to go along with the concrete concerns of its everyday existence, yet find itself taken over by sudden visitations from the past. At such moments, the subject catches a glimpse of a peculiar psychic reality that may momentarily seem more viscerally compelling than its actual life. In this manner, melancholia produces its own distinctive set of artifacts and representations (cf. Eng and Kazanjian, p. 5). This is to say that although melancholia on one level arrests the individual's ability to make meaning, the fiery reverence for the past that it exhibits also generates its own idiosyncratic world of meanings.

I will return below to the question of how these idiosyncratic meanings can be translated into more conventionally creative forms of imaginative production. Here I would merely like to hold open the possibility that the individual's immersion in melancholia may at times be a necessary step in preparing the ground in which inspiration later takes root. It is, in other words, conceivable that melancholia may in certain circumstances function as a basis of added imaginative prowess in that the subject may need the silence, solitude, and contemplative stillness of melancholia to access deeper forms of insight. Indeed, if melancholia expresses the psyche's more reclusive side, it may be because it is only by working its way through the sources of its despair—by digging deeply into the tender terrain of its losses—that the subject is able to access aspects of its life that normally remain hidden in the remote corners of its consciousness, and therefore to accede to the kind of intuition that leads to self-understanding. From this perspective, melancholia represents a pause before the leap, a moment of hesitation, an appraisal and an assessment—the psyche's signal to proceed mindfully, with prudence and affective discrimination.

Melancholia therefore challenges the distinction between creativity and pathology, ingenuity and symptom, love and death. This intrinsic ambiguity of melancholia may well be why the "noonday demon"—as melancholia was commonly called during medieval times—has historically held such a strong fascination, and why it continues to do so today. I myself admit to being endlessly fascinated. Yet the considerable allure of the various romantic notions that surround melancholia should not prevent us from recognizing that, on a rather fundamental level, melancholia signals the psyche's inability to move forward. Consequently, as much as I appreciate the idea that melancholia contributes to the psyche's potentialities, I think we need to pay equal attention to the psychoanalytic claim that melancholia can only give rise to imaginative insight once the subject is able to see past its melancholy fixations. While it may well be that creativity lies buried in melancholia—that the potential for creativity within melancholia is so palpable as to infuse the subject's entire existence with its weighty presence—it is also the case that creativity as a tangible outpouring of psychic energy can take place only at the moment when melancholia is transcended. This instance of transcendence does not have to be—and rarely is—permanent, yet it is absolutely necessary for the subject's ability to mobilize its inner resources in such a way as to be able to translate melancholia into meaning; the melancholy subject may reside at the threshold of innovation, but it is the very essence of melancholia to block and inhibit the subject's access to its innovative capacities as long as it is incapable of finding its way out of the labyrinth of its melancholy investments.

Kristeva (1987) asserts that though the imagination feeds on sadness, the work of art emerges only when the sorrow that triggers it has been repudiated and overcome. This is why the artist consumed by melancholia is at the same time absolutely relentless in his struggle against "the symbolic abdication that blankets him" (p. 9). The artist, in other words, recognizes that yielding to melancholia will lead to inertia rather than productivity, making it impossible for the work of art to materialize in any concrete form. The artist also knows that whereas melancholia may function as a potentially generative foundation of the imagination, the opposite is also the case in the sense that the imagination in turn serves as one of the most effective means of fending off melancholy moods. This is precisely why creative activity is for many individuals a way of getting the better of their melancholy tendencies. What this implies is that although melancholia may on one level beget creativity in that it fuels the imagination with vivid fantasies and imaginary wanderings, on another level its persistence signals the subject's inability to draw upon its creative resources to counterbalance the sadness of loss. As Kristeva explains, melancholia implies not only an intolerance for object loss, but also the signifier's failure "to insure a compensating way out of the states of withdrawal in which the subject takes refuge to the point of inaction (pretending to be dead) or even suicide" (p. 10).

Kristeva's discussion of melancholia functions as a useful addendum to the Lacanian argument that I developed in the previous chapter. Not only does Kristeva discuss loss and the processes of coming to terms with loss much more concretely than Lacan, but she takes the question of creative capacity and psychic potentiality beyond the analytic setting, ushering us into the ever-seductive terrain of art and artistic production. Like Lacan, Kristeva believes that lack is a necessary underside of meaning, and that loss is consequently a precondition for the emergence of symbolization. As she puts it, "let us note that 'lack' is necessary for the *sign* to emerge" (p. 23). The human infant, Kristeva maintains, is forced into the realm of signs precisely because it has lost something unbelievably precious. What Lacan theorizes as the loss of imaginary wholeness, Kristeva conceptualizes as the loss of what she calls the "Thing." The Kristevian Thing shares a close conceptual affinity with the Lacanian *das Ding* as the archaic nonobject of desire whose loss propels the subject on the particular path of its desire. Kristeva explains that ever since the violent severance of its attachment to the Thing, the subject suffers from the impression of having been deprived of a "supreme good"—of something that remains unnameable and unrepresentable but that persistently resurfaces as the cause of its desire. The loss of the Thing therefore gives rise to a deeply melancholy yearning that causes the subject to wander in pursuit of loves and adventures that it hopes will compensate for what it has lost. But as with the Lacanian *das Ding*, there is no object that can begin to adequately approximate the missing nonobject (p. 13).

The loss of the Thing thus gives rise to a primordial melancholia that is by definition incurable. But it also activates the subject's capacity for signification by motivating it to look for a means of reincarnating what it has lost. As Kristeva states, "In the place of death and so as not to die of the other's death, I bring forth—or at least I rate highly—an artifice, an ideal, a 'beyond' that my psyche produces in order to take up a position outside itself" (p. 99). In this manner, the subject's participation in the universe of signs and symbolic creations allows it to evoke and bring to life the lost nonobject through symbolization. This, in turn, enables it, momentarily at least, to triumph over its sadness:

> How can I approach the place I have referred to? Sublimation is an at-tempt to do so: through melody, rhythm, semantic polyvalence, the so-called poetic form, which decomposes and recomposes signs, is the sole "container" seemingly able to secure an uncertain but adequate hold over the Thing. [p. 14]

> Sublimation's dynamics . . . weaves a *hypersign* around and with the depressive void. This is *allegory*, as lavishness of that which *no longer is*, but which regains for myself a higher meaning because I am able to re-make nothingness, better than it was and within an unchanging harmony, here and now and forever, for the sake of someone else. Artifice, as sub-lime meaning for and on behalf of the underlying, implicit nonbeing, re-places the ephemeral. Beauty is consubstantial with it. Like feminine finery concealing stubborn depressions, beauty emerges as the admi-rable face of loss, transforming it in order to make it live. [p. 99]

Symbolization therefore constitutes a valiant attempt to manage loss, to mold a new "object"—an object composed of signs and signifiers—in place of the missing one. As a result, it functions as a kind of "lucid" counterdepressant (p. 25) that possesses the power to weave a web of meaning around the subject's inner void, and therefore to alleviate the pain that arises from this void. Sublimation, Kristeva maintains, gives the subject an uncertain yet adequate "hold" over the absent Thing, allow-ing it to come to terms with the inerasable imprint of sorrow that no amount of grieving will exorcise; creation, as a means of externalizing sadness—of turning tears into poetry, as it were—enables the subject to cope with the bitterness of loss by transforming this loss into a site of beauty and possibility. In this manner, beauty bears witness to the idea that "there is survival after death" (p. 98), seducing the subject to con-tinue living despite the fact that it always inexorably carries within itself the trace of loss as the very condition of its being.

Like Lacan, Kristeva believes that primordial loss is our opportu-nity to become subjects of signification. This is because the loss of the original object (the Thing) can only be mediated and survived through "an unbelievable symbolic effort" (p. 28). Indeed, it is precisely when the subject becomes interested in the life of signs that it discovers "the royal way through which humanity transcends the grief of being apart." In this sense, it is "nameable" melancholia—melancholia that has been given body in symbols—that makes subjectivity possible. Kristeva points out that the economy of discourses that the Western tradition (from Greek and Roman antiquity to Judaism and Christianity) has produced is marked by the peculiar fact that these discourses "are constituently very close to depression and at the same time show a necessary shift from depression to possible meaning." There exists then a "tense link between Thing and Meaning, the unnameable and the proliferation of signs, the silent affect and the ideality that designates and goes beyond it" (p. 100). The Western imagination, Kristeva concludes, owes a great deal to "the ability to transfer meaning to the very place where it was lost in death and/or nonmeaning" (p. 103).

In Kristevian terms, creativity therefore always bears witness to the melancholy trace of loss and separation even as it marks the ecstatic "beginning of the symbol's sway" (p. 22). Creativity, in other words, invariably carries the imprint of melancholia even as it offers the subject a remarkably powerful means of sublimating its losses. This in turn suggests that the transition from melancholia to creativity can frequently be quite perilous and unreliable. If the individual's creative capacities reside in, and arise from, the volatile space between melancholia and its sublimatory overcoming, then melancholia cannot but introduce a strong element of risk into any imaginative undertaking. That is, if Kristeva is correct in arguing that archaic object loss results in melancholia, and if creativity is aimed at surmounting this melancholia, then creativity is by necessity only one step removed from sadness, and two steps removed from the existential void that houses the subject's constitutive losses. This implies that if the imagination often prevails over melancholia, the reverse is also frequently the case in the sense that melancholia inescapably dwells coiled up within the imagination in ways that threaten to overflow with every manifestation of creativity. As a result, creativity calls for the subject's capacity to meet the melancholy roots of its identity without succumbing to the pull of sadness—a pull that, as those artists and other creative individuals who are racked by melancholia have discovered, can be overwhelmingly intense. Paradoxically, then, even though sublimation is meant to rescue the subject from its constitutive losses, it cannot but place it in danger of being devoured by these very same losses. As Kristeva states, the emptiness within the subject that the signifier induces is "also the barely covered abyss where our identities, images, and words run the risk of being engulfed" (1983, p. 42).

Kristeva in fact proposes that individuals who are incapable of breaking the cycle of melancholy attachments remain victim to the "flimsiness" of the signifier (1987, p. 20)—to its occasional failure to accomplish the desired transition from melancholia to meaning. The subject who is mired in melancholia is a mute prisoner of affect, unable to find a way of articulating its sorrow. That melancholia often gets the better of us testifies to the fragility and precariousness of human existence—to the fact that much of our lives are spent battling against "symbolic collapse" (p. 24). In extreme instances, sadness becomes the sole object of psychic cathexis because the subject cannot find another mode of compensating for its losses. In such cases, sadness functions as the only means of providing the self with a degree of cohesion: "The depressive mood constitutes itself as a narcissistic support, negative to be sure, but nevertheless presenting the self with an integrity" (p. 19). In this manner, suffering as a generalized state of being can become eroticized (p. 19)—can become the individual's only reason for living. When sublimation succeeds, in contrast, sadness is folded into the creases of the signifier, allowing the subject to develop a less libidinally charged relationship to its losses. That is, in instances where creativity triumphs over melancholia, sadness is integrated into the signifier's trajectory of meaning and, in this indirect manner, becomes articulable (even if this articulation radically changes and/or distorts its original shape).

LACAN VS. KRISTEVA

Kristeva's commentary on sublimation shares a great deal with Lacan's argument regarding signification and the poetic function of language (see Chapter 3). Both consider the imaginary as a site of the kind of primordial loss that gives rise to melancholy yearning. Both similarly consider the signifier as what potentially delivers the subject from this yearning. If the task of the Lacanian subject is to conjure meaning out of a void (to borrow from Silverman), the goal of the Kristevian subject is to bind energies and affects into words. Both thinkers are preoccupied with the idea that the subject's existential enablement depends on its capacity to compensate for the loss that founds its being—on its capacity to translate loss into signs, meanings, and, in those rare and auspicious moments when the shape of creation matches the shape of emptiness in a perfect and radiant manner, beauty and inspiration.

What distinguishes the two arguments, however, is that Kristeva has a lot more respect for the nostalgia that the subject feels for what it has lost. We have already seen that Kristeva posits melancholia as the generative underlining of creativity. While Kristeva on the one hand views the imagination as a means of overcoming melancholia, she at the same time maintains that there is "no imagination that is not, secretly or overtly, melancholy"; rather than seek the meaning of despair, Kristeva asserts, we need to recognize that "there is meaning only in despair" (pp. 5–6). What is more, Kristeva believes that the semiotic as a site of melancholy fixation functions as an invaluable source of "nutritive nonmeaning" (p. 101) that feeds the possibilities of signification. The imaginary for Lacan is what keeps the subject immersed in the melancholy (and dangerous) mirages of its fantasy life, enslaving it to the *objet a* and to the repetition compulsion; the semiotic for Kristeva is what holds the subject close enough to the melancholy roots of its identity for it to be able to utilize this melancholia as a potent wellspring for its imaginative undertakings. Lacan regards the subject's preverbal cathexes primarily as a threat to its ability to exploit the poetic potential of the signifier; Kristeva views these cathexes as the very precondition of such creative capacity. The intrusion of the imaginary within the symbolic for Lacan represents a regressive force that carries an existential risk; Kristeva deems this risk worth taking because, in her assessment, it remains the only effective means of ensuring that the symbolic remains open to transformation instead of solidifying into hegemonic patterns of meaning.

Whereas Lacan is mainly focused on the signifier, Kristeva believes that creativity invariably takes place at the intersection of language and drives—that it is the signifier's ability to productively harness the subject's semiotic energies that constitutes the basis of all imaginative activity. The subject's relationship to the semiotic is therefore quite complex in that if it wishes to retain a degree of imaginative agility, it must continually bring itself within a striking distance of the chaotic impulses of this semiotic— impulses that, terrifyingly enough, contain the residue of loss. From this perspective, creativity is a function of the subject's capacity to assimilate and refine the disruptive semiotic energies that provide the raw materials for its symbolic productions.[7]

Kristeva in fact argues that the signifier in itself represents a relatively sterile and mechanical component of meaning-making—one that, if it is to remain transformative, calls for the infusion of the more rhythmic, melodic, and primordial semiotic impulses. Kristeva concedes that the semiotic impulses in themselves do not amount to anything that could be considered creative; however, she insists that it is always the irruption of the unruly semiotic within the symbolic that provides the innovative force of any imaginative endeavor. Imaginative forms of signification are distinctive precisely in that they, unlike the more prosaic processes of our everyday meaning-making, are capable of transgressing the boundary between the semiotic and the symbolic so as to forge an opening for new and polyvalent meanings. In this sense, it is the dynamic interaction between the semiotic and the symbolic that brings about all the alterations of the signifying practice that are commonly called "creation" (1974, p. 62).

Kristeva has always been interested in how it is that individuals come to generate meanings that surpass the significatory conventions of the symbolic order. The semiotic is where Kristeva finds her answer. Yet although Kristeva contends that it is the semiotic drives that generate the necessary energy for all of the subject's innovative acts of meaning-making, she is not interested in fleeing the symbolic in search of some uncorrupted space of marginality that would provide a means of attacking the dominant order; Kristeva's theory of the imagination certainly suggests that there is something about the semiotic that by definition resides beyond the disciplinary power of the symbolic, but she is at the same time insistent that creativity is always a symbolic matter (even as it draws upon semiotic energies).

Critics such as Butler (1990) have found Kristeva's vacillation between the semiotic and the symbolic problematic because it appears to uphold the hegemony of the symbolic at the very moment that it seeks to subvert

---

7. Kristeva's argument reminds me of Nietzsche's contention that it is the delicate balancing act of the Apollinian and Dionysian components of ancient Greek culture that gives rise to Attic tragedy. Nietzsche and Kristeva both imply that creativity feeds on the unruly and unrefined elements of existence yet simultaneously demands the disciplining influence of what is calm, controlled, and cultivated. Whereas the Dionysian (or semiotic) provides the vitality that underlies creative acts, the Appollinian (or symbolic) offers the limits within which this vitality can productively be expressed.

it. However, I would argue that Kristeva is not necessarily invested in up-holding the hegemonic dimensions of the symbolic, but rather in illuminating the processes of regeneration that allow the signifier to renew itself like a snake shedding old skin. By maintaining that the psyche is not exclusively a province of signifiers, but also includes drives, energies, and affects that both figure into signification and exceed it, Kristeva offers us a theory of how it is that the signifier manages, over and over again, to revitalize itself in ways that allow meaning to evolve in rebellious and promiscuous directions.

In the previous chapter, I argued that it would be a mistake to conflate the Lacanian symbolic with Foucault's notion of disciplinary power. Kristeva offers us one way of understanding why symbolization is not fully containable by power and why systems of signification can shift considerably over time. The only reason the signifier does not grow hopelessly tired and insipid by the end of the day, Kristeva maintains, is that the semiotic continues to provide the erratic, capricious, and deeply unsettling, yet highly necessary, "fit of delirium" (1995, p. 31) within the signifying chain that incites changes in the symbolic. In forcing the symbolic to continuously encounter what exceeds its realm, the semiotic prevents it from congealing into static forms of meaning. In this manner, it becomes possible to comprehend how what has been marginalized by the symbolic order possesses the power to modify the very economy of this order by subverting its normative operations.

Another reason I find Kristeva's theory of the imagination useful is that it highlights the fundamental similarities between clinical practice on the one hand and artistic and sublimatory endeavors on the other. This is to say that putting a Kristevian spin on the Lacanian notion of the poetic function of language is valuable because it makes explicit the possibility that the processes of narrativization that take place in analysis[8] and the processes of innovation that take place in artistic and other forms of creative activity are closely aligned. Kristeva implies that both analysis and creativity depend on the signifier's ability to effectively bind drives and affects without at the same time immobilizing these drives and affects in overly inflexible patterns that would block the path to future development. As a result, she suggests that the inner impasses that make it difficult for the analysand to overcome symptomatic behavior are in many ways similar to the impasses that thwart the fluid unfolding of artistic potentialities.

---

8. I will discuss these in more detail in Chapter 5.

We have seen that the Kristevian signifier functions much like a crocheting needle that is able to pull the disorganized energies of the semiotic into the more structured domain of the symbolic in ways that weave novel patterns of meaning. As a consequence it is when something interferes with the signifier's ability to capture the semiotic in a satisfactory manner that the symptom ensues and that creativity becomes belabored. Analysis and artistic creativity are therefore analogous in that they both depend on the signifier's capacity to incorporate what resides outside of itself and, in so doing, to renew and revitalize itself.

Highlighting the parallels between analysis and artistic practice allows us to discern how Lacan and Kristeva, while disagreeing on many of the details, share some basic similarities, such as the fundamental belief that the trauma of originary loss is what makes the subject capable of signification and creative agency. One reason Lacan and Kristeva have been regarded as saying such vastly different things is that whereas Lacan puts literature and philosophy in the service of psychoanalysis, Kristeva frequently uses her psychoanalytic acumen to analyze the processes at work in poetry, literature, religion, philosophy, and other human productions that are operative outside the analytic situation. Lacan's focus is therefore more narrow in that he is primarily preoccupied with the *raison d'être* of psychoanalysis. We have seen that Lacan's chief objective is to detach the signifier from the primordial energies of the imaginary so as to help the subject overcome its repetition compulsion. Kristeva, in contrast, while also seeking ways to compensate for the loss of imaginary wholeness, is interested in creative pursuits much more broadly. As she explains, artistic activities and representations have been used in various societies throughout the ages as a therapeutic and cathartic device. As a result, psychoanalysts "owe it to themselves to enrich their practice by paying greater attention to these sublimatory solutions to our crises" (1987, pp. 24–25). If Lacan is first and foremost looking for ways to free the subject from its imaginary "mirages," Kristeva endeavors to understand the links between the imagination and the imaginary (or the semiotic). If Lacan regards the imaginary as what needs to be carefully contained, Kristeva views it less as an enemy than as a potential source of creative energy. And though both value analysis as a means of dealing with pathological formations, Kristeva is on the lookout for other forms of healing (art, literature, religion, and philosophy) as well. Lacan and Kristeva thus share the same aim, but their points of emphasis and methodology differ considerably.

CIXOUS ON LOSS AND WRITING

Throughout this book I have sought ways to think about loss affirmatively, as a potential source of creativity and psychic possibility. Loss is a peculiar form of suffering that connects us to our past, and I have outlined the similarities between Lacan and Kristeva in part because I believe that they can help us in the often quite difficult task of learning how to bring our past into our present in dynamic and vitalizing ways. We have seen that Lacan argues that it is because the subject is from the onset constituted as a being of loss that the "passion" of the signifier flows through it, animating its representational resources and enabling it to create meaning out of its lack. Kristeva in turn maintains that while loss draws the subject toward the stillness and deep silences (as well as the sensuality) of melancholia, it also propels it into the realm of imaginative and inspired productions.

I would like to add yet another layer to our understanding of the connection between loss and creativity by considering the description that Cixous (1977) provides of her rather tumultuous "coming to writing." Cixous posits that loss—"having once lost everything" (p. 38)—is the condition upon which writing becomes conceivable. Writing, Cixous proposes, is where life and death hurl into a fierce combat, and where—at least during those intoxicating moments when words flow without effort—life conquers death. "At first I really wrote to bar death," Cixous explains. "To see my loss with my own eyes; to look loss in the eye . . . Still here, I write life. Life: what borders on death" (p. 5). Writing is where life brushes against death even as it momentarily defeats it. Writing wells up from loss, traverses the body, and (as in Lacan and Kristeva) conveys the subject to a place "beyond lack" (p. 39). In this manner, writing sustains life by making it possible for the subject to survive its losses without falling into the abyss.

But Cixous does not stop at survival. Inspiration is what she is after. Writing for her is not merely a means of defying death, but of creating an over-abundance of life, of bringing the psyche acutely alive. This creation of life is necessary because the world is filled, particularly if one is a woman (and one might add, a member of any "marked" identity category), with impediments to life and creativity: "There are so many boundaries, and so many walls, and inside the walls, more walls. Bastions in which, one morning, I wake up condemned. Cities where I am isolated, quarantines, cages, 'rest' homes. How often I've been there, my tombs, my corporeal dungeons, the earth abounds with places for my confinement. Body in solitary, soul in silence" (p. 3). This is Cixous's attempt to articulate what Freud talks about in terms of the "strangulation" of affects, the repetition compulsion, and symptomatic behavior, namely the fact that psychic vitality can easily be lost under the pressures of navigating the complexities of the world. Freud regards psychoanalysis—particularly the processes of narrativization that characterize analysis—as a means of fending off this type of bodily and psychic death; Cixous implies that writing is one of the most efficient means of reanimating a lifeless psyche, and therefore of protecting soulfulness. Writing, Cixous in fact specifies, allows the subject to "stretch" its soul (p. 7)—to take pleasure in its body, mind, and spirit.

Cixous writes in order to work her way to a sense of possibility. The thrill of writing is for her corporeal as well as intellectual and spiritual, entailing the breaking down of the various "bastions" that freeze up and imprison the body. As a result, she talks about writing as a kind of violent transport that changes one's normal rhythms:

> Writing was in the air around me. Always close, intoxicating, invisible, inaccessible. . . . It came to me abruptly. One day I was tracked down, besieged, taken. It captured me. I was seized. . . . The attack was imperious: "Write!" Even though I was only a meager anonymous mouse, I knew vividly the awful jolt that galvanizes the prophet, wakened in midlife by an order from above. . . . An urge shook my body, changed my rhythms, tossed madly in my chest, made time unlivable for me. I was stormy. "Burst!" "You may speak!" And besides, whose voice is that? The Urge had the violence of a thunderclap. Who's striking me? Who's attacking me from behind? And in my body the breath of a giant, but no sentences at all. Who's pushing me? Who's invading? Who's changing me into a monster? Into a mouse wanting to swell to the size of a prophet? [pp. 9–10]

> Write? Me? Because it was so strong and furious, I loved and feared this breath. To be lifted up one morning, snatched off the ground, swung in the air. To be taken by surprise. To find in myself the possibility of the unexpected. To fall asleep a mouse and wake up an eagle. What delight! What terror. And I had nothing to do with it, I couldn't help it. [p. 11]

Cixous portrays writing as a tempestuous force that takes her unawares, that attacks, invades, and shakes her, and that—in making her defiant and stormy—energizes her from within. What is brilliant about this depiction of inspiration is the extent to which it manages to combine the exuberant sensation of coming to life (of, quite literally, regaining one's breath) with the realization that there is much about this process that remains beyond one's control. It also manages to convey the terror and frustration of the subject who is caught up within a creative impulse that in many ways exceeds its actual capacities. Writing comes as a liberation that is also a compulsion; it revives the self, yet it also demands the self's absolute surrender; it invades even as it gives life. Writing, in Cixous's rendering, requires the self to yield to a force outside of itself that speaks its meaning through the trembling body of the one who is being urged to swell to a size of a prophet.

I like to think of Cixous as a postmodern visionary, for she talks about writing very much along the same lines as some mystics describe their experiences of divine "rapture" or "transport." I am here reminded of an argument made by Evelyn Underhill in the beginning of the twentieth century (around the same time as Freud was trying to unearth the mysteries of the unconscious). Underhill maintains that the form of altered consciousness that characterizes states of mystical ecstasy is in many ways similar to the strong fixity of attention that underlies various forms of creative and inspired activity as well. Underhill points out that mystical experience entails a complete unification of consciousness—an exalted and expanded form of perception that causes the mystic to become entirely absorbed in her quest. This state of entrancement can be so profound that none of the messages of the outside world—even bodily pain—are able to break through its boundaries. The result, Underhill explains, is "not merely a mind concentrated on one idea, nor a heart fixed on one desire, nor even a mind and a heart united in the interests of a beloved thought: but a whole being welded into one, all its faculties, neglecting their normal universe, grouped about a new centre, serving a new life, and piercing like a single flame the barriers of the sensual world. Ecstasy is the psycho-physical state which generally accompanies and expresses this brief synthetic act" (1911, pp. 437–438). This same "machinery of contemplation," Underhill posits, is employed more or less successfully by creative individuals from inventors to poets, artists, musicians, and philosophers; the same altered consciousness, the same focus of attention, accompanies, in less violent form, all inspired endeavors. As the mystic is "caught up" in the divine, the artist or philosopher is "caught up" in her unique vision of reality. The "blanking out" of consciousness that is characteristic of the mystical state is equally typical of the creative state. Moreover, the mingling of pleasure and pain that someone like Saint Teresa depicts in great detail can take place in the context of creative efforts as well.

Underhill's depiction of creativity, like that of Cixous, may be too fanciful for many of us. However, I would venture to say that even if we are not capable of the kind of remaking of consciousness that Underhill describes, the aspiration for such a transformed state may well be what (at least sometimes) drives us as creatures of creative capacity. Many of us are familiar with the experience of being totally present "in the moment"—of allowing the past and the future to temporarily fade from consciousness, of losing track of our surroundings, of no longer needing to think things through in any measured manner—that accompanies our most important endeavors. What Underhill is arguing is that our best creative accomplishments are translations or concrete renderings of this type of absolute absorption.

The acute concentration that Underhill describes asks the subject to allow itself to be swept up in a reality that exceeds the self. Yet this act of surrendering the self to the task at hand should not be confused with a lack of discipline, for it is precisely discipline that creates the conditions under which such surrender becomes possible in the first place. In Chapter 1, I mentioned that Nietzsche argues that creativity has less to do with the act of letting oneself go than with gaining a certain mastery over the self. I would now like to modify this by proposing that it may well be that it is the self's mastery over itself that constitutes the boundaries of possibility within which surrender can profitably take place. The same way as Bataille maintains that losing one's footing within erotic experience calls for some sort of a guarantee that one will not fall irrevocably (see Chapter 2), self-surrender within artistic or other types of creative endeavors may only be feasible within securely established limits. This may also explain why mystical experience tends to take place within the strict regimen of monastic life. Those of us doing creative work know that inspiration rarely results from the efforts of will and self-control alone—that it is often precisely when we relinquish our will and self-control that things begin to flow—yet it seems that will and self-control are a necessary precondition for those treasured moments when exertion ceases and beauty slides out from underneath the shadows.

I find Underhill's conceptualization of the creative process intriguing because it presents surrender as a dynamic state which, rather than implying submission, victimization, or humiliation, sustains our capacity for inspiration. It also lends a fresh perspective on Lacan's assertion that the signifier speaks through us in ways that transcend our control by suggesting that in opening ourselves up to the signifier, we can attain realms of meaning that would otherwise remain inaccessible to us. Yet Underhill also acknowledges that the absolute concentration that characterizes the exalted state of creativity carries the risk of pathology in that it is always possible to become *too* fixated on an idea or activity. She proceeds to point out—and this reveals her to be a contemporary of Freud—that the alteration of consciousness that wings creative endeavors can also be found in hysterical patients. The state of hypnotic fixity can, in other words, surface in a more problematic form as a hysterical tendency to dwell upon one governing idea or intuition. Such pathological manifestations aside, however, the act of concentrating one's efforts in one place can potentially make the individual "more living than before" (p. 451).

Cixous approaches the theme of creative surrender by connecting writing with love. Whereas Kristeva claims that "there is no writing other than the amorous" (1987, p. 6), Cixous states:

> I write for, I write from, I start writing from: Love. I write out of love. Writing, loving: inseparable. Writing is a gesture of love. *The Gesture*. . . . Writing: making love to Love. Writing with love, loving with writing. Love opens up the body without which Writing becomes atrophied. For Love, the words become loved and read flesh, multiplied into all the bodies and texts that love bears and awaits from love. Text: not a detour, but the flesh at work in a labor of love. [p. 42]

> Love made a gesture, two years ago, a fluttering of eyelids and the text rises forth: there is this gesture, the text surges from it. . . . The text is always written under the sweet pressure of love. My only torment, my only fear, is of failing to write as high up as the Other, my only chagrin is of failing to write as beautifully as Love. [p. 43]

Love opens the body so that writing can surge forth; writing originates from love, and it is also a gesture of love—a gesture that weaves the beloved other into a text. In *A Lover's Discourse*, Barthes (1977) talks about the manner in which the lover's text is haunted and animated by the ever-present trace of the loved object. Likewise, Cixous affirms that a text is always written under the pressure of love, and that her only fear is failing to write well and beautifully enough to do justice to this love. The pressure of love is, moreover, irresistible. As Cixous explains: "Under the blows of love I catch fire, I take to the air, I burst into letters. It's not that I don't resist. It speaks, and I am what is uttered" (p. 44). Love speaks and the subject is what is uttered; the subject's very being as well as its capacity to make meaning exist merely as a kind of utterance of love.

Writing is, moreover, an indirect means of keeping the loved object alive even in its absence. As Cixous states, "I write and you are not dead. The other is safe if I write" (p. 4). The loss of a loved being can therefore be generative in that it gives rise to a certain kind of representational urgency. Because the subject needs something—words, images, sounds, or movements—to take the place of the lost other, longing and inspiration become one and the same thing. In the words of Cixous, the other is "the one who is always there, the one who is never exhausted, the one who never runs out, but whose every phrase calls forth a book—and whose every breath inaugurates a song . . ." (p. 43). Every step that the subject takes, every question that it asks, every sentence that it writes, all of its dreams, actions, creations, and aspirations, are aimed at making good the loss that it has suffered. In this sense, the subject's sense of incompleteness can engender an almost compulsive creative impulse. Yet the other's persistent trace exceeds the subject's every effort to exhaust it. On the one hand, then, writing is an act of generosity that sustains the absent other as a living presence. On the other hand, writing pours out of the subject because it is the only way the subject can contain the longing within; writing gives structure to the subject's longing, therefore making it more manageable. Either way, the subject owes its inspiration to the other who is missing but who nevertheless infuses its texts with a certain impalpable energy.

Cixous writes from the absence of the loved other. The same way that the Kristevian subject engages in creative endeavors to compensate for loss, Cixous believes that writing functions as "the assault of love on nothingness" (p. 4). Writing transcends death in that it serves as a means of transfiguring the lost object into something that endures in an altered state. Whereas melancholia embalms the object into an ageless and unchanging image, writing reworks it into an ever-mobile web of meaning. Lacan and Kristeva both imply that this is one of the better ways of coping with loss. This is because the sublimatory working-through of loss gives the subject the agency to rename what it has lost without at the same time making any demands on the object itself. This renaming is where something affirmative takes place—a certain kind of renarration or inner metamorphosis that allows the subject to rewrite the losses of its past into a psychically manageable present. I have already implied that psychoanalysis functions as one technique of such rewriting (I will return to this in greater detail in

Chapter 5). But we have also learned that creative activities are an especially effective means of bringing about this type of psychic transformation. For Cixous, it is writing in particular that fends off melancholia. It is as if the stringing together of words somehow directly compensates for the hollow space left by the lost object. This may be why the blank page can be so uncanny. While writing fills the subject's inner void, the blank page stares back with a relentless intensity, and seems only to widen the void; it seems only to deepen the well of the unspeakable.

BEYOND MELANCHOLIA: WELCOMING THE OTHER AS OTHER

Insofar as melancholia marks the kind of desire that is by definition unspeakable, it brings the subject against the experience of the Lacanian real. The real is what has not yet been put into a narrative, and it consequently represents an unmediated form of encountering reality. As such, it confronts the subject as a potentially shattering enigma that can only be "solved" by finding the appropriate signifiers with which to contain it (see Feher-Gurewich and Tort 1996, p. 33). In some instances, such as mystical ecstasy (see Lacan 1975), the real is experienced as a transcendent union with a mysterious unknown. In others, such as melancholia, the real is experienced as an engulfing return to the swampy terrain of the imaginary. One of the main reasons it is so difficult for the subject to burrow its way out of the morass of melancholia is that melancholia reactivates its imaginary fantasy of being able to reunite with what it has lost. This implies that as long as there exists no narrative with which to transform the silences of melancholia into communicable meaning, it remains impossible for the subject to access the creative potentialities that melancholia may contain.

But if it is narrativization that reclaims the subject from the real, then what is the mechanism that gives it access to narrativization? In Kristevian terms, if the imagination is lodged in the inscrutable space between the semiotic and the symbolic, then what is the psychic lever that jolts the subject from melancholia to meaning? Those who have tried to conquer melancholia without success know that the experience can be like poking at the sturdy canvas of a circus tent with one's bare fingers. Without a weapon of some sort, it is impossible to pierce the canvas so as to gain access to the world beyond. What then is the weapon that cuts the canvas?

From a Lacanian perspective, the subject's ability to move from melancholia to meaning entails a process that is quite similar to the one that constitutes it as a subject of signification in the first place. As we saw in the previous chapter, Lacan maintains that the process of subject formation demands that a psychic limit be placed on the subject's fantasy of everlasting union. We saw that it is when the subject encounters resistance to its fantasmatic mirages or misrecognitions—when the experience of symbolic castration cuts into its sense of plenitude and wholeness—that it is able to exchange the *jouissance* of the imaginary for the creative capacities of the signifier. As long as the subject adheres to the fantasy of fusion—and as long as it blames the other for always disappointing it—it will spin in circles. In contrast, it is when something in the other's discourse provides a definite limit to the subject's fantasy—when the other forecloses all hope of absolute satisfaction—that it becomes possible (and imperative) for the subject to accede to meaning.

The paradigmatic limit of this kind is the oedipal prohibition, but the subject obviously encounters countless such limits—various disappointments and disillusionments—throughout its existence. This implies that creativity materializes in very different ways in different individuals because it is bound up with the specific manner in which the other deflates the *jouissance* that the subject derives from its melancholy fantasies. But this variability does not change the basic fact that it is only when the other's limit has been firmly set—when there is no longer a convenient place for the subject's fantasies to attach themselves to—that melancholia begins to give way to narrativization, interpretation, and application.

If Lacan spent his lifetime shaking people out of their imaginary fantasies, it is because he believed separation to be the engine of creativity.[9] He also believed separation to be the precondition of the individual's capacity for love. As I mentioned in Chapter 3, Lacanian analysis has frequently been criticized for pathologizing love because it presents subject formation as a matter of differentiation rather than of reciprocity and intersubjectivity. However, as I have tried to illustrate, Lacan is not necessarily denying the possibility of love as such, but merely explaining the

---

9. Separation of course is not a one-time psychic event, but rather an ongoing process of working through loss. To put the matter differently, mourning can be thought of as a process of coming to understand one's melancholia. One needs to mourn, precisely, to "know" one's melancholia, and therefore to (for the time being at least) transcend it.

failures of fusion-love. It is therefore not the absence of love that Lacan advocates, but rather a different understanding of what love is and what its place should be in our lives.

We have seen that Lacan believes that it is only when the subject is able to accept its status as a being of lack—when it recognizes that there is no object capable of providing it with a definitive sense of psychic restoration—that it can begin to treat others with a degree of responsibility. The problem with melancholia is that it represents the subject's absolute refusal to accept lack. Melancholia clings to the promise of wholeness, which means that it holds the subject caught in the narcissistic circuit of imaginary fantasy and the *objet a*. The melancholy subject may "love" its object with infinite faithfulness, yet it is utterly incapable of relating to this object without drawing it into its own psychic economy in ways that leave it no space to exist as an independent entity. The object is in fact fixed within the subject's inner world in ways that cannot acknowledge its radical alterity as a continuously evolving entity. In this sense, melancholia is by definition a self-serving psychic phenomenon in that though it may facilitate the subject's own inner growth, it cannot allow for the growth of the lost object. Against this backdrop, Lacan's valorization of separation opens onto a surprisingly ethical understanding of love, for it touches upon the basic question of whether desire can tolerate the alterity of the other without losing its vibrancy.

Lacan suggests that non-narcissistic love becomes possible only when the subject is able to extricate itself from the web of melancholy fantasy that consistently subsumes the other to the self, and therefore annihilates what is most vital about the other. Separation, in other words, is not a matter of forsaking love, but rather of laying the groundwork for a psyche that is able to transcend melancholia enough to love without cannibalizing the other. Lacan here has an unlikely ally in Luce Irigaray (1994) who argues that a loving connection survives only to the extent that the two lovers are able to protect a sense of mystery between themselves—to the extent that they are able to preserve a gap, distance, or difference that ensures that they always remain irreducible to each other.[10] Love, Irigaray posits, is not about possession or appropriation, but rather

---

10. Irigaray's analysis of love is disturbingly heterocentric, but it does offer a useful contrast to the narcissistic paradigm that so often predominates psychoanalytic accounts. While Irigaray criticizes phenomenological thinkers such as Lévinas and Merleau-Ponty, her approach is primarily phenomenological.

about cultivating an opening within the self that invites the other to enter while simultaneously respecting its integrity and distinctiveness. Irigaray describes this inner opening as a "place of silence" (p. 62)—as something similar to the Heideggerian "clearing" that creates a space for the "presencing" of other people, objects, and things (see Chapter 3). This place of silence, like the Heideggerian notion of "letting-be," is meant to facilitate the other's process of becoming without interfering with its course. It can be thought of as a space where desire stands still so as to allow the other to approach without being ambushed—as something akin to the act of hiding in the bushes and holding one's breath in order to induce a nearby deer to come to the watering hole. If one gets too impatient, if one permits one's desire to get the better of oneself, the deer will flee. Reining in one's desire, in contrast, creates the conditions for the other's advance.

The purpose of love, Irigaray suggests, is to create a bridge that enables the lovers to approach each other, but that can never be entirely crossed; while the bridge allows for the flow of energies, perceptions, and communications between the lovers, it is constructed in such a way as to prevent the lovers from ever collapsing into each other. The problem with imaginary fantasies in the Lacanian sense is that the subject who is caught up in the melancholy folds of its fantasy life not only wants to cross this bridge, but wishes to burn it once it has been crossed so as to ensure its enduring union with the loved other. This implies that it is only when the subject is able to resist that attraction of melancholy fantasy that it is able to hold open its inner clearing in such a way as to begin to truly respond to the other. Irigaray recognizes this, which is why she specifies that her aim is to preserve the "twoness" of the two individuals in love. As she explains, "I will never agree with those who say that in love, including carnal love, it is possible or desirable to overcome the two" (p. 62). Irigaray, moreover, goes further than Lacan in describing what the alternative to fusion-love might actually look like:

> I am sensible with you, each of us remaining ourselves. . . . Leaving both of us to be—you and me, me and you—never reducing the other to a mere meaning, to my meaning, we listen always and anew to each other so that the irreducible can remain. . . . Between us is something which will never be mine or yours. . . . I want to live in harmony with you and still remain other. . . . To be two would allow us to remain in ourselves, would permit gathering, and the type of safeguarding which does not

> restrain, the kind of presence which remains free of bonds: neither mine
> nor yours but each living and breathing with the other. It would refrain
> from possessing you in order to allow you to be—to be in me, as well.
> [pp. 9, 13, 16]

Between lovers there exists something that belongs to neither of them, and
that consequently allows them to exist alongside each other, in harmony
yet separate from each other. To "be two" in Irigaray's sense means to "leave
the other to be . . . to contemplate him as an irreducible presence, to relish
him as an inappropriable good, to see him, to listen to him, to touch him,
knowing that what I perceive is not mine. Sensed by me, yet remaining
other, never reduced to an object" (p. 46).

Western philosophy is notoriously incapable of thinking about difference outside of paradigms of objectification, violation, and appropriation. When the other is not conceptualized as a narcissistic double, it is
often thought of as a vaguely hostile force that is somehow to be defeated
or overcome. Irigaray counters this type of thinking by theorizing difference as a means of creating connections between individuals rather than
as what divides them. Irigaray in fact argues that the subject's very existence is protected by the other's irreducibility:

> But is my existence not protected by your irreducibility? Is the total other
> that you are not my guardian? Does such a distance not allow me to
> remain tangible? . . . Each remote from the other, we are kept alive by
> means of this insuperable gap. Nothing can ever fill it. But it is from
> such nothingness that a spring of the to be is derived for us. Is it not
> because I do not know you that I know that you are? [p. 9]

> Consuming does not produce one's existence. Instead, difference can
> protect this existence. I am if you are, to be together with you allows
> me to become. The two, this two, is the bit more which is indispens-
> able if I am to be. Closing myself up in consumption, in posses-
> sion, in production, does not make me one. What makes me one,
> and perhaps even unique, is the fact that you are and I am not you.
> [p. 16]

The irreducibility of the two is what creates the possibility of "being" in
the first place—and this not only in the sense that the other's unknowability
guarantees its existence as a separate entity ("Is it not because I do not know
you that I know that you are?"), but also in the sense that the subject's own
capacity to "be" is sustained by the other's radical otherness ("What makes

me one, and perhaps even unique, is the fact that you are and I am not you"). It is thus the distance between the two that allows each of them to exist as a viable entity; each is kept alive and nourished by the gap between them. In classically phenomenological texts, such as Hegel's, it is by fixing the other as an object that the self realizes itself as a subject capable of transcendence. For Irigaray, in contrast, it is the subject's ability to preserve the subjecthood of the other that protects its own ability to actualize itself as a subject.

The fact that the other always remains enigmatically other is also what sustains love over time. As Irigaray puts it, it is only by leaving "an extra cloud of invisibility" (p. 46) between themselves that the lovers are able to defend their separateness, and therefore to protect their love. It is the fact that there is always something about the other that remains invisible and inaccessible that allows love to evolve. As a result, it is important for the subject to safeguard a space of silence and mystery within itself: "I who am visible to you must also protect a certain reserve. Within the intention of appearing to you, there must also exist the intention of remaining invisible, of covering life and love with the shadow of a secret" (p. 47). To cover a part of oneself in the cloak of invisibility, to hold a part of oneself undisclosed, is to cultivate one's clearing of silence, and therefore to offer oneself to the other. In contrast, when one makes oneself completely visible and transparent, when one clutters one's interiority with incessant noise and chatter, when one smothers the mystery within one's being, one closes off the inner space that is capable of accommodating the other as other. One, in short, destroys the possibility of love.

GIVING THE GIFT OF LOVE

The question of how to love without subsuming the other to one's narcissistic economy resides at the heart of learning how to relate to others with a degree of generosity. Kaja Silverman (1996) argues that this kind of generosity is a matter of bestowing upon the other what she calls an "active gift of love." What Silverman means by the active gift of love is the act of elevating the beloved other to a position of such magnificent ideality that it becomes impossible for the subject to appropriate or approximate the other's perfection. To love in such a manner, Silverman explains, is "to confer ideality upon an object in contradistinction to the self—or, to state the case more precisely, in contradistinction to that image or object which one attempts to assimilate to the self" (p. 74). Such love guarantees that the subject returns from its encounter with the other empty-handed "not only because the return journey is made without the *objet a*, but because the outward journey is synonymous with a certain bequest, which has been made at the expense of the self, with the conferral of ideality on the *objet a*" (p. 76).

Silverman's argument may at first seem counterintuitive in that it relies on the very mechanism of idealization that characterizes the subject's narcissistic relationship to the *objet a* in the first place. It may, in other words, be difficult to discern immediately how the active gift of love differs substantially from the dynamic of identification and idealization that, according to Lacan, leads the subject, over and over again, to annihilate the other's alterity. Silverman asserts, however, that the active gift of love makes it impossible for the subject to conflate the beloved object with the self because it raises this object to such extreme heights that the object must by definition remain external to the self. "The gift of love is loving in the most profound sense of the word," Silverman maintains, "not because it abolishes identification, but because it involves idealization, and hence identification, at a distance from the self—because it strives to keep the cherished 'image' outside" (p. 76). While identification normally assimilates the other to the self, "the active gift of love works to inhibit any such incorporation by maintaining the object at an uncrossable distance" (p. 77). Since any idealization is always inherently and necessarily identificatory— since there is no way for the subject to avoid identifying with what it idealizes—the only way to avoid repeating the incorporating gesture of narcissistic love is to distance the idealized object from oneself to such an extent that there remains no possibility of equating the two. The solution to the problem of narcissistic love, Silverman thus suggests, is not to pretend that it would be possible to forgo idealization, but rather to idealize in such a way that this idealization ends up working "to the 'credit' or enrichment of the object rather than the ego" (p. 75).

Silverman emphasizes that idealization translates to an active gift of love only when it is rendered from a distance. To fully appreciate what Silverman means by "distance," it is necessary to understand the distinction that she draws between active and passive forms of idealization. Passive idealization, Silverman explains, "involves misrecognizing the ideality which one has conferred upon the other as the other's essence" (p. 77). Active idealization, in contrast, demands the subject's self-consciousness regarding its role in the production of the idealized object:

[T]o give someone the active gift of love implies assuming a *productive* relation to him or her. It means not only to "crystallize" the other, as Stendhal would say—to encrust that other with the diamonds of ideality— but to do so knowingly, and without forgetting for a moment that he or she is also a subject of lack. The active gift of love consequently implies both idealizing beyond the parameters of the "self," and doing so with a full understanding of one's own creative participation with respect to the end result. [p. 78]

Active idealization demands the subject's full consciousness of its participation in the creation of the idealized object—a consciousness that makes it impossible to forget that, beyond idealization, the object is always also a subject of lack (and therefore less than ideal). This is to say that the active gift of love "implies epistemological access to what would otherwise remain occluded in the mists of the imaginary." This epistemological access guarantees that the subject knows that if something about the other dazzles it, it is because it "has rendered it dazzling" (p. 80). In this manner, active idealization prevents the subject from mistaking the object's ideality for its intrinsic character; the subject retains its awareness of the act of idealization so that "the newly created image does not congeal into a tyrannizing essence" (p. 2). The "luster" that the subject bestows upon the other through the active gift of love should therefore not adhere to the other seamlessly, but should always be recognized as a quality that emanates from the subject's own desire. This is important because without this attentiveness to the distinction between the object's ideality on the one hand and its alterity beyond this ideality on the other, the subject wishing to give the active gift of love would not be any different from the narcissistic subject who, caught in its melancholy fantasies of omnipotence and self-completion, sees in the other only the idealized image of itself. This is why Silverman insists that the active gift of love "means to *confer* ideality, not to *find* it" (p. 78).

The subject's ability to remain conscious of its active role in the production of ideality is especially important because of its strong tendency to idealize in ways that conform to preexisting cultural conceptions of ideality. Silverman points out that objects "which are repeatedly portrayed by a particular society as 'the ideal' can exercise an almost irresistible attraction," with the result that "the subject more often than not libidinally affirms what is culturally valorized" (p. 80). In this context, the active gift of love refers most emphatically to those processes of idealization that confer ideality upon individuals who are commonly aligned with debased and denigrated images. This process of active idealization, rather than passively and blindly upholding cultural norms of ideality, "conjures into existence something genuinely new," and provides a means of conceptualizing "how we might put ourselves in a positive identificatory relation to bodies which we are taught to abhor and repudiate" (p. 79). Such an active gift of love utilizes what Silverman calls "productive vision"—the kind of vision that is able to see "something other than what is given to be seen"—as a basis of imparting visibility and value upon culturally invisible or devalued bodies and identities. Active idealization, in this sense, sidesteps the narrow mandates of cultural ideality to grant validity "upon bodies which have long been accustomed to neglect and disdain" (p. 227).

Silverman's notion of the active gift of love thus presents idealization as a potentially transformative force—a force capable of giving rise to new sparkling ideals, intensities, and sites of appreciation. In Chapter 1, I argued that Nietzsche regards the metaphoric or untruthful nature of the world as what allows us to take advantage of the fact that, as human beings, we are capable of brilliant fables. The solution to the lack of truth then is not to intensify our search for facts, but rather to cultivate our talent for constructing world-altering fictions. Silverman is saying something very similar, namely that it is as active producers of ideality that we can begin to change the world. Silverman's analysis, moreover, offers a compelling attempt to reconcile the subject's tendency to idealize the beloved other with the necessity of finding a way to allow this other to remain irreducibly other. Silverman thus provides a psychoanalytic solution to Irigaray's question of how to protect the "twoness" of the two individuals in love. If Irigaray goes further than Lacan in conceptualizing what love beyond the narcissistic circuit might entail, Silverman in turn goes further than Irigaray in being able to give shape to one psychic mechanism that might allow the subject to love without losing track of the other's alterity. As such, Silverman's active gift of love is also an ethics of love.

The question that Silverman's analysis raises is the extent to which the active gift of love can survive the ideal's undoing. It seems to me, in other words, that if the active gift of love is to retain its ethical charge, it must be able to accommodate the collapse of the ideal along with its flawlessness. If there truly is to exist, in the mind of the idealizing subject, a conscious awareness of the difference between the object as an ideal on the one hand and the object as a site of irreducible alterity on the other, the gift of love must be able to withstand a fissure in the structure of idealization; it must allow the other's alterity to reveal itself in ways that have nothing whatsoever to do with the ideal. In Chapter 3, we saw that Barthes proposes that the death of desire begins the moment the ideal shatters. This is undoubtedly the case even when the ideal has been actively and deliberately constituted. Consequently, it is only when the subject's affection endures beyond the dynamic of idealization that we approach the full significance of what it means to actively bestow the gift of love.

If, as Lacan suggests, the creative unfolding of the subject's psychic potentialities demands that it come to terms with its own lack and castration, its capacity for love in turn depends on its ability to accept the lack and castration of the other. Silverman touches upon this by positing that since no one can ever embody the ideal in any absolute sense, we must allow for the possibility of a "good enough" (in Winnicott's sense) approximation.[11] I would like to propose that one way the subject might preserve the other's integrity as a "good enough" object is by opening a space for its surrender. In Chapter 2, I considered the possibility that surrender may be a mode of self-actualization. I was interested in the idea that the subject's capacity to surrender itself in the presence of a loved other gives it access to layers of its being that under normal circumstances remain concealed. I would now like to add that insofar as the active gift of love must be able to tolerate the breakdown of the ideal, it calls for the loving subject's ability to facilitate and bear witness to the other's surrender. This is because facilitating the other's surrender requires the subject, for the time being at least, to suspend the ideal so as to allow an alternative, and perhaps less immaculate, reality to emerge. Without this possibility of a less immaculate reality, the burden of ideality on the object can become too heavy to endure.

Here it is useful to evoke Irigaray's notion of the caress. Irigaray endeavors to develop an ethics of the caress that is meant to sidestep the idea—advocated by Lévinas (1961), among others—that the caress is primarily a means of fixing the other in the kind of state of passivity that hinders its ability to realize its potentialities. While Lévinas describes the caress as a kind of profanation, as a surrender to tenderness that evacuates the body of its status as a transcendent being by making it inert in ways that prevent its processes of becoming, Irigaray envisions it as a site of self-awakening.

---

11. Silverman, moreover, emphasizes that we need to recognize that the "good enough" ideal is "triumphant in exact proportion to the adversity it overcomes—that it counts most when circumstances most conspire against it, when it is, from a social standpoint, most *impossible*" (p. 225).

The caress, Irigaray (1994) maintains, has nothing to do with ensnarement or possession. Rather than violating the other's mystery or reducing the other to passivity, the caress "gives the other to himself, to herself, thanks to an attentive witness":[12]

> The caress is an awakening to you, to me, to us. The caress is a reawakening to the life of my body: to its skin, senses, muscles, nerves, and organs, most of the time inhibited, subjugated, dormant or enslaved to everyday activity, to the universe of needs, to the world of labor, to the imperatives or restrictions necessary for communal living. The caress is an awakening to intersubjectivity, to a touching between us which is neither passive nor active. . . . The caress is an awakening to a life different from the arduous everyday. It is a call to a return to you, to me, to us: as living bodies, as two who are different and co-creators. [pp. 25–26]

The caress is an offering of an altered state of consciousness. It ushers the lovers into a different realm of existence, a realm that is divorced from the everyday realm of work and responsibility, and that allows for a calmer psychic and emotional reality to surface. As Irigaray puts it, the caress is "an invitation to rest, to relax, to perceive, to think and to be in a different way: one that is more quiet, more contemplative, less utilitarian." The caress, in other words, is a "gift of safety" that the subject grants to the other in order to allow it to "return" to itself in the sense of being able to shed the multiple layers of worry that characterize everyday existence (p. 27). Whereas Foucault's care of the self asked the subject to "return" to itself in moments of solitary contemplation, Irigaray conceptualizes this "return" as an intersubjective event. For Irigaray, the caress is an awakening to a peacefulness beyond the everyday that is made possible by the presence of a loving other.

Irigaray's notion of surrender is less violent than the kind of mystical abandon or creative surrender that Underhill describes (as well as the kind of erotic surrender that I discussed in Chapter 2), but it is similar in that it conceives of surrender not as a form of submission, but rather as a different way of seeing and inhabiting the world. Surrendering oneself to the other's touch is not about losing one's sense of agency, but rather about entering a mode of being that allows one to access a version of oneself that one does not ordinarily reveal to the world. As such, surrender is by defi-

---

12. Note the similarity to Oliver's notion of witnessing (see Chapter 2).

nition an initiation to what resides beyond the ideal (including Silverman's ideal). By this I do not mean that surrender necessarily unearths aspects of being that are somehow more fundamental than those that provide the materials for idealization—although I do think that this is an open question—but merely that it reveals an alternative subjective reality that is inherently resistant to idealization. Idealization tends to fixate on and take hold of what is readily discernible on the surface. Surrender in turn activates recesses of the individual's being that are not visible on the exterior, and that have consequently not been available to idealization. As a consequence, surrender foregrounds the distinction between the ideal and whatever is "other" than the ideal—whatever has not yet been assimilated to the ideal. In this sense, surrender is the moment when we actually hear the sound of the tear in the iconography of idealization.

Insofar as surrender precipitates the ideal's undoing, it provides a test of the kind of love that endures beyond the ideal. As a result, giving the gift of love must entail the loving subject's willingness to take a step back in order to create the clearing (in Irigaray's sense) necessary for the unraveling of the other's ideality. It must allow the other's alterity to surface in all of its strange—and perhaps even threatening—intensity. Enabling the other to surrender tells this other that it is loved both in its attempt to approximate the ideal and in its absolute failure, at the moment of surrender, to do so. It therefore represents the active gift of love in its purest form because it communicates to the other that what escapes ideality still remains "good enough" to elicit the subject's love. Moreover, insofar as surrender makes the other's lack visible to the subject, it tests the degree to which the subject has, or has not, managed to transcend melancholia. We have seen that the subject of melancholia cannot tolerate lack either in itself or in the other, but that the subject who has moved past its melancholy fixations thrives in the opening created by lack. This implies that the subject whose love survives the other's surrender (and therefore the other's lack) also survives its own lack (and therefore the specter of its own surrender). This is one way to understand what it entails to move from melancholia to meaning, for what is meaning if not the necessity of having to face one's barely deferred—and therefore always imminent—surrender.

5

Pain

> You must be ready to burn yourself in your own flame: how could
> you become new, if you had not first become ashes?
>
> Friedrich Nietzsche, *Thus Spoke Zarathustra*

MYTHOLOGIES OF BEING

One of the underlying themes of my analysis thus far is the idea that there
exists a connection between suffering and psychic multidimensionality—
that the pain of the past can somehow be redeemed by the wisdom and
creativity of the present. Throughout my discussion, I have singled out
specific techniques—such as Nietzsche's stylistic self-fashioning, Foucault's
care of the self, Oliver's notion of witnessing, Heidegger's ideal of poetic
dwelling, Lacan's analysis of the poetic function of language, Kristeva's
theory of the imagination, and Cixous's account of writing—as examples
of the various ways in which lack, absence, constraint, limitation, and even
melancholia can contribute to the subject's creative agency. What remains
to be accomplished in the pages of this concluding chapter is to offer a
more sustained discussion of the task of forging a rewarding present out of
a less-than-perfect past. I will do this by bringing Nietzsche into conversation with psychoanalysis.

I would like to specify right away that the suffering I will be talking about in this chapter has more to do with the human predicament—
with the fact that life is inherently demanding and anxiety-inducing—than

with circumstantial forms of hardship. I will, in other words, for the most part be referring to the kind of suffering that is an integral part of the human condition rather than to the kind of suffering that is caused by oppressive social conditions. Yet this division is sometimes difficult to uphold, and if my discourse occasionally slides between these two registers of psychic pain, it is because I can no longer meaningfully distinguish between them. Within this framework, I will consider the psychoanalytic implications of Nietzsche's argument that suffering is an important component of a meaningful life. I am interested in what psychoanalysis, which is centrally concerned with alleviating psychic pain, can learn from a philosophy that regards pain as a basis of existential nobility. I am also interested in what Nietzsche's notion of *amor fati*—of loving one's fate even when this fate causes pain—can add to our understanding of inner potentiality.

Throughout this book, I have presented psychoanalysis as a particularly powerful technique of cultivating the subject's inner potentialities.[1] Analysis is of course not the only means of such cultivation. All activities that somehow stir the imagination—falling in love; creating or taking pleasure in art, poetry, or literature; thinking philosophically; inventing a mathematical formula; partaking in communal activities; conversing with one's friends; doing work that one enjoys; engaging with the world in ethical or political ways; cooking a delicious meal; running through the rain; or simply daydreaming with one's back against the wall and one's face toward the sun—can contribute to a sense of psychic richness. How and where a particular individual finds fulfillment depends on a largely idiosyncratic intersectionality of personal, familial, and societal factors. Yet I would maintain that analysis is quite uniquely positioned to promote the expansion of the individual's psychic life. This is because it can change how the individual relates to others.

I have sought to demonstrate that the manner in which we fit into interpersonal, societal, or even international structures of power can wound

---

1. This chapter opens with two sections that rearticulate some of the main psychoanalytic themes that I have developed in this book. This is in part because I would like this final chapter to function as a summary of sorts, and in part because I hope that by revisiting some of the principal preoccupations of my analysis, and by focusing on slightly different aspects of these preoccupations than before, I will be able to offer a fresh perspective on why psychoanalysis has been so central to my investigation. Readers who wish to proceed with entirely new materials are invited to skip ahead to p. 205.

us in profoundly debilitating ways. Yet I have also emphasized that it is because our psyches open to the world that they possess the capacity for restoration and revitalization. From this perspective, there is no better way to alleviate the suffering caused by others than by inventing new and better forms of intersubjectivity.

The power of psychoanalysis resides in part in the fact that it is particularly effective in generating new forms of intersubjectivity. Although analysis can obviously not change societal or international structures of power—and while it is consequently far from being an all-purpose solution to our crises—it can alter how we relate to others on the interpersonal level, and consequently how we understand our place in the world. All of our social relationships possess the potential to transform us; however, the influence that others have over our psychic states is usually quite unpredictable. There is, in other words, no established set of rules according to which such relationships develop. This is where analysis is distinctive, for it was Freud's genius to have built a highly ritualized form of intersubjectivity into the very technique of analysis. The point of transference, after all, is to allow the analysand to experience and experiment with various modes of relating without the perils that under normal circumstances accompany such interpersonal undertakings. By this I do not mean that matters between the analyst and analysand always evolve in safe and predictable directions, or that there are no moments of affective intensity, but merely that because analysis functions on the level of discourse rather than of "raw" affect, it by definition follows a less treacherous path than do most other relationships. Describing the difference between passionate love and transference love, for instance, Kristeva (1983) states that transference love is an "optimum" form of interrelation because it avoids the chaotic dimensions of passionate love while at the same time allowing the analysand to experience some of its revitalizing aspects (p. 15). This is to say that transference enables the analysand to access the sensation of self-awakening that frequently accompanies passionate love without exposing herself to the threat of self-dissolution that equally often hovers on the edges of real-life passion; if the experience of passionate love makes the subject feel fully alive, analysis is able to approximate this feeling in a much less volatile setting. If analysis works, Kristeva suggests, it is because Freud was the first in the history of the Western world to turn "love into a cure" (p. 8).

Kristeva maintains that insofar as the analyst is interested in lessening the pain of her patients, she is "duty bound to help them in building their own proper space. Help them not to suffer from being mere extras in their lives." By this Kristeva does not mean that analysis aims to fill the patients' sense of lack, emptiness, or displacement with secure meaning, but rather that it triggers the kind of polyvalent discourse that helps them "speak and write themselves in unstable, open, and undecidable spaces" (p. 380). What I have tried to suggest in this book is that the process that Kristeva is referring to is best understood as one of self-mythologization. In Chapter 1, I argued that subjectivity is always inevitably a mythology of being—a depository of socio-symbolically and discursively constituted personal meanings that have over time solidified into existentially convincing psychic structures. I moreover proposed that like Nietzschean self-stylization and Foucault's care of the self, psychoanalysis can be thought of as a practice of subjective remythologization. By this I do not mean that psychoanalysis aims to "refine" or "improve" the individual's character in the manner that Nietzsche and Foucault outline. I also do not mean that analysis shares the emphasis on self-mastery that the other two accounts foreground. Rather, I mean that analysis allows the analysand to accept—and make the most of—its status as an ever-evolving entity that possesses the power to intervene in the unfolding of its destiny.

The Freudian practice of free association lifts the demand for self-mastery (as well as for rationality and consistence) in ways that are closer to the type of creative self-surrender that I described in Chapter 4 than to anything that either Nietzsche or Foucault delineate. In *The Interpretation of Dreams*, Freud quotes a letter that Schiller wrote to a friend who was complaining of insufficient productivity:

> The ground for your complaint seems to me to lie in the constraint imposed by your reason upon your imagination. . . . It seems a bad thing and detrimental to the creative work of the mind if Reason makes too close an examination of the ideas as they come pouring in—at the very gateway, as it were. Looked at in isolation, a thought may seem very trivial or very fantastic; but it may be made important by another thought that comes after it, and, in conjunction with other thoughts that may seem equally absurd, it may turn out to form a most effective link. Reason cannot form any opinion upon all this unless it retains the thought long enough to look at it in connection with the others. On the other hand, where there is a creative mind, Reason—so it seems to me—relaxes its watch upon the gates, and the ideas rush in pell-mell, and only then does it look them through and examine them in a mass. [Quoted in Freud 1900, p. 135]

The similarities between Schiller's depiction of the relaxation of rationality that facilitates the outpouring of creativity and Freud's request that the analysand report all of its thoughts as they arise, without censorship or any attempt at coherence, are striking. What makes both creativity and free association possible is the subject's capacity to slacken its watch upon the gates of reason so as to allow an alternative reality to reveal itself. As a result, both Schiller and Freud regard the tendency to "reject too soon and discriminate too severely" as an impediment to the emergence of insight. While Schiller complains that critics are often "ashamed and frightened of the momentary and transient extravagances which are to be found in all creative minds," Freud remarks that one of the challenges of analytic practice is that patients often find it difficult to abandon their critical faculties, and consequently put up a whole fortress of resistances that make it impossible to access unconscious meaning (pp. 135–136).

By positing psychoanalysis as a process of self-mythologization I do not then mean to downplay the centrality of unconscious forms of meaning-production—indeed, as I have tried to indicate all along, it is precisely because the subject is driven by unconscious desire that it is capable of signification in the first place—but merely to emphasize that the analytic experience offers the individual the kind of imaginative agility that opens up the possibility of alternative existential mythologies. Freud, like Schiller, stresses the value of allowing thoughts to surface freely, without any critical intervention. Nevertheless, as in artistic practice, these "involuntary thoughts" (p. 135) do eventually become the raw materials for interpretation and reworking (or working-through). This is the point at which processes of subjective remythologization become possible. Although these processes obviously take place within the conventions of cultural intelligibility that govern meaning-making at any particular point in history, they nevertheless provide the subject with an innovative relationship to itself that allows it to gradually reinvent its foundational myths. We are here not in the realm of agency in any traditional sense of self-possession or control, but rather in the sense of the subject's capacity to creatively bring to life the metaphors of its existence. This is one way of thinking about psychic potentiality and self-actualization in the constructivist context.

LIVING THE PAST IN THE PRESENT

Analysis posits the subject as a historical being, conditioned by the specifics of kinship and culture, and it is this personal history—the impact of the subject's past on its present—that it endeavors to uncover. Analysis seeks to disclose the complex ways in which the subject's history plays into its capacity to meaningfully live in the present, highlighting the various obstacles that may interfere with its ability to adequately explore the possibilities of its being; in conceptualizing subjectivity as a phenomenon in which the subject's past, present, and future are strung together by a more or less continuous thread of desire, analysis reveals how the subject can remain chained to its past in ways that effectively block the unfolding of its potential in the present. The symptom marks precisely such a blockage of potentiality, and it is then the task of analysis to enable the subject to work its way through the symptom to a more free-flowing space of self-constitution.

In the previous chapter, I proposed that an important part of the analytic process is to empower the subject to approach its past in such a way that this past does not arrest its psychic life but rather feeds the myriad potentialities of its present. While analysis is oriented toward the past in that it is interested in the history of the subject's desire, its purpose is to resurrect this past in ways that vitalize rather than suffocate the present; the point of releasing the subject from its compulsion to repeat self-undermining patterns is to try to ensure that when its past desires resurface in the present, they do so in a non-destructive manner. There is obviously no infallible means of accomplishing this goal, for desire is always inherently destructive as well as generative, and therefore cannot be domesticated without a significant amount of repression. Nor does analysis aim at such domestication. It does, however, seek to mobilize the play of signifiers so as to enhance the subject's ability to represent its desire in psychically valuable ways. Indeed, since there is no ultimate signifier that would extinguish the subject's desire, meaning-making in the analytic context remains the kind of infinitely fluid process which, ideally at least, teaches the subject that its past is never irrevocably fixed or closed off, but instead remains permeable to retrospective acts of reinterpretation. The past always casts a shadow over the present, but the present also in many ways holds the key to the past in the sense that the subject's actions in the present can help it reconfigure the past in ways that allow it to affirmatively "own" this past. The past, like the future, thus represents a continually evolving space of imaginative possibility that remains highly responsive to the subject's attempts to read it in constructive ways.

In Chapter 1, I talked about the psyche as a sedimented site of metaphoric meanings, and wondered whether it might be possible for us to retroactively rework our earliest socio-cultural interpellations. I wondered whether recent layers of psychic meaning possess the power to alter earlier layers. Psychoanalysis reveals that they do. Because we possess the capacity for memory, we inevitably live in the past as much as the present. Not only are our present experiences infused with past meaning, but we constantly rewrite our past along mythological lines. The people and experiences that have meant the most to us, we wrap in special significance. In this manner, life is transformed into narratives, yet these narratives—and therefore how we understand our experiences—shift with each telling. Indeed, the usefulness of our narratives rests in part precisely in their instability—the fact that each retelling provides an opportunity for a new story to emerge. Over time, our stories begin to eclipse the original experience. Sometimes it even happens that we come to view our entire life in relation to a single mythological moment—a turning point or a sea change—and the rest of our lives, what we do, experience, and dream about, comes to be interpreted in relation to this moment.

On the most basic level, a myth is a story whose "accuracy" does not matter nearly as much as its power to evoke moods and sensibilities that add meaning and flavor to our existence. Although myths obviously cannot give us the "truth" of the self, they possess the power to provide an imaginatively convincing rendering of its potential. As such, they shift our attention from what we lack to what we might be able to accomplish. This is one reason that I believe in the continued relevance of psychoanalysis to contemporary critical theory, for this shift from lack to potentiality is what this theory also needs to achieve. What psychoanalysis shows us is that it is by inserting our past and present experiences into the myths or narratives that make up our existence that we create the psychic foundations for this existence. Psychic depth is consequently not a function of an inner essence, but rather of a gradual layering of stories that become compelling over time. This is a psychoanalytic rendering of the Nietzschean self that I outlined in Chapter 1.

We of course know that the unconscious always exceeds the limits of what is rationally knowable or narrativizable. We also know that the accuracy with which we remember and interpret our lives is always suspect in the sense that the narratives we generate rarely provide a faithful interpretation of experience. Yet it is precisely this narrative "inauthenticity" that opens the space for psychic enablement by allowing us to tell our stories in ways that vitalize rather than diminish us. Although the agency that arises from such acts of narrativization can never grant us a stable sense of ontological wholeness, it provides us with the kind of discursive flexibility—the kind of interpretative entitlement over the parameters of our being—that suggests we might not be wholly and hopelessly subjected after all, but that there might remain, within the confines of the socio-symbolic order, spaces in which creativity can still take place. In this manner, the signifier, which itself refuses the comforts of plenitude—which in fact thrives in the rift between desire and its (non)fulfillment—functions as the purveyor of a certain kind of existential fullness; while the signifier can never offer us a definitive sense of psychic repair, it can engender a strong sense of creative agency.

I have emphasized in this book that psychoanalysis exploits our capacity to reinvent our lives through such creative agency. While analysis cannot provide an infallible solution to our existential dilemmas, it can help us treat our life as a fluid and multifaceted space where reassessment and revision, and sometimes even a strong sense of adventure, are possible. If narrativization is so important to analysis, it is because narratives make it possible not only to gain a glimpse of the unconscious terrains that motivate our behavior in the world but also to manipulate this behavior so as to modify it over time. Since it would be entirely possible for us to further disempower ourselves by the incessant retelling of past injury, the processes of self-mythologization that take place in analysis cannot be merely reassuring or stabilizing, but must be able to change the customary course of our psychic responses. By rupturing the patterns that hold us imprisoned in inert modes of behavior, analysis brings about internal movement and, potentially at least, creates an opening for some sort of enlightenment—for new ways of living and relating. The power of analysis is in fact such that it can nudge us from a past experienced as a living death to a present that is lived ardently, with a profound appreciation for the astonishing beauty of life's unpredictability. There can be something so intensely poignant about this experience that when we, after a long period of inner paralysis, resurface in the world of the living, we hardly recognize ourselves. We have finally, through some mysterious process of self-renewal, learned how to live.

Psychoanalytic acts of self-mythologization teach us how to live not only because they rework the past, but also because they—*precisely insofar as they rework the past*—free us to engage with the present in a more dynamic manner. Walter Pater (1873) reminds us of the "awful brevity" of existence, emphasizing that life is but a short interval between birth and death, and that our task is to exploit this interval to the best of our capacity. As Pater famously puts it:

> A counted number of pulses only is given to us of a variegated, dramatic life. How may we see in them all that is to be seen in them by the finest senses? How shall we pass most swiftly from point to point, and be present always at the focus where the greatest number of vital forces unite in their purest energy? To burn always with this hard, gem-like flame, to maintain this ecstasy, is success in life. [p. 152]

If a counted number of pulses only is given to us of life, how do we live this life to the fullest? With the greatest possible attention? How do we see in each transient moment all that is to be seen in it? If to burn with a "hard, gem-like flame" is what constitutes "success in life," how do we best tend this flame? Psychoanalytic acts of self-mythologization, I have suggested, enable us to better answer these questions.

Pater likens existence to "a tremulous wisp" constantly forming and reforming on the surface of a stream. Pointing out that life is a sequence of unstable, flickering, and inconsistent impressions that, somewhat tragically, are extinguished the moment they are consciously apprehended, Pater stressed the importance of rousing the human spirit "to a life of constant and eager observation." Not to engage in such observation—not to invite the dyes, colors, tones, forms, and moods of the world to stir our senses— is, Pater explains, "on this short day of frost and sun, to sleep before evening" (pp. 151–152). Pater thus reminds us of the value of remaining cognizant of the complex texture of our experiences. Indeed, for Pater, the texture of our experiences and "success in life" appear to be one and the same thing: it is by allowing ourselves to savor the full-bodied singularity of our experiences that we are able to insert passion into our lives. If Nietzsche urges us to become the poets of our life, Pater asks us to approach the particularities of our existence with the ardor of the artist's keen vision. In one of the most startling passages of her memoirs, Saint Teresa describes her rapturous states as an effort to see the color of God's eyes (1565, p. 205). Pater, it seems to me, is asking us to try to see the color of the world's eyes—to remind ourselves that it is not always the outcome of our experiences but rather the process of experiencing itself that offers us the kind of "quickened" (Pater 1873, p. 153) sense of life that makes it worth living.

For Pater, evanescence is what keeps life moving. The key to existential intensity, Pater argues, is to keep the evanescence of life in the forefront of our consciousness, for it is when we forget about this evanescence that we become complacent and neglectful of our surroundings. More specifically, Pater suggests that the best way to feed the "gem-like flame" of existence is to guard against the tendency to form habits that dull our experiences by making us relate to the world in worn-out and unimaginative ways. It is by defending the fleeting impression against the pacifying effects of habit, Pater posits, that we are able to mine the uniqueness of each instant without at the same time closing ourselves off to those ensuing instants that are always already crowding our horizon.[2]

What I have proposed in this book is that psychoanalytic processes of self-mythologization and renarrativization liberate us from the soul-deadening habits of the past. It is obvious that we cannot survive in the world without a certain degree of habitual behavior. It is also obvious that forgetting the evanescence of life is sometimes the only way to avoid despair, and therefore to continue living. I am therefore not saying that self-actualization is primarily a matter of sidestepping habits. At the same time, resisting habits may allow us to encounter the world in more discerning ways.

To the extent that psychoanalysis allows us to undo habitual and repetitive patterns of behavior, it invites us to consider what it might mean, outside of traditional teleological models of self-actualization, to live up to our potential. It in fact encourages us to regard the goal of fulfilling our potential as inherently unfulfillable, yet no less attractive for this unfulfillability. As the ever-enigmatic trope of future possibility, "potentiality" as an ideal only survives to the extent that it is able to defer its realization. Our existential possibilities can therefore never be entirely consumed. Indeed, psychoanalysis implies that rather than seeking to arrive at a definitive moment of transcendence, we would do well to recognize that it is precisely the impossibility of transcendence that enables us to attain the "quickened" sense of life that infuses our experiences with the desired intensity. It is the impossibility of transcendence that ensures that the future remains open. In this manner, psychoanalysis theorizes the impossibility of transcendence as empowering, even exhilarating, rather

---

2. I am here reminded of Kierkegaard's (1843a) contention that if boredom is "the root of evil" (p. 287), habit in turn is the root of boredom. The solution to the problem, Kierkegaard posits, is to continually "vary" oneself (p. 294) through a process akin to the agricultural method of rotating crops that consists of repeatedly changing the method of cultivation as well as the crops used.

than traumatic. This, I would maintain, is a valuable means of envisioning self-actualization in the posthumanist context. And it may also be an important way of caring for the soul.

ALMS THROWN TO A BEGGAR

From an analytic perspective, living up to one's potential entails coming to terms with the particularity of desire. In Chapter 3, we saw that Lacan suggests that it is by developing a more active relationship to our desire that we can begin to relate to the world in an enabled manner. We also discovered that Lacan gives a new and powerful spin to what various philosophers have said throughout the centuries, namely that we risk ourselves in exceedingly dangerous ways whenever we turn to external objects for our happiness. Some thinkers, such as Schopenhauer, have taken this insight to the extreme, proposing that because desire causes suffering, only a compete annihilation of desire can offer a permanent release from affliction. Along lines that bear a startling resemblance to Lacanian theory, Schopenhauer (1851) defines desire as an "unquenchable thirst" (p. 312) without the possibility of lasting satisfaction. Each fleeting moment of fulfillment, Schopenhauer explains, is "like the alms thrown to a beggar, which reprieves him today so that his misery may be prolonged till tomorrow" (p. 196). In this manner, human life swings like a pendulum to and fro between desire and attainment, making satisfaction ultimately elusive. Because desire is a form of suffering, and satisfaction is merely a temporary suspension of desire, each moment of fulfillment is always merely the foundation of a new form of striving. Happiness is therefore essentially a negative rather than a positive state, signifying the absence of pain rather than the fullness of being.

Existence for Schopenhauer is therefore something for which the individual must pay by constant suffering. Moreover, like Lacan, Schopenhauer argues that each object of desire retains its value only insofar as it manages to evade the subject's grasp. As a result, those for whom abundance and satisfaction come too readily, who find their wishes fulfilled before they have had time to experience the sting of desire, suffer from a lack of want and become burdensome to themselves, aimless wanderers in search of stimulation, drifting from pleasure to pleasure, from one diversion to the next, always ultimately disappointed, always in the end frustrated with themselves. These wanderers, cursed with an overfullness of life, seek only to "kill time" so as to consume the hours that separate them from death; in them bore-dom has become despair, an intense existential affliction.

Schopenhauer maintains that the fact that suffering will inexorably find its way into our lives should lead us to adopt an attitude of indifference to-ward the particulars of our suffering. The poignancy of our misfortunes, he contends, stems from our belief in their accidental nature—from our con-viction that happiness would be possible had fate dealt us a better hand. In contrast, the acknowledgment of the inescapability of suffering should lead us to recognize that only the form in which our suffering manifests depends on chance. This is to say that our present suffering merely fills a slot that would, in its absence, be immediately occupied by some other mode of suf-fering. Although we constantly search for explanations for our distress, these explanations only gloss over the fact that were it not for a specific external cause of our suffering, the pain "would appear in the form of a hundred little annoyances and worries over things we now entirely overlook" (p. 317). Con-sequently, Schopenhauer finds a certain dignity in the kind of stoic equa-nimity which, recognizing the universality of affliction, does not dwell on the particulars of its own hardship. Schopenhauer moreover speculates that such nobility of character often arises from the experience of a "single great suffering" that is so intense that it inoculates the individual against all lesser forms of sadness; once the will is broken by such an overwhelming blow, the subject by necessity shows itself mild, resigned, and able to reconcile itself to its plight (p. 396).

The only way to break the cycle of suffering, Schopenhauer suggests, is to voluntarily commit oneself to a path of asceticism and self-renunciation. As long as the subject desires, it will not be able to attain the state of calm contentment that it seeks. As a result, the subject's goal should be the con-stant mortification of its desire. The individual who has chosen a life of asceticism deprives himself of every pleasure so that the "satisfaction of desires, the sweets of life, may not stir his will, of which self-knowledge has conceived a horror" (p. 382). In this manner, the individual gradually smothers his desire until his former life stands before him as indifferently "as a fancy dress cast off in the morning, the form and figure of which taunted and disquieted us on the carnival night" (p. 390). Nothing can now move, alarm, or distress him, for he has cut all the threads of desire that hold him immersed in the world; instead of "the constant transition from desire to apprehension and from joy to sorrow," we witness a life of "ocean-like calmness" and "deep tranquillity" (p. 411).

Schopenhauer's mistrust of desire thus arises from his recognition of the enormous magnitude of psychic pain that can result from its notoriously capricious trajectory. From a Schopenhauerian perspective, it is more prudent to curb, control, and curtail one's desires than it is to follow their unruly and disobedient demands. By annihilating the subject's desires to the extent that they no longer possess the power to agitate or disconcert, Schopenhauer's ideal of self-renunciation is meant to protect it from forms of suffering that result from its passionate commitments to the external world; the severing of worldly attachments reduces the level of affective engagement to a minimum, and over time numbs the disagreeable along with the agreeable.

There is a certain similarity between Schopenhauerian self-renunciation on the one hand, and the strategies of self-limitation that we looked at in the context of Nietzsche and Foucault in Chapter 1. The difference, however, is that whereas Nietzsche's self-stylization and Foucault's care of the self focus on the creative potentialities of self-limitation, Schopenhauer regards self-renunciation primarily as a means of eliminating the subject's will-to-life. The obvious problem with Schopenhauer's scenario is that since desire sustains the subject's relationship to the world, the subject who extinguishes its desire simultaneously loosens its bonds to life until, as Schopenhauer himself admits, all that remains is "a mild foretaste of the death that proclaims itself to be the dissolution of the body and of the will at the same time" (p. 396). Furthermore, even when asceticism does not bring about such an extreme outcome, its self-negating impulse can lead to a radical constriction of the subject's life-world, depriving it of the type of experiential variety that contributes to existential fullness. Though it may be less painful to approach the world with an attitude of acquiescence than with the kind of inquisitive ardor that Schopenhauer condemns, self-renunciation can easily degenerate into a defensive tentativeness toward the world's offerings. As such, it serves as a means of hiding from the world rather than of productively working through the anxieties and opportunities that ensue from encountering the world in an open manner.

The tragedy of Schopenhauerian asceticism is that it cannot free the subject from pain without simultaneously eradicating its capacity for pleasure. Nietzsche recognizes this, which is why his interest in self-limitation never takes the form of advocating self-renunciation for its own sake. Nietzsche in fact consistently ridicules the self-mortifying asceticism of the Christian priest, and goes to great lengths to distinguish his own "cheerful" asceticism from monastic forms of self-discipline which, in his view, are merely invented to better "slander" life (1872, p. 23). More generally speaking, Nietzsche has little patience with forms of constraint or self-limitation that are designed to break the confidence of the spirit rather than to enhance its vitality.[3] Moreover, though Nietzsche shares Schopenhauer's distrust of unbridled passions, he believes in the transformative power of suffering. As a result, rather than focusing on how to evade suffering, Nietzsche outlines the various ways in which suffering can be translated into a source of insight for the life-affirming spirit.

One of the main points that I have tried to communicate in this book is that Freudian (and Lacanian) psychoanalysis aims at a similar translation. Like Schopenhauer, Freud recognizes that desire causes suffering. However, because psychoanalysis considers desire to be foundational to subjectivity, its goal cannot be to eradicate suffering through the repudiation of desire, but rather to enable the subject to develop an interpretative relationship to this desire. This is why I have accentuated the importance of taking responsibility for one's desire by learning to actively listen to its messages rather than remaining a passive bystander to the unfurling of its drama (e.g., the repetition compulsion). It is also why I have emphasized that desire is what connects the subject to the world, and consequently sustains its capacity to form meaningful and ethical relationships with the people, objects, and things of this world. Since desire from the analytic perspective forms the very "stuff" of life—what animates the human subject and makes the world go round—analysis cannot regard it as the enemy of subjectivity, but must instead seek to harness it in constructive directions.

---

3. See *The Birth of Tragedy*: "Christianity was from the beginning, essentially and fundamentally, life's nausea and disgust with life, merely concealed behind, masked by, dressed up as, faith in 'another' or 'better' life. Hatred of the 'the world,' condemnation of the passions, fear of beauty and sensuality, a beyond invented the better to slander this life, at bottom a craving for nothing, for the end, for respite, for 'the sabbath of sabbaths' . . . at the very least a sign of abysmal sickness, weariness, discouragement, exhaustion, and the impoverishment of life" (1872, p. 23). Christianity is thus in Nietzsche's view a religion that arises from a profound hatred of the world in that it condemns the passions, mortifies the body, and invents God "as a counterconcept of life" (1908, p. 334). As he puts it in *Beyond Good and Evil*, "The Christian faith is from the beginning sacrifice: sacrifice of all freedom, all pride, all self-confidence of the spirit, at the same time enslavement and self-mockery, self-mutilation" (1886, p. 75).

Freud and Nietzsche share the insight that artistic and creative activity is a particularly productive means of redirecting or sublimating desire. As we have seen, Nietzsche is interested in art not only as object of contemplation, but as a way of life. His ideal of living one's life as poetry turns art into a tool of character building. Similarly, Freud not only regards art, literature, and philosophy as powerful devices for binding desire, but develops the techniques of free association and transference as an "art" (as well as a science) of character modification. By drawing this parallel, I do not wish to imply that Freud necessarily endorses Nietzsche's ideal of existential nobility. I am merely saying that Freud developed psychoanalysis as a very precise method for what Nietzsche, as well as many other philosophers before him, had also sought to accomplish, namely a psychic transformation that allows the human subject to attain a more rewarding relationship both to itself and to its surroundings. Nietzsche's approach may seem more proactive in that he seeks to actively build new layers of character while Freud is primarily interested in undoing pathologies that undermine the individual's well-being. Yet in the end, the two methods amount to something quite similar in that the undoing of pathologies by necessity reconfigures the individual's psyche, and consequently, like Nietzsche's stylistic self-fashioning, generates an altered inner reality.

If Nietzsche's ideal of self-stylization arises from artistic principles, Freud's attempt to revitalize the psyche also unmistakably follows an "artistic" path. Lacan capitalizes on this insight, which is one reason that he is so interested in shifting the subject's desire from the *objet a* to the poetic dimensions of language. As we have seen, the purpose of this shift is to awaken the subject from the fantasy world of its narcissistic misrecognitions. We have also determined that the stakes of this shift are nothing less than a radical transformation of the subject's understanding of itself as a being of psychic potentiality. Like Schopenhauer, Lacan believes that living by our wants is unlikely to grant us happiness. At the same time, like Nietzsche and Freud, he realizes that the solution to this predicament cannot be to eradicate desire, but rather to modify its trajectory. The conundrum that Lacanian analysis, like much of earlier Western philosophy, faces is how the human being can live in the world in a reasonably contented manner despite the fact that it is inherently a creature of lack and alienation. As I have stressed, Lacan's response is to insist that it is only by embracing its lack, and by learning to cope with its alienation (and the suffering that this alienation may generate) in constructive ways, that the subject can begin to realize its potential.

LETTING SUFFERING LIE UPON ONESELF

Schopenhauer wishes to abolish suffering. Psychoanalysis aims to work through suffering until it yields to interpretation. Nietzsche in turn tells us that there are times when it is best to let suffering "lie upon" oneself. Nietzsche, in other words, insists that it is possible to banish suffering too fast, before one has had time to process the insights that it might yield. Because Nietzsche regards suffering as a potentially transformative experience, he believes that to annihilate suffering would be to cheat ourselves of something fundamental. As a result, he derides those who pity others for their suffering, and particularly those who are prone to pity themselves when suffering strikes:

> If you . . . have the same attitude toward yourself that you have toward your fellow men; if you refuse to let your own suffering lie upon you even for an hour and if you constantly try to prevent and forestall all possible distress way ahead of time; if you experience suffering and displeasure as evil, hateful, worthy of annihilation, and as a defect of existence, then it is clear that besides your religion of pity you also harbor another religion in your heart that is perhaps the mother of the religion of pity: the *religion of comfortableness*. How little you know of human *happiness*, you comfortable and benevolent people, for happiness and unhappiness are sisters and even twins that either grow up together or, as in your case, *remain small* together. [1882, pp. 269–270]

If happiness and unhappiness are twin sisters and only grow together, then trying to prevent and forestall unhappiness leads to the constriction of happiness as well. This temperance of both joy and sorrow—this "smallness" of both happiness and unhappiness—is, Nietzsche insists, the destiny of those who fail to recognize the creative potential of suffering:

> The whole economy of the soul and the balance effected by "distress," the way new springs and needs break open, the way in which old wounds are healing, the way whole periods of the past are shed—all such things that may be involved in distress are of no concern to our dear pitying friends; they wish to *help* and have no thought of the personal necessity of distress, although terrors, deprivations, impoverishments, midnights, adventures, risks, and blunders are as necessary for me and for you as are their opposites. It never occurs to them that, to put it mystically, the path to one's heaven always leads through the voluptuousness of one's own hell. [1882, p. 269]

Nietzsche thus promotes the "personal necessity of distress," for he believes that such distress is what most effectively perpetuates the soul's cycle of regeneration in the sense that it induces the subject to reassess and readjust the outlines of its existence. As new misfortunes cover over and exorcise the traces of older agonies, longstanding wounds undergo a process of healing that generates an opening for new forms of life. To fail to understand this, Nietzsche maintains, is to interpret suffering superficially, without recognizing that the risks, blunders, terrors, and deprivations of a lifetime are as important for the soul's ability to develop as are its more pleasurable experiences.

It is important to emphasize the distinction that Nietzsche draws between debilitating and transformative forms of suffering, for otherwise it would be all too easy to fetishize suffering by suggesting that it is invariably a constructive experience. Nietzsche scorns the fact that dominant society often manages to inculcate resignation, persuading individuals to accept suffering and lack of fulfillment as an inevitable part of their existence—even as a sign of their basic "humanness"—when they should in fact be resisting. As a result, Nietzsche is careful to assert that "noble" forms of suffering have nothing to do with masochistic sentiments of duty or humility. Noble suffering is not a matter of internalizing pain or punishment, but rather of knowing how to make the most of one's suffering. The noble recognizes the frightfulness of life, yet chooses to proceed in spite of this frightfulness because it appreciates the initiatory value of suffering—the way in which the economy of the soul, balanced and rebalanced through each new encounter with hardship, undergoes an alchemical process that induces the individual to evolve and therefore, paradoxically, to become "younger, fuller of future" (p. 331).

The Nietzschean noble creates out of its inner abyss, indeed requires this abyss to fully realize its potential. As I already emphasized in Chapter 1, Nietzsche's vision of existential nobility is problematic in that it assumes the subject's capacity to control its inner states. It is also quite unnerving in that it tends to rank individuals according to their capacity to withstand the pressure of dominant culture (thus the distinction between the noble and the herd). At the same time, I feel that Nietzsche explores quite compellingly the enigmatic relationship that at times exists between destruction and resurrection, for he recognizes that for new forms of life to emerge, something within the subject's inner life must be shaken to the core so as to shatter the well-established structures that hold it immersed in, and therefore confined to, outmoded psychic conditions and conventions. Insofar as Nietzsche believes that existential nobility is a function of how well and deeply an individual "knows" to suffer, he implies that those who have learned to exploit their suffering have attained a more complete understanding of the world. Mistakes are painful, but they can also induce the subject to reevaluate and correct its path in ways that may otherwise be inconceivable. Because suffering forces the subject to cast off those of its inner attitudes that no longer serve a purpose, it can reward it with greater levels of awareness and a more evolved way of approaching the world.

Nietzsche suggests that to try to protect the subject from suffering is to deprive it of experiences that in the long run add substance to its life. For Nietzsche, those who have plunged to the depths without destroying or unduly humbling themselves have gained access to distant worlds—to haunting visions that give them the privilege of the kind of wisdom that cannot be learned in ordinary ways, or passed on by a master to a disciple, but must instead be earned through the immediate experiencing of affliction. Such individuals realize that by virtue of their suffering they are instinctively familiar with the kinds of mysterious inner landscapes that others will never be able to visit (1886, p. 209). In this sense, by providing a test for the spirit's resoluteness, for its capacity to see and experience deeply, as if through a magnifying lens, everything that there is to see and experience in the world, suffering "fixes and hardens a type" (p. 200).

Nietzsche asserts that it is the subject's sustained struggle against unfavorable conditions that has generated every advancement the world has ever known. He in fact believes that there exists a profoundly symbiotic relationship between suffering and creativity, that creativity by definition entails a great deal of "bitter dying" (1892, p. 111) on the part of the creator. As he writes:

> You want if possible—and there is no madder "if possible"—*to abolish suffering*; and we?—it really does seem that *we* would rather increase it and make it worse than it has ever been! . . . The discipline of suffering, of *great* suffering—do you not know that it is *this* discipline alone which has created every elevation of mankind hitherto? That tension of the soul in misfortune which cultivates its strength, its terror at the sight of great destruction, its inventiveness and bravery in undergoing, enduring, interpreting, exploiting misfortune, and whatever of depth, mystery, mask, spirit, cunning and greatness has been bestowed upon it—has it not been bestowed through suffering, through the discipline of great suffering? [1886, p. 155]

Nietzsche depicts a soul tense in misfortune, terrified of destruction, yet able to take advantage of its suffering to create "something for the sake of which it is worthwhile to live on earth, for example virtue, art, music, dance, spirituality—something transfiguring, refined, mad and divine" (p. 111). Maintaining that it is the "discipline" of great suffering that has brought about everything that is inspired and innovative about human life, Nietzsche contends that abolishing suffering would be to stifle the creative spirit. In this sense, the existential "cheerfulness" of the noble—its legendary light-ness and liveliness—is always in the final analysis a reward for a "long, brave, industrious, and subterranean seriousness" (1887, p. 21). For Nietzsche, there can be no happiness without the meticulous mining of the depths. It is only those who have known gravity who have earned the right to skid the surface of things—only those who have peered into the terrifying abysses of existence who can aspire to the highest peaks of self-actualization. The noble spirit's unwavering capacity for self-renewal—its ecstasy of becoming—is therefore always purchased at the price of suffer-ing. In this manner, rebirth for Nietzsche, as perhaps rebirth everywhere, is founded on and evokes death in the sense that the radiance of the new self can arise only from the ashes of the old one.

I have already noted that although Nietzsche disagrees with Schopen-hauer's views of ascetic self-renunciation, his own ideal of existential nobil-ity relies on an ethos of self-limitation that borders on asceticism. Such self-limitation, Nietzsche believes, provides the basis for a productive and joyful kind of spirituality, and accordingly characterizes the lives of all genuinely inventive individuals. Nietzsche in fact maintains that it is the spirit's "secret self-ravishment"—the "labor of a soul voluntarily at odds with itself"—that constitutes the cradle of all imaginative capacity (p. 87). Nietzsche describes this process of subjective refinement via the image of the sculptor's capacity to turn his creative talent—the "hardness" of his hammer—against himself so as to rescue out of the chaos and madness of life the shape or design that best approximates the sought-after ideal (1886, p. 155). The point is not to arrive at a perfect statue but merely to release from the captivity of the raw materials the form that best fulfills the potential that lies dormant within. This can be visualized as the practice of gradually hollowing out a marble block by drawing away excess marble from the nooks and recesses of the newly emerging figurine. Suffering, Nietzsche proposes, is one of the most efficient tools of such molding, for it extracts the dross out of existence, washes away surplus matter, and distills the subject's sensibilities.

In this manner, suffering acts like a fine sieve that separates the gold from the grains of sand.

AMOR FATI: LOVING ONE'S FATE

Nietzsche's affirmative understanding of suffering culminates in his philosophy of *amor fati*—of being able to love one's fate regardless of what this fate holds in store:

> My formula for greatness in a human being is *amor fati*: that one wants nothing to be different, not forward, not backward, not in all eternity. Not merely bear what is necessary, still less conceal it—all idealism is mendaciousness in the face of what is necessary—but *love* it. [1908, p. 258]

> I want to learn more and more to see as beautiful what is necessary in things; then I shall be one of those who make things beautiful. *Amor fati*: let that be my love henceforth! . . . all in all and on the whole: some day I wish to be only a Yes-sayer. [1882, p. 223]

The Nietzschean lover of fate not only endures what is necessary in life, but chooses to welcome this necessity even when it frustrates, disappoints, or causes pain. The proponent of *amor fati* learns to see as beautiful what is necessary in things, learns, in other words, to appreciate the preciousness of each and every moment even when the value of that moment remains shrouded in mystery. Nietzsche explains that the lover of fate is first and foremost a "yes-sayer" who has faith in the erratic and slippery path of its existence in the sense that it trusts that everything happens for a reason—that its destiny, left to its own devices, will in the end turn out exactly as it "should"; the fate-loving subject accepts experiences as they come, without any attempt to deny or negate them, for it knows that what appears unbearable in the present moment may in the future turn out to be a source of existential wonder.

It should be emphasized right away that *amor fati* as a philosophy of life does not imply a fatalistic resignation to adversity. It does not, for instance, demand that those who find themselves constrained by external circumstances submit to their predicament without trying to ameliorate their situation. If this were the case, Nietzsche's conception of the self could hardly be considered affirmative but would signify the kind of static and defeatist attitude toward life that Nietzsche regards as the very antithesis of nobility. What *amor fati* does call for, however, is the subject's ability to meet the hardships of its life in such a way that they do not destroy its inner resolve. Instead of allowing the mishaps and calamities of its existence to paralyze its psychic resources, the Nietzschean noble takes these mishaps and calamities as one component—momentarily inevitable perhaps but not necessarily life-determining in the long run—of a much larger existential design. As Nietzsche explains, the noble knows how to bring together "what is fragment and riddle and dreadful chance" in life so as "to create the future, and to redeem by creating" (1892, p. 216). The noble turns accidents to its advantage, mobilizes disappointments in the service of its imagination, and collects from everything that it sees, hears, and lives through, the sum of its destiny. The noble does not fight its fate, but rather reworks this fate until it is able to say: "But I willed it thus!" (p. 216). This is what Nietzsche means by the bravery of the noble spirit in the face of affliction: the noble affirms its fate, says "yes" to the abyss, yet simultaneously looks for a means of turning this abyss into an existential opportunity.

While the distinction between fighting one's fate on the one hand, and attempting to transform it into an existential opportunity on the other, may seem difficult to discern, it is the essence of *amor fati* to be able to tell the difference. In waging war against one's destiny, one squanders one's energy in useless endeavors to change what is inherently unchangeable. *Amor fati*, in contrast, implies the subject's capacity to meet the challenges of life in such a way that they do not crush or deplete its spirit, but rather become a source of revelation, guiding it to a wholly different set of meanings, values, and goals. The noble spirit who affirms its existence affirms it in its entirety. This is ultimately the meaning of *amor fati*: that one is able to accept, even love, life in its totality, including what causes sadness and sorrow, because one knows that pain is a necessary component of pleasure, indeed that pleasure is only recognizable as pleasure because of one's familiarity with pain. Precisely because the noble understands that all things in life are "chained and entwined together" (p. 332), it knows that the spirit that has borne "the heaviest fate, a fatality of a task, can nevertheless be the lightest and most transcendent." That is, the noble recognizes that the spirit that has had "the hardest, most terrible insight into reality . . . nevertheless does not consider it an objection to existence, not even to its eternal recurrence—but rather one reason more for being himself the eternal Yes to all things" (1908, p. 306).

Amor fati is therefore connected to Nietzsche's notion of the "eternal recurrence" of things—to his cyclical vision of existence that dictates that the spirit who wishes the return of what has brought joy must also invite the return of what has brought pain. As Nietzsche puts it, "if ever you wanted one moment twice, if ever you said: 'You please me, happiness, instant, moment!' then you wanted *everything* to return" (1892, p. 332). The noble, who comprehends and lives by this principle of eternal recurrence, "believes neither in 'misfortune' nor in 'guilt': he comes to terms with himself, with others; he knows how to *forget*—he is strong enough; hence everything *must* turn out for his best" (1908, p. 225). The noble thus knows not only how to extract value out of suffering, but also how to forget what it cannot change; it is strong enough to shrug its shoulders in the face of what is inevitable. Although it unflinchingly stares into the deepest, most bottomless of abysses, it is decidedly not a self-negating subject, but one that is intensively in love with the potentialities of its destiny.

The elitism of Nietzsche's vision is undeniable, for it is only the select few—the strongest of spirits—who could ever fully follow the principles of *amor fati*. The goal of fashioning out of oneself an eternal "yes-sayer," though seemingly calling for an attitude of resignation, for a radical unwilling of the will, is at the same time the most willful of acts. There are times when it is difficult not to fight one's fate, when it is virtually impossible to bide one's time instead of charging ahead with one's retort. In these situations, *amor fati* amounts to a deliberate act of self-assertion whereby the subject, in a magnificent display of self-sufficiency, "wills" itself *not* to will; the noble knows how to suspend its will so as, paradoxically, to amplify the power of this will.

SUFFERING AND SOULFULNESS

Amor fati is in many ways the pinnacle of Nietzsche's philosophy of the self. It reveals that existential nobility for Nietzsche has little to do with customary markers of privilege—such as wealth or social power—but rather revolves around the subject's ability to translate pain into meaning, value, and beauty. As such, it has a great deal in common with the ideal of soulfulness that I have tried to articulate in this book. Nietzsche in fact suggests that suffering and soulfulness often inhabit the same psychic landscape, not in the masochistic sense of self-mortification but in the dynamic sense of self-transformation. In this manner, Nietzsche offers us a discourse that speaks about the soul—and speaks to the soul—in ways that provide an evocative model of what it might mean to take seriously the call of one's destiny as a seat of psychic opportunity.

Nietzsche's *amor fati* connects strength to the subject's capacity to differentiate what it can control from what it cannot, thereby circumventing struggles that are by definition unwinnable. In this manner, *amor fati* strikes a delicate balance between desire and detachment in that it calls for the subject's passionate pursuit of its path while at the same time demanding its absolute indifference to those aspects of this very same path that reside beyond its control. *Amor fati*, in other words, insists on the distinction between love and command—between the subject's ability to embrace its destiny on the one hand and its inclination to try to control it on the other. Nietzsche understands that what we wish to own and manipulate wields a tremendous power over us: that on which we have set our hearts can exhilarate us, but it can also wound and disempower us. It is for this reason that *amor fati* instructs us that it is only when we have overcome the temptation to try to master what resists our powers of mastery that we reach the state of freedom. Yet this stance of nonmastery does not imply the lack or impossibility of love; on the contrary, it is precisely when we relinquish our compulsion to possess that we learn how to love. This is the notion of loving one's fate that Nietzsche submits to us.

Interpreting fate in this Nietzschean sense should make us reluctant to pass judgment on painful life episodes on the basis of what seems readily apparent on the surface. We all enter this world devoid of depth and understanding, and the course of individuation that takes place throughout our lives entails the gradual integration of the various experiences that are designed to teach us how to live. What Nietzsche shows us is that this course of individuation remains incomplete without the individual's ability to process pain. Even if existential lightness is the goal toward which the noble moves, Nietzsche makes it clear that this lightness can only be attained through a familiarity with the sadder and more solemn side of existence. This implies that to the extent that our culture insists on contentment, and tries to weed out the slightest traces of sadness, it might actually be hindering the psyche's ability to realize its full potential. Yet it must also be recognized that there is a world of difference between the kind of fertile grief or sadness that holds the promise of its own creative overcoming and the kind of apathetic stupor that descends upon the subject as a result of its abduction into the whirlwind of its daily troubles and tensions. From a Nietzschean point of view, the subject's ability to live up to its potential in many ways depends on its capacity to hear and honor the messages of the former without getting entangled in the latter.

By positing that it is at times important to let suffering "lie upon" oneself, Nietzsche suggests that self-cultivation calls for the patience to decode the subtle messages of sadness so as to determine why it emerges, what it means, and what it might want. If sadness results in the momentary dissolution of the subject's psychic structures, if it makes it difficult for the subject to proceed with its customary concerns, then what is it trying to tell it about the state of its soul?

We have seen that psychoanalysis endeavors to transform the subject from someone who is passively spoken by its desire to someone who actively speaks it. What Nietzsche reveals is that becoming an active speaker of one's desire may sometimes require the humility to admit that one is not yet fully able to interpret the myriad meanings of this desire. Because the psyche's archaeology often takes unforeseen directions, we have little choice but to allow the intricacies of our destiny to emerge gradually, according to their own inner design. There are some psychic events that take decades to develop and disclose their meaning for the simple reason that they only become significant over time, at specific points in the individual's existential trajectory. To reveal them prematurely would be to squander their message. To repress them altogether would be to prevent them from maturing. To listen to them respectfully, without attempting to coerce them into yielding what they may not yet be ready to yield, gives them the time and space to grow into wisdom.

The goal of psychoanalysis is to unravel the psychic aporias reflected in the symptom. But it is also conceivable that the persistence of certain kinds of symptomatic behavior is the psyche's means of preserving those of its mysteries whose existential significance has not yet fully materialized. Nietzsche's commentary on suffering suggests that it is not always that cure that should interest us but rather the hidden meaning of pathology. From this point of view, the symptom represents a nexus of psychic energy where the subject's past continues to speak with particular urgency. The fact that the subject does not fully understand the meaning of this speech does not necessarily mean that it is entirely valueless or unimportant, but rather that it is inviting the subject to listen to its desire with a wholly different ear. The task of interpreting symptomatic behavior (as Lacan understood) should therefore be regarded as a poetic one—attentive to the subtle and multifarious meanings encoded within the symptom.

Freud emphasized that the symptom is a metaphor for what the individual is unable to express directly. As a result, the process of deciphering psychic fixations should not be viewed exclusively as an attempt to neutralize their power, but also as an occasion to become better acquainted with the affective undercurrents that animate the individual's existence. Insofar as the symptom urges the subject to pay closer attention to what ails or encumbers its spirit, it would be a mistake to dismiss it too hastily, without first understanding what it is trying, so awkwardly and uncomfortably, to communicate about the larger needs of the psyche. In this sense, the symptom is not merely what needs to be eliminated, but also what should be carefully decoded so as to gain insight into repressed, rejected, or unrealized aspects of the subject's psychic life; since the symptom does not exist without a reason, it may serve as an invaluable guide toward those aspects of the self that are foundering under neglect or denial. This implies that healing in any deep sense cannot take place without a vigorously imaginative engagement with the idiosyncratic messages of the psyche's pathologies. The point, after all, is to work "through" rather than "against" the symptom. This, to me, is a profoundly consoling manner of understanding what it might mean to fail to cure or be cured in a "timely" fashion— with the kind of speed that is demanded by our efficiency-oriented culture.

Nietzsche demonstrates that the value of our experiences often reveals itself slowly, over extended landscapes of inner complexity that make it impossible to accurately assess, at any given point in time, the full significance of a particular psychic event. This is one reason that Nietzsche's *amor fati* places suffering in a cyclical framework where it can happen that the sorrow of yesterday becomes the joy of tomorrow, the despair of the past catches up with us as the gratitude of the future, and the weakness of the moment spurs us to cultivate the strength of the days to come. *Amor fati* demands our patience in the face of the fickleness of fortune, asking us to have confidence in the idea that what is meant to happen always will in the end, however unpredictably, happen. Conversely, it teaches us that sometimes we are not ready to go where our desire would take us, that there are times when we need an obstacle, a hindrance, or a stumbling block—time and space to experiment, deliberate, and grow.

Amor fati encourages us to appreciate the more irrational contours— the shifting sands—of our psychic landscapes so as to become reconciled to the idea that sometimes we are misled only be to initiated in breathtaking ways. It also reminds us that the various torments of life, its losses and discontents, its thousand tiny deaths, are a sign that something within our being is aspiring to a fresh mode of encountering the world. In inviting us to approach existence with a more reflexive attitude, *amor fati* mellows out the sharp edges of want and desire, enabling us to recognize the times when the best we can do is to allow the events and episodes of our life to develop without any urgency, struggle, or resistance. *Amor fati* thus asks us to slow down, to trust the rhythm of life, and to create space for experiences to emerge without attempting to rush or force their course. This is what loving one's fate means, in the most profound sense.

FINDING (THE) CONSOLATION IN NIETZSCHE

This was a difficult book to write in part because I found myself constantly called upon to justify the fact of being a constructivist thinker who (nevertheless) feels the need for consolation. I have not found an adequate justification for my "transgression" beyond the vague intuition that the idea that consolation is somehow inherently problematic is linked not only to the (sometimes quite justifiable) aversion to sentimentality that characterizes posthumanist theory, but also, in some intangible manner that is difficult to articulate, to the politics of class as well. Who has the luxury of arguing that the search for consolation represents a lapse of critical insight? Perhaps even more fundamentally: What is being disavowed through the vehement denial of the need for consolation? I think that it is certainly wise to remain conscious of the particular shape taken by our yearning for consolation. The search for consolation could, for instance, get us in trouble if it translated into a desire for a unitary and fully integrated self. But to completely disengage ourselves from the very idea of consolation seems pathological (too obsessively dissociative) rather than progressive. I had always read Nietzsche for consolation—both to find the consolation in Nietzsche, and to be consoled by him. I cannot see the harm in this.

The Nietzschean noble combines existential lightness with adversity in ways that resonate with my wish to comprehend how the subject might be able to translate its abjection into a psychically livable reality. Nietzsche implies that a subject who has suffered possesses immense potential not only for creativity, but also for wisdom, pleasure, and laughter. In this manner, Nietzsche invites us to consider misfortune in terms other than despair. Although it may seem that Nietzsche's vision of *amor fati*, centered as it is around the distinction between the noble and the herd in ways that explicitly align strength with aristocratic notions of self-overcoming, is irreconcilable with an ethical understanding of abjection, the fact that he interprets hardship as a means of attaining a more multidimensional self provides a curiously reassuring account of what it means to encounter less than ideal circumstances. As I have already implied, existential nobility for Nietzsche revolves around the subject's ability to fashion an empowering mythology of being out of the variable constituents of its existence, however bleak or uncompromising these constituents may on the surface appear. This may seem like a small (or even a misleading) consolation, but I would argue that there are (unfortunately) instances when it is just about the only thing that makes psychic survival possible.

One of my aims in this book has been to show that the posthumanist subject, no less than its humanist forerunners, would benefit from the kinds of mythologies of being that provide a sense of psychic possibility. Contemporary constructivist theory has exploited to great advantage the insight that the inherently social nature of subjectivity implies a high degree of subjection to the dominant norms that govern collective life. My objective, on the other hand, has been to highlight the enabling and creative dimensions of sociality without at the same time losing sight of its more hegemonic aspects. In a way, my goal has been to show that the glass is half-full rather than half-empty, and that as human beings, we possess a much greater measure of agency (including imaginative agency) than posthumanist theory ordinarily allows for. This is one reason that I have been so interested in questions of inner potentiality and self-actualization—in how individuals come to lead rewarding lives even when their external circumstances seem to war against the possibility of such lives. Although it would obviously be impossible to define self-actualization—to determine how each individual is to inhabit the space of possibility—I have endeavored to enlarge the conceptual space within which to discuss the question from a constructivist perspective.

Freud and Nietzsche have been so central to my undertaking because they both understand that we are all creatures of return and repetition—of what Freud calls the repetition compulsion and Nietzsche theorizes as the eternal recurrence of things. We have seen that while Freud focuses on the pathological aspects of repetition, and seeks ways to break the cycle, Nietzsche is interested in the individual's capacity to surrender to the cycle. *Amor fati* as the "eternal Yes to all things" is a matter of the subject's ability to affirm its fate to the extent that it would choose the same fate over and over again, even if it knew full well that it would have to endure the hardships as well as the pleasures of this fate. However, as I have endeavored to illustrate, affirming one's fate in the Nietzschean sense is not the same thing as being overruled or immobilized by this fate. Quite the contrary, *amor fati* implies the subject's readiness to love not only the variable ingredients of its fate but, more importantly, the *process* of encountering this fate—of creatively wrestling with whatever opportunities or obstacles that this fate may bring. Nietzsche's *amor fati* therefore shares with Freudian psychoanalysis the willingness to sort through whatever wreckage life (wave after wave) washes ashore. Because both thinkers recognize life's repetitive logic, both admit the likelihood of the past's painful return. Yet both also believe in the possibility of a more promising revisitation; both possess a keen eye for the sparkle of precious stones amid the rubble.

I have in this book looked for (and found) consolation; however, there has also been a certain hard edge to my discussion in the sense that I have insisted that psychic revitalization demands the subject's willingness to confront those parts of its past that it has pushed aside because they are too painful or disappointing to bear. I have emphasized that psychoanalysis can revive an impoverished psyche by helping the subject break out of formulaic patterns of representation that threaten to imprison it in states of inertia and complacency. By lifting the obstacles to self-representation, and by opening the path to self-mythologization, analysis puts the subject's psychic fixations in motion in ways that potentially give rise to a more agentic inner reality. However, since the logic of these fixations—the reason that they exist at all—is to preserve the status quo and to shield the subject from having to face past traumas, the process of loosening them can be quite challenging; the subject can suffer considerably when its adaptive defenses begin to shake and repressed aspects of its personality present themselves to be reassimilated into its psychic structures. Freud explains that the symptom often reaches its highest pitch of intensity when its determining cause is being approached (1910, pp. 14–15). This implies that the subject may live the painful parts of its repetition compulsion in a very powerful manner during analysis. Yet it is only through such a process of reenactment that the psyche is able to renew itself.

Nietzsche's *amor fati* similarly demands the subject's ability to face those elements of its existence that are difficult to withstand. Moreover, like psychoanalysis, *amor fati* highlights the value of admitting uncertainty and unpredictability as an important part of what makes us human. Poststructuralist theory has taught us to recognize the violence that inheres to attempts to arrest the instability of life and meaning. Freud and Nietzsche reveal that we are violent with *ourselves* (as well as with others) when we fail to tolerate life's inevitable ambiguities. This is why the understanding of the posthumanist soul that I have advanced in this book includes the idea that soulfulness is a matter of learning to live with the volatility and unknowability of existence without falling into states of psychic rigidity. I have done my best to demonstrate that while our impulse might be to demand clarity from the world as well as from ourselves, soulfulness implies knowing how to experience states of non-mastery as enabling rather than threatening.

Soulfulness then entails a degree of resourcefulness in negotiating the frequently quite confused outlines of our lived experience. This is the main reason that processes of psychic negotiation and transformation—Nietzschean self-stylization, Foucaultian care of the self, psychoanalytic acts of self-narrativization, and so on—have been at the forefront of my discussion. Such processes compel us to look for answers to the all-important question about the best way to live (to ask ourselves: "What do you *really* want?"). They, in other words, invite us to read the signifiers of our desire so as to attain a higher degree of self-understanding. As we have learned, at times reading the signifiers of our desire tells us how to encounter the world in more creative, engaged, or responsible ways. At other times, it unearths the ways in which we might long, momentarily at least, to be released from the banalities of everyday existence so as to be transported into mythical domains where larger-than-life narratives of epic passion still reign. The signifiers of our desire allow *jouissance* to erupt in the realm of symbolization. This is why they might be able to guide us in our search for a more affirmative—less fragile and vulnerable—vision of psychic life; they might help us reinvent the soul.

I was prompted to write this book because I kept asking myself how I should live my life so as not to squander the brief existential interval that I so miraculously possess. I am now no more capable of answering this question than I was at the beginning of my inquiry, yet I am closer to comprehending how it becomes possible for the subject to reclaim its past in ways that yield not only meaning, value, and beauty, but also a degree of consolation. Although I may never be able to arrive at an adequate understanding of how I should live, I now possess a better sense of how I *have* lived. Perhaps even more significantly, I recognize how the past continues to speak in the present, how the desires of today reinterpret the losses of yesterday, and how the strengths that I now wield stem from the weaknesses that I have had to overcome. I recognize, in other words, that even if the past continues to animate the present, it is equally the case that the present animates the past, and therefore holds it open to reinterpretation. It may well be that we can never fully know how to live in the present (living in the present is sometimes very difficult). But we *can* learn how to live our past in the present—how to appropriate our past in such a way that it stands not merely as a record of our failures, but as a vibrant foundation for our efforts to redefine our future.

T. S. Eliot once wrote that a poet "is not likely to know what is to be done unless he lives in what is not merely the present, but the present moment of the past, unless he is conscious, not of what is dead, but of what is already living" (1917, p. 44). My argument in this book has in many respects been similar, namely that as human beings we do not always know how to meet the future unless we are familiar with how the past makes itself present in our psyches. To look to the past is therefore not merely to confront what is dead (although this can be a part of it—as an act of farewell to something that has been outlived), but also to discover our potential in what is "already living" within us. The main thing that writing this text has revealed to me is that I have a profound attachment to the notion of psychic potentiality, to that acute conviction that at times stirs and perturbs the human spirit—and that can vex and chafe like a pebble in a shoe—that there is an entire reservoir of riches within us. Much of this book was written under the mundane conditions of scholarly exertion. But there are parts—perhaps the best, perhaps the worst—that were written in the rare and enchanting state of inspiration. If this makes me terribly antiquated, I do not mind a bit. Critics may take from me whatever else they wish, but I will not relinquish the bliss of the written word.

Amor fati.

References

Anzaldúa, G. (1987). *Borderlands/La Frontera: The New Mestiza*. San Francisco, CA: Aunt Lute Books.

Barthes, R. (1957). *Mythologies*, trans. A. Lavers. New York: Noonday Press, 1993.

———— (1977). *A Lover's Discourse*, trans. R. Howard. New York: Hill and Wang, 2001.

Bataille, G. (1957). *Eroticism: Death and Sensuality*, trans. M. Dalwood. San Francisco, CA: City Lights Books, 1986.

Baudelaire, C. (1859). Salon of 1859. In *Baudelaire: Selected Writings on Art and Artists*, trans. P. E. Charvet. London: Penguin, 1972.

Benhabib, S. (1992). *Situating the Self: Gender, Community, and Postmodernism in Contemporary Ethics*. New York: Routledge.

Benjamin, J. (1988). *The Bonds of Love: Psychoanalysis, Feminism, and the Problem of Domination*. New York: Pantheon.

———— (1998). *Shadow of the Other: Intersubjectivity and Gender in Psychoanalysis*. New York: Routledge.

Berlant, L. (2004). *Capitalism, the Children, and Compassion*: La Promesse and Rosetta. Presentation at the Harvard Humanities Center Gender and Sexuality Studies Seminar, Cambridge, MA, March 19.

Bornstein, K. (1994). *Gender Outlaw: On Men, Women, and the Rest of Us*. New York: Routledge.

Brennan, T. (1992). *The Interpretation of the Flesh: Freud and Femininity*. New York: Routledge.

———— (1993). *History After Lacan*. New York: Routledge.

———— (2000). *Exhausting Modernity: Grounds for a New Economy*. New York: Routledge.

Butler, J. (1990). *Gender Trouble: Feminism and the Subversion of Identity*. New York: Routledge.

———— (1993). *Bodies That Matter: On the Discursive Limits of "Sex."* New York: Routledge.

———— (1997). *The Psychic Life of Power: Theories of Subjection*. Stanford, CA: Stanford University Press.

———— (2000). *Antigone's Claim*. New York: Columbia University Press.

———— (2004). *Undoing Gender*. New York: Routledge.

Butler J., and Scott J., eds. (1992). *Feminists Theorize the Political*. New York: Routledge.

Cheng, A. A. (2000). *The Melancholy of Race: Psychoanalysis, Assimilation, and Hidden Grief*. Oxford: Oxford University Press.

Cixous, H. (1977). *Coming to Writing and Other Essays*, trans. S. Cornell, D. Jenson, A. Liddle, and S. Sellers. Cambridge, MA: Harvard University Press, 1991.

Cooper, D. (1999). *Existentialism: A Reconstruction*. Oxford, UK: Blackwell.

Das Dasgupta, S., and DasGupta, S. (1997). Bringing up baby: raising a "third world" daughter in the "first world." In *Dragon Ladies: Asian American Feminists Breathe Fire*, ed. S. Shah, 182–199. Boston, MA: South End Press.

Davidson, A. (2001). *The Emergence of Sexuality: Historical Epistemology and the Formation of Concepts*. Cambridge, MA: Harvard University Press.

de Beauvoir, S. (1949). *The Second Sex*, trans. H. M. Parshley. New York: Vintage, 1989.

de Lauretis, T. (1987). *Technologies of Gender: Essays on Theory, Film, and Fiction*. Bloomington: Indiana University Press.

———— (1994). *The Practice of Love: Lesbian Sexuality and Perverse Desire*. Bloomington: Indiana University Press.

Deleuze, G., and Guattari, F. (1980). *A Thousand Plateaus: Capitalism and Schizophrenia*, trans. B. Massumi. Minneapolis: University of Minnesota Press, 1987.

Dor, J. (1997a). *The Clinical Lacan*, ed. J. Feher-Gurewich. Northvale, NJ: Jason Aronson.

———— (1997b). *Introduction to the Reading of Lacan: The Unconscious is Structured Like a Language*, ed. J. Feher-Gurewich. Northvale, NJ: Jason Aronson.

Durkheim, E. (1915). *The Elementary Forms of the Religious Life*, trans. J. W. Swain. New York: Free Press, 1965.

Eliot, T. S. (1917). Tradition and the individual talent. In *Selected Prose of T. S. Eliot*, ed. F. Kermode, 37–44. San Diego, CA: Harcourt, 1975.

Eng, D. L. (2001). *Racial Castration: Managing Masculinity in Asian America*. Durham, NC: Duke University Press.

Eng. D. L., and Han, S. (2000). A dialogue on racial melancholia. *Psychoanalytic Dialogues,* 10(4):667–700.

Eng, D. L., and Kazanjian, D., eds. (2003). *Loss: The Politics of Mourning*. Berkeley: University of California Press.

Fausto-Sterling, A. (2000). *Sexing the Body: Gender Politics and the Construction of Sexuality*. New York: Basic Books.

Feher-Gurewich, J. (2003). Lacan and American feminism: Who is the analyst? In *Beyond French Feminisms: Debates on Women, Culture and Politics in France 1980–2001*, ed. R. Célestin, E. DalMolin, and I. de Courtivron, 239–246. New York: Palgrave Macmillan.

Feher-Gurewich, J., and Tort, M. (1996). *The Subject and the Self: Lacan and American Psychoanalysis*. Northvale, NJ: Jason Aronson.

Flax, J. (1990). *Thinking Fragments: Psychoanalysis, Feminism, and Postmodernism in the Contemporary West*. Berkeley: University of California Press.

Foucault, M. (1976). *The History of Sexuality: An Introduction*, vol. 1, trans. R. Hurley. New York: Vintage, 1990.

——— (1984). *The Care of the Self: The History of Sexuality*, vol. 3, trans. R. Hurley. New York: Vintage, 1988.

Freud, S. (1900). *The Interpretation of Dreams*, trans. J. Strachey. New York: Avon.

——— (1910). *Five Lectures on Psycho-Analysis*, trans. J. Strachey. New York: W. W. Norton.

——— (1917). Mourning and melancholia. *Standard Edition* 14:239–258.

——— (1923). *The Ego and the Id*, trans. J. Strachey. New York: W. W. Norton.

——— (1930). *Civilization and Its Discontents*, trans. J. Strachey. New York: W. W. Norton.

Garber, M. (1992). *Vested Interests: Cross-Dressing and Cultural Anxiety*. New York: Routledge.

Ghent, E. (1990). Masochism, submission, surrender. *Contemporary Psychoanalysis* 26(1):108–136.

Green, A. (1986). *On Private Madness*. Madison, CT: International Universities Press.

Grosz, E. (1990). *Jacques Lacan: A Feminist Introduction*. New York: Routledge.

——— (1994). *Volatile Bodies: Toward a Corporeal Feminism*. Bloomington: Indiana University Press.

——— (1995). *Space, Time, and Perversion*. New York: Routledge.

Halberstam, J. (1998). *Female Masculinity*. Durham, NC: Duke University Press.

Haraway, D. (1991). *Simians, Cyborgs, and Women: The Reinvention of Nature*. New York: Routledge.

Hegel, G. W. F. (1807). *Phenomenology of Spirit*, trans. A. V. Miller. Oxford, UK: Oxford University Press, 1977.

Heidegger, M. (1927). *Being and Time*, trans. J. Macquarrie and E. Robinson. New York: Harper & Row, 1962.

———— (1971). *Poetry, Language, Thought*, trans. A. Hofstadter. New York: Harper & Row.

Hill Collins, P. (1991). *Black Feminist Thought: Knowledge, Consciousness, and the Politics of Empowerment*. New York: Routledge.

hooks, b. (1994). *Outlaw Culture: Resisting Representations*. New York: Routledge.

Horkheimer, M., and Adorno, T. W. (1944). *The Dialectic of Enlightenment*, trans. J. Cumming. New York: Continuum, 1994.

Irigaray, L. (1994). *To Be Two*, trans. M. M. Rhodes and M. F. Cocito-Monoc. New York: Routledge, 2001.

Jakobson, R. (1987). *Language in Literature*, ed. K. Pomorska and S. Rudy. Cambridge, MA: Harvard University Press.

Jardine, A. A. (1985). *Gynesis: Configurations of Woman and Modernity*. Ithaca, NY: Cornell University Press.

Kant, I. (1790). *The Critique of Judgment*, trans. J. C. Meredith. Oxford, UK: Oxford University Press, 1991.

Kierkegaard, S. (1843a). *Either/Or*, trans. D. F. Swenson and L. M. Swenson. New York: Anchor, 1959.

———— (1843b). *Fear and Trembling*, trans. A. Hannay. London: Penguin, 1985.

Kristeva, J. (1974). *Revolution in Poetic Language*, trans. M. Waller. New York: Columbia University Press, 1984.

———— (1983). *Tales of Love*, trans. L. S. Roudiez. New York: Columbia University Press, 1987.

———— (1987). *Black Sun: Depression and Melancholia*, trans. L. S. Roudiez. New York: Columbia University Press, 1989.

———— (1993). *New Maladies of the Soul*, trans. R. Guberman. New York: Columbia University Press, 1995.

———— (1996). *The Sense and Nonsense of Revolt*, trans. J. Herman. New York: Columbia University Press, 2000.

Lacan, J. (1966). *Écrits: A Selection*, trans. A. Sheridan. New York: W. W. Norton, 1977.

———— (1975). *The Seminar of Jacques Lacan, Book XX: On Feminine Sexuality: The Limits of Love and Knowledge*, trans. B. Fink. New York: W. W. Norton, 1999.

———— (1986). *The Seminar of Jacques Lacan, Book VII: The Ethics of Psychoanalysis*, trans. D. Porter. New York: W. W. Norton, 1992.

Lasch, C. (1984). *The Minimal Self: Psychic Survival in Troubled Times*. New York: W. W. Norton.

Layton, L. (1998). *Who's That Girl? Who's That Boy? Clinical Practice Meets Postmodern Gender Theory*. Northvale, NJ: Jason Aronson.

Lear, J. (1990). *Love and Its Place in Nature: A Philosophical Interpretation of Freudian Psychoanalysis*. New Haven, CT: Yale University Press, 1998.

———— (1999). *Open Minded: Working Out the Logic of the Soul.* Cambridge, MA: Harvard University Press.

Lévinas, E. (1961). *Totality and Infinity*, trans. A. Lingis. Pittsburgh, PA: Duquesne University Press, 1969.

Lingis, A. (1985). *Libido.* Albany, NY: SUNY Press.

Lorde, A. (1984). *Sister Outsider: Essays and Speeches.* Freedom, CA: Crossing Press, 2001.

Lu, L. (1997). Critical visions: the representation and resistance of Asian women. In *Dragon Ladies: Asian American Feminists Breathe Fire*, ed. S. Shah, 17–28. Boston, MA: South End Press.

Lyotard, J-F. (1979). *The Postmodern Condition: A Report on Knowledge*, trans. G. Bennington and B. Massumi. Minneapolis: University of Minnesota Press, 1984.

Marcuse, H. (1955). *Eros and Civilization.* Boston, MA: Beacon.

———— (1964). *One-Dimensional Man: Studies in the Ideology of Advanced Industrial Society.* Boston, MA: Beacon.

Marx, K. (1846). The German ideology. In *The Marx-Engels Reader*, ed. R. C. Tucker, 146–200. New York: W. W. Norton, 1978.

Modell, A. (1993). *The Private Self.* Cambridge, MA: Harvard University Press.

Nehamas, A. (1985). *Nietzsche: Life as Literature.* Cambridge, MA: Harvard University Press.

Nietzsche, F. (1872). *The Birth of Tragedy*, trans. W. Kaufmann. New York: Vintage, 1967.

———— (1873). Truth and falsity in an ultramoral sense. In *Critical Theory Since Plato*, ed. H. Adams, 634–639. Orlando, FL: Harcourt Brace Jovanovich, 1992.

———— (1882). *The Gay Science*, trans. W. Kaufmann. New York: Vintage, 1974.

———— (1886). *Beyond Good and Evil*, trans. R. J. Hollingdale. London: Penguin, 1990.

———— (1887). *On the Genealogy of Morals*, trans. W. Kaufmann and R. J. Hollingdale. New York: Vintage, 1989.

———— (1892). *Thus Spoke Zarathustra*, trans. R. J. Hollingdale. London: Penguin, 1969.

———— (1908). *Ecce Homo*, trans. W. Kaufmann. New York: Vintage, 1989.

Oliver, K. (1997). *Family Values: Subjects Between Nature and Culture.* New York: Routledge.

———— (2001). *Witnessing: Beyond Recognition.* Minneapolis: University of Minnesota Press.

Pater, W. (1873). *The Renaissance*, ed. A. Phillips. Oxford, UK: Oxford University Press, 1998.

Plato (385 B.C.). *Symposium*, trans. R. Waterfield. Oxford, UK: Oxford University Press, 1994.

———— (370 B.C.). *Phaedrus and Letters VII and VIII*, trans. W. Hamilton. London: Penguin, 1973.

Prosser, J. (1998). *Second Skins: The Body Narratives of Transsexuality*. New York: Columbia University Press.

Saint Teresa (1565). *The Life of Saint Teresa of Ávila by Herself*, trans. J. M. Cohen. London: Penguin, 1957.

Sartre, J-P. (1940). *The Psychology of Imagination*. London: Methuen, 1974.

Schiller, F. (1795). *Letters on the Aesthetic Education of Man*, trans. R. Snell. New York: Frederick Ungar, 1977.

Schopenhauer, A. (1851). *The World as Will and Representation*, vol. 1, trans. E. F. J. Payne. New York: Dover, 1969.

Silverman, K. (1996). *The Threshold of the Visible World*. New York: Routledge.

———— (2000). *World Spectators*. Stanford, CA: Stanford University Press.

Stendhal. (1822). *Love*, trans. G. Sale and S. Sale. London: Penguin, 1975.

Stone, S. (1997). The empire strikes back: a posttranssexual manifesto. In *Writing on the Body: Female Embodiment and Feminist Theory*, ed. K. Conboy, N. Medina, and S. Stanbury, 337–359. New York: Columbia University Press.

Underhill, E. (1911). *Mysticism: A Study in the Nature and Development of Man's Spiritual Consciousness*. London: Methuen.

West, C. (1993). *Race Matters*. Boston, MA: Beacon.

Wilde, O. (1891). The critic as artist. In *The Artist as Critic*, ed. R. Ellmann, 340–408. Chicago: University of Chicago Press, 1982.

Willett, C. (2001). *The Soul of Justice: Social Bonds and Racial Hubris*. Ithaca, NY: Cornell University Press.

Winterson, J. (1987). *The Passion*. New York: Grove.

———— (1996). *Art and Lies*. New York: Vintage.

Woolf, V. (1929). *A Room of One's Own*. San Diego, CA: Harcourt, 1989.

Žižek, S. (1989). *The Sublime Object of Ideology*. New York: Verso.

Index

Printed in the United States
By Bookmasters